BLACK SUPERMAN

BLACK SUPERMAN

A CULTURAL AND BIOLOGICAL HISTORY OF THE PEOPLE WHO BECAME THE WORLD'S GREATEST ATHLETES

Patrick Desmond Cooper

With a Foreword by Dr. Errol Morrison

First Sahara Enterprises • Austin

First Sahara Enterprises

10602 Little Wind Cv.

Austin, TX 78730 USA

www.patrickdesmondcooper.com

© 2003 by Patrick Desmond Cooper

All rights reserved.

Printed in the United States of America.

ISBN 978-0-9822372-0-5

Cover design by Tony Pierre-Louis

Editorial support and design by

Silent Partners, Inc.

8727 Shoal Creek Blvd.

Austin, TX 78757-6815 USA

www.silentpartners.com

Contents

Acknowledgments vii

Foreword ix

Author's Notes xi

Introduction: A Most Vexing Debate xiii

Part One: The Greatest Athletes

1. Not Just Statistically Dominant but Stylistically Different 3

2. The Great Debate: Nature or Nurture? 17

3. The Turning Point 49

Part Two: The Performance Evidence

4. In Baseball, Race Has Always Been a Factor 59

5. Basketball: A Showcase for Black Athletic Talent 81

6. In Football, Quotas Kept Blacks off College
    and Professional Teams 91

7. An Extraordinary Dominance of Sprinting, Jumping, and Hurdling .. 99

8. Other Africans: Champions of Distance Running 117

9. Boxing: White Champions Avoided Fighting Blacks 121

Part Three: The Biological Evidence

10. Disease, Biological Superiority, and Athletic Ability 133

11. Body Structure, Physiology, and Athletic Performance 149

12. Natural Selection and the West African Biological Miracle 169

13. The Biology of Speed 187

Part Four: The Implications

14. Standard Tests and the Definition of Intelligence 199

15. A Clearer View of African History 215

16. The Pure Race Myth and the African Origins of Modern Humans..... 245

Selected Bibliography 273

Acknowledgments

To the memory of my wonderful parents, Herman and Zetty Cooper; and for my wife, Juin; my sons, Greg and Charlie; my daughter, Rachel; and my sisters, Marcia and Marlene. Thanks particularly to Juin and Greg, without whose help and support this book would not have been possible.

Foreword

It is not often that one reads of the positives and the achievements of the sons and daughters of the African Diaspora against a setting of thorough evidence-based discourse and distanced objectivity. It is not often that those of the African Diaspora are grouped on the basis of that genetic umbilical cord and treated as such, irrespective of their current geographical distribution or varied phenotype, the latter being the result of centuries-long interracial admixture. Nonetheless, the scientific underpinnings for that hereditary trail are now being elucidated and becoming clearer as the investigations gather momentum.

Indeed, it is not often that we pause to revisit, examine and explain the tremendous physical attributes of the diasporal descendants and to group them within the pages of one exhaustive tome as occurs in *Black Superman.*

Herein, the author, Patrick Desmond Cooper, who hails from the Caribbean island of Jamaica, puts together an admirable account of the black sports individual, and without rancor or diatribe has outlined how despite earlier constraints and adversity, the physical prowess of the black athlete has surfaced and has now become legendary.

He not only carefully documents the historic data, which eloquently speaks to this, but delves into an underlying scientific dissertation, ferreting out all the available research that has relevance and bearing on the subject.

The research is exhaustive and the scientific details enunciated are sound. It is indeed a tribute to the author's thoroughness in preparation that he has taken rather esoteric research and translated it for the easy reading of the interested public. I say esoteric in that much of the post-Darwinian evolutionary concepts surrounding the terms 'survival of the fittest' and 'selection of the species' have been shrouded in misunderstandings and have fallen more or less out of public scrutiny.

It is of interest that the current work on transmission of mitochondrial DNA vis-à-vis nuclear DNA is elucidated and outlines the possible biblical correctness of a 'mother Eve,' no matter how basic and prototypic.

An explanation is adduced for the 'selection' of the black phenotype for physical prowess, and herein the author demonstrates a remarkable grasp of the anatomical, physiological, and biochemical alterations that have resulted in part from this 'selection' and of the relative advantage bestowed on the metabolism of those populations that historically suffered from sickle cell disease—an adaptation to malaria—which was once endemic in the mother country.

BRAVO!

The concept that the abnormal sickle hemoglobin carries less oxygen to the tissues but that the oxygen is more rapidly released there, as an asset to overcome any oxygen debt built up during physical exertion, is an idea that has been bandied about for some time among medical scientists. Patrick Cooper has woven this concept into the other anatomical findings that all contribute evidence to support the potential physical superiority of the diasporic descendants. He even helps to clinch his hypothesis by pointing out that these biomedical advantages have been further enhanced by the concentration of the genetic pool of those displaced from the motherland and born, bred, and nurtured in and through adverse fortunes.

This book, *Black Superman,* is a must read for every man, woman, and child of the Diaspora. It is brilliant, breathtakingly accurate, and incisively written. It should be on the reading list for all schools' literature texts as well as those who marvel at the supremacy of black athleticism.

It ends on a very philosophical note akin to the view expressed by Old Chief Seattle on the signing of the peace treaty, in the 18th century, between the native and the conquering American. In a speech titled 'we may be brothers after all', he said, inter alia….

"All things are connected...!"

PROF. THE HON. ERROL Y ST.A. MORRISON OJ

MD, PHD, FRCP (Glasg), FACP, FRSM (UK)

PRO VICE CHANCELLOR AND DEAN

SCHOOL FOR GRADUATE STUDIES AND RESEARCH

THE UNIVERSITY OF THE WEST INDIES

Dr.Morrison is the leading authority on diabetes in the Caribbean; in addition to his administrative responsibilities he is also Professor of both Biochemistry and Endocrinology.

Author's Notes

Black Superman was written to extol the genes and genius of African and African-descended populations, to comprehensively explain the disproportionate athletic power of genes designed in Africa, and to forcefully expose and debunk the myths and lies that undergird the historic slander of black intellectual inferiority. Despite its title, it is not a paean to black racial superiority, but rather a confirmation of the essential equality of the entire human race.

It has been almost five years since *Black Superman* was first published. Since then, time and events have lent credibility to some of the book's most important claims. One such claim—that the athletic superiority of men and women of West African descent in athletic activities involving speed and power is genetically based—has been highlighted by results from a lab in Scotland. In addition, the recently concluded Beijing Olympics shone the spotlight on the extraordinary success of the Jamaican sprinters, led by the remarkable Usain Bolt.

After more than ten years of research, I concluded that the disproportionate success of West African-descended athletes was due to (1) biomechanical and biochemical differences between themselves and White and Asian athletes, and (2) biochemical differences between themselves and all other Africans. I argued that the biochemical differences—essentially differences in glucose conversion rates—between West Africans and all other populations, including other black Africans, was linked to their development of biological defenses against falciparum malaria. In the uniquely lethal West African malarial environment, individuals with sickle cell trait (those with one sickle gene) possessed a significant selective advantage.

I explained that although sickling is caused by a single amino acid substitution on the beta chain of the hemoglobin molecule, the mutation had triggered a series of physiological adjustments which, incidentally, had favorable athletic consequences. That the adjustments or compensatory mechanisms, all of which have been scientifically tested and evaluated, include a higher percentage of fast-twitch muscle fibers; greater activity in the phosphagenic, glycolytic, and lactate dehydrogenase metabolic pathways; and a greater rate of ventilation. That they altered how the affected individuals process, store, and utilize energy for skeletal muscle contraction, and enhanced their ability to build lean muscle mass.

I also explained that the sickle cell trait and the biological adaptations it set in motion would have considerable medical and physiological consequences. And I detailed those consequences.

Following the publication of *Black Superman,* I invited my friend of several decades, Professor Errol Morrison (who also wrote the foreword to this book) to co-author the article, "Some bio-medical mechanisms in athletic prowess," which was published in the *West Indian Medical Journal* in 2006. These two publications triggered a major research project by the International Center for East African Running Science, Institute of Biomedical and Life Sciences, University of Glasgow; the School of Graduate Studies and Research, The University of West Indies, Mona Campus; and the Faculty of Medicine, University of Sydney, Australia.

Their study, titled "Can genetics explain the dominance of athletes of West African ancestry in international sprint events," collected saliva samples from more than 200 national standard Jamaican athletes. The early results indicate that the fast-twitch muscle fibers of more than 70% of the Jamaicans, as compared to 30% of elite Australian athletes, contain the Actinen A protein, which significantly improves the performance of those fibers.

Black Superman is not just about sports and science. It is, as the full title implies, a cultural and biological history of the West African peoples. It covers a wide range of subjects, including history, biology, anthropology, and linguistics, which are not usually found in a single book. With very little fanfare it has found its way into libraries and onto bookshelves around the world. I invite you to read further and to participate in the great debate this book was written to address. Why are people of West African descent so disproportionately represented among the greatest athletes in the world?

Patrick Desmond Cooper
September 2008

Introduction

A Most Vexing Debate

This book was written to address one of the most vexing and controversial debates in recent American history. Why are African Americans and other people of African descent so disproportionately represented among the greatest athletes in the world? What is the source of their athletic success; is it culture or is it biology? And, perhaps even more importantly, what are the implications, if it is the latter? Indeed, it is my contention, that on this question, because of America's shameful racial history, the answer and the implications are two sides of a single coin.

I will argue that black athletes such as Michael Jordan, Muhammad Ali, Carl Lewis, Barry Bonds, Serena Williams, Tiger Woods, Jim Brown, Pele, and the cricketer Garfield Sobers rank not only among the very greatest performers of all time in their respective athletic activities, but that they are also athletes of such tremendous raw physical ability that they could only have been black and of West African origin. The extraordinary fact that the greatest athletes the world has ever known have all descended from one relatively small area of the world, I will prove, is not mere chance.

I will also argue that contrary to established European and American history Africa was both the birthplace of modern man and of modern civilization. It is now scientifically incontrovertible—I will make clear— that Africa's designation as the "dark" continent and the reputation of its people as intellectually inferior to all other populations was not just unjustified but the result of a long, massive, deliberate and organized campaign to justify the sins of slavery and segregation. Since it is now widely agreed—as I will explain— in the scientific community that modern man emerged from Africa as recently as 50,000 years ago, any continuing claim that civilization began in the Middle East must be dismissed for what it is, a mere remnant of a thoroughly discredited racist propaganda campaign. Clearly, the contention that civilization emerged from non-African sources and the established fact that the direct ancestors of Europeans and Asians lived in Africa until fairly recently, are, clearly, mutually exclusive concepts.

The concept that black Africans were incapable of creating civilizations was a logical and necessary extension of the theory that slavery, despite its manifest cruelties, had rescued black Africans from what one contemporary commentator described as "the profoundest depths of savage barbarity." If that was not true, if black men and women had created great civilizations, had originated, promulgated, and contributed mightily to the world, then slavery was a sin of such enormity, of such monstrosity, that even God himself may never forgive those, and their generations, who had been responsible for such a sin against his African children. Such a fate was far too awful to contemplate. Far preferable, was imagining that it was God himself who had first cursed the children of Ham and made them black.

During the past decade or so, a prime-time television program and a couple of books have examined the question of black athletic dominance. But these attempts have been restricted to raising questions and pointing out intriguing anatomical and physiological differences between the races. *Black Superman* is the first comprehensive effort not only to fully document the anatomical and physiological differences between the races, but also to explain the historical environmental conditions that created these differences, detail precisely how they influence athletic performance, and examine the scientific and social implications of those differences.

Black Superman takes the position that the athletic superiority of black athletes of West African descent in athletic activities involving speed and power is based on (1) biomechanical and biochemical differences between themselves and white and Asian athletes, and (2) biochemical differences between themselves and all other Africans. The biochemical differences— essentially differences in glucose conversion rates—between West Africans and all other populations, including other black Africans, developed as a result of uniquely hostile environmental conditions in at least some parts of West Africa. Blacks from other parts of the African continent, led by the Kenyans, are now the greatest distance runners in the world. And while those other Africans share some athletically advantageous physical qualities, like low subcutaneous fat, narrow hips, and long arms and legs, with their West African cousins, it appears that they are similar to Europeans and all other racial groups in muscle fiber distribution—the basis of the great speed, quickness and leaping ability of the great black athletes of West African origin. So it is clear that the source of the athletic ability of West Africans is not peculiar to all or even most African populations and cannot therefore be seen as an African trait.

Specifically, I contend that the athletic superiority of people of West African descent is linked to their development of biological defenses against falciparum malaria. In the uniquely lethal West African malarial environment, individuals with sickle cell trait (those with one sickling gene) possessed a significant selective advantage. Although sickling is caused by a single amino acid substitution on the beta chain of the hemoglobin molecule, the mutation triggered a series of physiological adjustments, which, incidentally, had favorable athletic consequences. The adjustments, all of which have been scientifically tested and evaluated, altered how the affected individuals process, store, and utilize energy for skeletal muscle contraction, and enhanced their ability to build lean muscle mass.

Despite its title, *Black Superman* is not a paean to the racial superiority of black athletes. To the contrary, by arguing that the athletic dominance of black athletes is due to biologically meaningless physical differences, I hope to demonstrate the essential equality of the human race. Perhaps nothing will make this clearer than the subject matter of the final chapter of this book: that modern man emerged from the African continent only 50,000 years ago and therefore, homo sapiens sapiens, is too young a species for biologically meaningful differences—such as in brain size and structure—to have developed between its various geographical groupings.

For many years, the theories that purported to explain black athletic success were rooted in crude and patently ridiculous racial biology. Not surprisingly, as a consequence, many Americans, led by the black intellectual community, have contemptuously rejected biological explanations of black athletic achievement and have attempted to ascribe black athletic success to a variety of sociological and psychological factors.

Also contributing to the current wide acceptance of environmental explanations for black athletic success in the general intellectual community is what has been described as "the dark history of eugenics"—a history that eventually provided the Nazis with the scientific rationale for the systematic slaughter of ten million European Jews, Gypsies, and other "undesirable elements." In the backlash against eugenics, environmentalism became the fashion. But the pendulum has swung again—this time, I believe, permanently. The evidence in favor of nature's superior role is clear and overwhelming. The emerging science of molecular biology is proving that heredity is primarily responsible for determining individual appearance, personality, behavior, and performance.

Clearly, the most important implication of any claim that people of African descent are biologically different in any way is the often unspoken but very real fear that such a difference can only be negative. There can be little doubt that—given the history of so-called scientific racism in the United States—a justifiable fear of racial biology has prevented Americans of all races from openly discussing the many obvious, scientifically documented, anthropometric and physiological differences between the races. The concept that physical superiority could somehow be a symptom of intellectual inferiority only developed when physical superiority became associated with blacks. Nevertheless, I was aware, almost as soon as I began thinking about this book, that it would be incomplete without an in-depth examination of the consequences of claiming that biological differences are responsible for the athletic success of black Americans.

I began thinking about the subject matter of this book shortly after arriving in this country in July of 1978, following more than two years in England. Growing up in Jamaica in a family that was proud of its mixed African and British ancestry, I had rarely thought of race. Until 1962 Jamaica had been a British colony and class and shade absorbed far more of our time and attention, and although there was more than some correlation between shade and class, they were never regarded as the same thing. In fact, I cannot recall having or overhearing even a single discussion on race at our home during all the years that I lived at my parents' home, and I lived at home until I was 21 years old. There was, however, lots of talk about class and what that meant.

In colonial Jamaica, social class was almost everything, far more important, for example, than mere money. Those who attempted to buy their way into "polite" society were usually unsuccessful. No group was seen as more obnoxious, and none were more despised than monied "hurry come-ups" who had not mastered the social graces, who were, obviously, lacking a proper family background. To be successful, social-climbing had to be accompanied by the careful—and preferably slow—acquisition of a range of anglicized cultural accoutrements. Included among these were mastery of

Standard English and social codes of conduct, and the adoption of acceptable forms of worship. In colonial Jamaica dark skin was acceptable, if it was not tainted by too close an identification with Africa. For the most part Afro-Saxons were perfectly acceptable.

Speech, was, and although to a lesser extent, is today, the most accurate indicator of social class in Jamaica. Until the social revolution of the 1980s, the ability to speak the "Queen's" English was a requisite skill for entry into the upper and middle classes. In stark contrast, the language of the vast majority of the population, a Creole stew of English with a smattering of Twi, superimposed on an African grammatical structure, is nearly incomprehensible to non-Jamaicans. As the Jamaican scholar, Patrick Bryan, explained in *The Jamaican People 1880-1902*: "The language of the Jamaican masses was the conduit through which they expressed their folklore, proverbs and songs, and the primary vehicle for religious expression as well. The ability to speak "good English" was a measure of the extent to which a citizen was conversant with British culture."

Since both my parents had white fathers of British ancestry who were married to their mothers, in our family conversance with British culture was, in a manner of speaking, genetic. My parents, particularly my father, were anglophiles and monarchists. Family lore has it that when George VI's death was announced my father shed more tears than the royal family. We were raised in what one of my sister's described as "a bubble," which kept us hermetically sealed off from almost all Afro-Jamaican cultural influences. While many members of the middle and upper classes sometimes used the Jamaican dialect as a way of demonstrating their social awareness, we were instructed to speak properly at all times.

Another important indicator of social class in Jamaica was how and where one worshipped. Among the black majority, Christianity, like every other aspect of cultural expression, had been, as Bryan put it, "consistently reinterpreted in African terms." Although they had absorbed some superficial aspects of Christianity, religious practices, such as pukkumina and myalism, were, fundamentally, expressions of African beliefs in obeah and magic. Even among members of traditional Christian churches, the appeal of emotional, evangelical religions was extremely strong and revivalist movements periodically swept through the island. The power of their appeal to the Jamaican masses was feared, as Bryan explained, because of their potential for generating social mischief, and despised because of their alleged primitivism.

Alexander Bedward, the instigator of the largest and most sustained of these movements, was quoted by the *New York Times* as telling his followers that the time had come "when the blacks must rise up and crush the whites and assume the government, as their brothers have done in Haiti." Eventually, and inevitably, Bedward was, Bryan wrote, "put away in the lunatic asylum which was the destination of many religious Afro-Jamaicans who were certified insane through revivalism, obeah or other religious excitement." Bedwardism, which obviously tapped into a longing for a more vital form of religious experience than was being offered by the established church, was denounced by the Anglican Bishop of the time as evidence of the "deep degradation" of the black masses.

For families like ours the raw emotionalism of Afro-Jamaican religious expression was absolutely verboten. We, my two sisters and I, were raised as observant Roman Catholics, my mother's faith. And while my mother in her later years would abandon the Catholic Church for a more emotionally satisfying "charismatic" denomination, a practice since duplicated by one of my sisters, my most religiously sublime moments were experienced standing under the soaring ceiling of a cathedral. Under that vast dome, conscious of my insignificance, transported by the ritual chanting of the Latin mass and the deep, sonorous roar of the organ, inhaling the mysterious scent of burning incense, something transcendent happened. For me, that was as close as I've ever been to the spiritual ecstasy that union with God promises. Seven of my most impressionable years were shaped by a rigid Jesuit education, which, piled on top of my Anglo-Saxon indoctrination, if the truth be told, left me completely incapable of responding, other than intellectually, to the siren call of mother Africa. That is why this book is, I have come to understand, this once good Catholic boy's way of making atonement.

In Jamaica, I never viewed athletic performance through the prism of race but by the time I arrived in the United States exposure to British racism had made me psychologically prepared to do so. I had begun my professional career as a staff reporter on the sports desk of the *Gleaner*, the largest and oldest daily newspaper in the English-speaking Caribbean. I had competed in and/or covered soccer, cricket, track and field, boxing, and swimming; but the rules and the stars of baseball, basketball, and what I then called American football were still mysteries to me.

One of the delights of living in England, for me, was the enormous amount of high-quality cricket and soccer—much of it international—that was available on television. Imagine, then, my mixed feelings when I came to the States and discovered that there were even more hours of televised sports available on television, but that almost all of them were devoted to sporting activities I did not understand. It was during the long hours that I watched and tried to decipher the intricacies of football, baseball, and basketball that I first became convinced that the differences between black and white athletes, in both substance and style, were too pronounced to be explained by culture alone.

Almost instinctively, perhaps because I had spent many hours as a teenager wondering why Africans had survived the conditions that had totally destroyed Jamaica's indigenous population, I knew that the explanation was probably to be found somewhere in Darwin's theory of the survival of the fittest. But, with a wife and three children, translating that insight or hunch into this book became a long and arduous process. As I became more familiar with American society, I became increasingly aware of just how explosive discussions of racial differences can be. So, by the time I was ready to begin the first draft of this book, I was aware that race would have to be a primary focus.

It is easy to believe, given its apparent ubiquity, that the concept that Africans are intellectually inferior to other racial groups is a natural law, as old as history itself. In fact, it is a fairly recent invention, the result of an intensive, systematic, decades-long campaign waged on both sides of the Atlantic to justify the sin of slavery. Seeking to reconcile the irreconcilable, Christian slaveholders and their supporters and apologists struggled to create a moral basis for excluding black Africans from the human family.

Alarmed by the success of the abolitionists in exposing the contradiction between slavery and the universal equality proclaimed both by the Declaration of Independence and the country's traditional religious teachings, the defenders of slavery decided that their position could only be justified by a clear demonstration that black inferiority was an unalterable fact of nature. "If this be not true," one defender admitted, "American slavery is a monstrous wickedness."

Initially, much of the defense of slavery was based on Scripture. But, as the writer and historian Drew Gilpin Faust explained, "For an age increasingly enamored of the vocabulary and methods of natural science, biblical guidance was not enough. The accepted foundations for truth were changing in European and American thought, as intellectuals sought to apply the rigor of science to the study of society and morality, as well as the natural world." The result of this growing dependence on science was the development of a new ideology, polygeny, that sought to establish moral authority by creating a scientific rationale for slavery and postbellum racial oppression. Polygeny claimed that human races were separate biological species, the descendants of different Adams.

One of the major goals of the campaign to justify slavery was to convince the world, including the Africans themselves, that they were a people without history—a race of such natural and inherent inferiority that they had contributed virtually nothing to the civilization of the world. Although the historian and statesman Eric Williams has convincingly demonstrated that "slavery was not born of racism, rather, racism was the consequence of slavery," the stunning success of proslavery propaganda, so-called "scientific racism," has deeply ingrained the mythology of natural black inferiority into the subterranean consciousness of the entire world.

It is this mythology, which even now retains much of its original power, which continues to disfigure the reputation of Africans and to distort and inhibit the debate about the source of the extraordinarily disproportionate athletic success of African Americans and other people of West African descent. *Black Superman* seeks therefore not only to explain the biological basis for African American athletic superiority but also to expose and debunk the myths and lies that undergird the historic slander of black intellectual inferiority.

In some ways *Black Superman* was a difficult, or more accurately, challenging, book to write. I am a journalist, not a scientist and much of what I've written here I learned as I read and researched. To do justice to the thesis it was necessary to cover a range of subjects, including sports, history, biology, anthropology and linguistics, which are not usually found in the same book. Because of my background as a journalist and advertising copywriter, *Black Superman* is, I am confident, as clear and as free of scientific jargon as is possible to make such a book. Nevertheless, it could be regarded by some with less than a strong interest in the subject matter of the book as challenging to read as I found it to write, at least in parts. Some may well claim that there is altogether too much information about too many subjects. The book is structured however in such a way that a pretty full understanding of the thesis can be gained without a full and detailed reading of every chapter, since much of the more "challenging" topics are outlined in the earlier chapters of the book and explored in greater detail in later ones.

Despite the challenges or perhaps because of it, researching and writing *Black Superman* was, for me, not just exhausting and enlightening but also exhilarating and extremely satisfying. For those of you, to whom the subject matter of this book is of some importance, I profoundly believe that the effort it may take to complete every chapter will be well worth every precious hour you devote to it.

Part One

The Greatest Athletes

1

Not Just Statistically Dominant but Stylistically Different

As he powered his way to the bar set almost two feet above his head, before gathering himself for that final mighty effort that would send him twisting backwards, headfirst, into the pit below, Javier Sotomayor knew that a special place in history had been reserved for him. He was always confident. Without confidence, what he did for a living would be impossible; the bar would seem too high, far too intimidating. But tonight it was more than that. Tonight he knew, as only those whose fortunes depend on understanding what their bodies tell them, could. Tonight he knew not even a bar set so high could defeat him. He was ready, in both mind and body, for this test.

When the competition began, the powerful young Cuban was already the greatest high jumper of all time and held the world record. But on that muggy Saturday night in August of 1989, he became a legend. What he did on the final day of the Caribbean Zone Track and Field Championship in San Juan, Puerto Rico, was thought—even after man walked on the moon—to have been beyond human accomplishment. To the thousands who were actually in the Sexto Escobar Stadium that night, it was the greatest physical feat they had ever witnessed.

More than a decade has passed since that fateful night, and during all of

that time the eight-foot mark has been reached on only one other occasion—
and that was some four years later by Sotomyor himself. No other jumper has
ever cleared eight feet, or indeed even come close. Although a giant leap (the
greatest high jump of all time), clearing eight feet was for Sotomayor only a
slight improvement on his existing world record, which stood at just a half-
inch less than the magical barrier of eight feet. But adding that final half-inch
and breaking through that physical and psychological barrier was, in its way,
as important a symbol of man's seemingly limitless potential as was the
shattering of earlier barriers, both physical and technological, that also
limited man's reach.

Sotomayor's great leap was also symbolic of the extraordinary athletic
ability of the descendants of the black Africans who were snatched from the
rain forests of West Africa and dragged in chains and shackles to the sugar
and cotton plantations of the New World. Sotomayor comes from the same
racial stock as Charles Dumas, the black American, who thirty-three years
earlier had broken the seven-foot barrier. And, of course, both Sotomayor
and Dumas share a common genetic background with the great black athletes
of North America, the Caribbean, Latin America, West Africa, and Europe.
Barry Bonds and Tiger Woods of the United States, Sammy Sosa and Pedro
Martinez of the Dominican Republic, Hakeem Olajuwon of Nigeria, Patrick
Ewing and Lennox Lewis of Jamaica, and almost all of the other great black
athletes in the world—with the notable exception of the unmatchable
distance runners from other areas of Africa—are all united by a common
bond to West Africa.

While these great distance runners from other regions of Africa, as
explained earlier, share some athletically advantageous characteristics with
West Africans—longer arms and legs, narrower hips, and lower
subcutaneous fat—they appear, based on the result of a number of studies, to
be similar to whites and all other groups, except those of West African
descent, in muscle fiber distribution, that is in the ratio of fast-twitch to slow-
twitch muscle fibers. Although it is possible, perhaps even likely-because
most live and train in mountainous regions-that they have unusually high
levels of hemoglobin and therefore exceptionally effective oxygen-
transporting systems, their athletic advantage appears to be primarily
biomechanical: longer legs and narrower hips increase stride length and
efficiency, and lower body fat improves power-to-weight ratios. These
advantages could be particularly meaningful in distance running, which is
where the great African runners from places like Kenya, Ethiopia, South

Africa, and Morocco excel.

It is especially instructive that the most successful African distance runners are from high altitude regions of Ethiopia and Kenya. The great Olympic champion, Haile Gebrselassie was raised in the highland region of Arssi in Ethiopia, and a significant majority of Kenya's greatest runners come from a relatively small area in that country's Nandi Hills. In addition to a running tradition, the countries share a common border and closely related peoples. Centuries of selection, in the relatively thin air and rugged terrain of the highland regions of these countries, have produced peoples remarkably adapted for distance running; low bodyweights, because of both size and extremely low subcutaneous fat percentages, long arms and legs, high levels of hemoglobin, and powerful hearts and lungs.

But no other racial or ethnic group has ever produced individuals with the combination of anatomical and physiological characteristics required to match the feats of the great black athletes of West African descent. Nor, given the very special environmental conditions that created the unique abilities of West Africans, is it likely to ever happen again. Not even the intensive efforts of the state-supported systems of the former East Germany and the former Soviet Union were able to produce male athletes capable of competing successfully against the best black male athletes from around the world. Those systems, because they combined early detection and selection of potential champion athletes with financial support and intensive and often scientifically innovative training methods, were able to turn out white athletes who were usually able to defeat other white athletes from less comprehensive systems. But training, however intensive and scientific, proved repeatedly to be an inadequate substitution for the genetic endowment of the great black male athletes.

For many years a striking feature of international track and field competitions, including the Olympics, was the considerable disparity between the performances of male and female athletes from the Soviet Union, East Germany, and other Eastern European countries. Soviet and European men had very little success in the explosive events—such as the 100-, 200-, and 400-meter sprints, 110-meter hurdles, and long jump—when competing against black athletes from the U.S., West Africa, and the Caribbean. But before the collapse of the Soviet Union, the women were often successful not only against black track and field athletes but against all comers in just about all Olympic events, including swimming and gymnastics.

However, this advantage over black women in both explosive and distance events, some of it due to the illegal use of performance-enhancing drugs, has disappeared. Tougher enforcement action against illegal drug use, considerably tougher training regimens for black women in the United States, and the continuing entry of black women (from around the world) into organized athletics will ensure that the role of black women in athletics will continue to grow in the years ahead. But it is doubtful that black women, for reasons related to both biology and culture, will ever be quite as athletically dominant as black males. However, an increasing number of physically dominant female black athletes will likely emerge, as the runner Marion Jones and the tennis player Venus and Serena Williams have demonstrated in recent times.

Biologically, black women generally do not possess the same physical advantages over white women that black men have over their white counterparts. Black women, undoubtedly, share some black male advantages, such as in the ratio of fast-twitch to slow-twitch muscle fiber. Although, as far as I am aware, all comparative tests of black and white athletes have been limited to males, there is no reason to believe that there would be any differences between the genders in fiber type proportion. But the demands of childbirth in physically challenging environments frequently selected females with physical characteristics—wide hips and high body fat are examples—that are not always suitable for intense athletic competition. This was particularly true in areas of high infant death rates, as the rain forests of West Africa undoubtedly were before the advent of modern medicine.

So while black men enjoy both anatomical (biomechanical) and physiological (biochemical) advantages over white males, black female advantage is probably, frequently, limited to the biochemical, such as the percentage of fast-twitch muscle fiber. Biomechanical factors such as hip width (which influences stride length and efficiency) and body fat percentage (which influences power-to-weight ratios) are significant if minor contributors to black male advantage and are not advantages black women, generally, also enjoy.

Culturally, black women have long been handicapped athletically by the difficulties of hair grooming, as well as by expectations that they would spend far less time enjoying physical activities outside and far more time indoors contributing, disproportionately, to household chores. Even today, as a consequence of this legacy, young black girls compete in organized athletics at far lower percentages than their white counterparts or black or white males. But as the emergence of exceptional black female athletes in tennis, basketball, and track and field attests, these cultural barriers are being eroded by the expanding financial opportunities now available to female athletes.

They are only a tiny percentage of the world's population. But, athletes of West African origin—whose ancestors evolved in the harshest environment on earth, survived the unspeakable horrors of the passage across the Atlantic, and multiplied—are now a clear majority of the greatest athletes in the world. Despite the brutality of slavery and the exposure to new diseases that had decimated the native populations of the New World, these hardy people, the sinews of the Industrial Revolution, overcame the cotton and sugarcane fields and conquered the playing fields. As the earlier lists of athletes indicate, black athletes of West African descent have been enormously successful in athletic activities like basketball, boxing, track and field, baseball, football, soccer, and cricket. Indeed, it is not an exaggeration to claim that black males have dominated and transformed every athletic activity they have entered in significant numbers. In recent years, the performances of the golfer, Tiger Woods, as well as those of the tennis players, the Williams sisters, are proving that black athletes of both genders can also significantly affect the playing style and training regimens of established sporting activities, even without entering them in significant numbers.

Then there is Barry Bonds, the magnificent outfielder of the San Francisco Giants, whose last four or five seasons have probably cemented his place as the greatest baseball player of all time. Mike Scioscia, the manager of the Anaheim Angels, whose team defeated Bonds' San Francisco Giants 4-3 to win the 2002 World Series, paid this tribute to Bond just before the series began. "He's in a league of his own as a hitter. He's incredible. There isn't any way you can overrate Barry Bonds. The last two years are the best of anyone in the history of baseball. Nobody's had better years when you combine all the numbers he's had the past two years." Bonds did not disappoint. Despite compiling a postseason record of 27 walks, Bonds also established postseason records for home runs (8) and, in series of more than four games, for slugging percentage (1.294) and on-base percentage (.700). Although not a record, Bonds' .471 postseason batting average was also one of the highest all-time marks.

Despite being a mere 12 percent of the American population, African Americans dominate America's major professional team sports, including basketball, football, and baseball. Currently about 90 percent of the players in the NBA (basketball), 70 percent of those in the NFL (football), and about one-third of those in Major League Baseball are black. But even these numbers, as impressive as they are, do not accurately reflect the real physical superiority of black athletes of West African origin in athletic activities based on speed, power, and quickness. Consequently, particularly in baseball, even a larger percentage of the greatest players than their representation would suggest are black.

The most explosive leapers and dunkers and the players with the fastest first steps and the nimblest footwork in basketball are black. The fastest wide receivers, cornerbacks, and linebackers, the most elusive running backs, and the quickest defensive ends in football are black. The outfielders and shortstops with the greatest range, the base stealers with the greatest foot speeds, and the hitters with the greatest natural bat speeds in baseball are black.

Blacks dominate boxing in every weight division in which they are a significant presence. In track and field, their control of the sprints, high hurdles, and long jump is almost total. Astoundingly, the two hundred fastest times in the 100 meters—all under 10 seconds, a barrier no white, Asian or East African runner has ever broken in recognized competition—are all held by athletes of West African origin. As impressively, all 40 finalists in the 100 meters in the 1984, 1988, 1992, 1996, and 2000 were of West African origin. Obviously, the statistical likelihood of these things happening, based solely on population numbers, is just about zero.

Black athletes are not just quantitatively better, they are also stylistically different. This stylistic difference is not merely cultural; it accurately reflects the differences in physical skills between the races. Michael Jordan played in the air because he could; Larry Bird stayed on the ground because he had to. Black running backs are swift and elusive; white running backs are big and powerful. There are some big, powerful black running backs, but there are no swift, elusive white ones. It is not because white kids do not wish to grow up to be like Mike or Barry Sanders. It is simply because, to succeed at the highest levels of athletic competition, athletes have to maximize their strengths and minimize their weaknesses.

In the United States, black athletes have already changed the way baseball, basketball, and football are played. Their speed, quickness, and leaping ability have revolutionized all three major American team sports, and the revolution is far from over. Anybody who was fortunate enough to watch Ali, Pele, Carl Lewis, and the great cricket player Gary Sobers at the height of their powers knows that speed and lightning-quick reflexes were the very essence of these athletes' extraordinary abilities. Speed, quickness, and leaping ability—which is vertical speed—clearly separate black athletes of West African origin from all others, including other blacks from other parts of the African continent.

The lightning-quick reflexes and tremendous acceleration of the great black base-stealers, along with the extraordinary range of the very best black outfielders, shortstops, and second basemen, have made baseball far more athletically challenging and exciting. Black world-class athletes, such as defensive end Lawrence Taylor and Olympic sprint champion-turned-wide receiver Bob Hayes, similarly transformed the National Football League. Taylor established passrushing as a potent defensive weapon and heralded the era of the mobile quarterback. Hayes' blazing speed, which forced teams to invent zone coverages and to recruit a new and faster class of defenders to contain him, also ushered in the era of the super-fast wide receiver and the all but complete demise of white receivers and cornerbacks. Until the late 1950s, the National Basketball Association was slow, predictable, and horizontal. The foot speed, vertical speed, and unparalleled quickness of the great pioneering black basketball players such as Bill Russell and Elgin Baylor revolutionized rebounding and shot blocking, unleashed the fast break, and transformed the NBA into what it is today: a showcase for the greatest athletes from all over the world.

Now, this unique gift is in the process of further transforming professional football. It is also having a major impact on golf, which until the advent of Tiger Woods (the first great athlete to play golf professionally) was dominated by white men of mediocre physical abilities. In addition, this gift is making women's tennis almost unrecognizably different from the game played by earlier stars like Chris Evert.

In the first Sugar Bowl of the 21st century, a 19-year-old sophomore quarterback from Virginia Tech, Michael Vick, with one extraordinary performance, finally destroyed the old 20th century prototype of the perfect quarterback and created a brand new one molded in his own image. Showcasing his 4.25 speed in the 40-yard dash, his ability to throw the ball 65 yards flat-footed with one flick of his left wrist, and his superhuman ability to avoid mayhem-minded defenders with one deft move, the 6-1, 214-pound Vick routinely accomplished the impossible.

Banished since that electrifying night, according to *ESPN Magazine,* was the old vision of "a 6-5, 225-pound rock who stands tall in the pocket, shrugs off linebackers and can throw a football through a brick wall." Because of what Vick accomplished that night in January 2000, "the dream quarterback is now highly mobile, as dangerous running the ball as passing it... and unlike the option quarterbacks of old, these guys have strong arms and direct offenses in which they are just as likely to throw as to run." What the magazine elected not to mention was that in the old prototype the quarterback was almost always white, and in the new one he will be increasingly black.

The truth is, as we know, Vick (brilliant as he is) did not destroy the old prototype by himself. He had plenty of help, especially from an earlier new prototype: linebackers, such as Lawrence Taylor, with 4.5 or better speed. As *ESPN Magazine* explained, "what has brought mobile quarterbacks to the fore is their effectiveness as an antidote to the faster, bigger defenders now crowding the line of scrimmage." The magazine quoted a number of college offensive coordinators to support their contention. According to George Deleone of Syracuse: "There was a day when the linebacker who ran 4.5 was a freak, now he's commonplace. Defensive linemen are also much faster. The classic drop-back guy who's immobile is so vulnerable now to the speed of a defense that can really rush the passer."

To emphasize just how much faster today's linebackers and defensive linemen are than their predecessors, Keith Gilbertson of Washington compared the timing of a quarterback's release a decade ago to what must be done today. "You'd count off, thousand and one, thousand and two, thousand and three, buzzz. Now it's thousandandone, thousandandtwo, throw it. It has to be gone." Again, what *ESPN* elected not to mention was that the new, faster, bigger defenders are overwhelmingly black.

Bobby Bowden, the legendary Florida State coach, claimed that the new acceptance of the mobile quarterback was the final barrier to overcome as the old, negative stereotypes of black quarterbacks were destroyed. "We've allowed these young men to compete, and they've shown they can do it. The high school coaches accepted it, and they developed these kids to where they know what to with the football," said Bowden. Unsaid but clearly implied was a refutation of the old dogma that blacks lacked the necessities to master an offense, remain calm and cool under fire, and rally the troops in adversity. The white football establishment long believed—with the rest of white America—that only special white men possessed such qualities.

To emphasize just how much the thinking of white coaches has evolved on the subject of black intellectual capacity, another veteran coach, UNLV's John Robinson, frankly addressed the sensitive matter of the tendency of white coaches to move athletic black quarterbacks to other positions. "A Marcus Allen—referring to the 1981 Heisman Trophy-winning and all-pro tailback who played for him at USC—coming out of San Diego now might play quarterback, which Marcus was in high school. Back in the '70s and '80s, if [an athletic] quarterback wasn't an accurate passer coming out of high school, a coach would move him. Now coaches are hanging in there and working with a good athlete, improving his passing skills as they go along."

Speed and power are also rocking the once staid world of golf. An understanding is dawning that the basis of Tiger Woods' powerful swing and mighty drives is the speed of his club head. For years *Golf Digest* published detailed photographic sequences that graphically displayed and dissected the swings of the game's best players. Since 1973, according to *The New Yorker*, "the magazine's photographers have shot their swing sequences with a high-speed camera called a Hulcher, which was originally developed, at the request of a government agency, to take stop-action photographs of missiles."

A few months after winning the Masters in 1997, the then 21-year-old Woods was asked by *Golf Digest* to perform for the Hulcher. To the amazement of the magazine editors, when the prints came back from the lab, only five frames of the hundreds taken had captured Woods' swing at the moment his club head connected with the ball—a problem they had never previously encountered. Attempting to explain what happened, executive editor Roger Schiffman told *The New Yorker*, "With other tour players, we almost always get a picture of impact with every swing." But, as *The New Yorker* described, "When Woods makes his normal swing, the head of his driver moves at about a hundred and twenty miles an hour—a good fifteen miles an hour faster than the club head of a typical touring pro, and about thirty miles an hour faster than the club head of an average amateur."

In a telling demonstration of the changing times, Woods' dominance is being described by white reporters as a product not only of a superior physical ability, but also of a superior work ethic and extraordinary intelligence, mental toughness, and focus. A notable example was a cover piece in *The New Yorker*, by David Owen. Owen reported that, "Woods spends almost as much time studying golf's history as he does making it. When Tiger was still a toddler... the child was able to identify the swing flaws of adult players... While his grade school contemporaries drew pictures of racing cars and robots, Tiger sketched the trajectories of his irons. From the moment he climbed down from that high chair, he seems to have been phenomenally well equipped—temperamentally, emotionally, intellectually—to exploit the physical gift he was born with."

The article also describes Woods' amazing decision to conduct a major overhaul of his game shortly after winning the Masters and the Western Open in 1997. Despite winning the Masters by a record margin with a swing that he admitted, "was almost perfect," Woods spent more than a year taking it apart and putting it together again. Woods' dissatisfaction with his swing in 1997, Owen reported, seemed "to an outsider, almost reckless—especially since it concerned a problem that is beyond the ability of most golfers to conceive of as a problem." The process of correction included "hitting thousands and thousands of practice balls, enduring countless hours of tedious drills, and adding several brick-size slabs of muscle to what was already a virtually fat-free physique."

Woods' enormous talent and unrivaled intensity has changed, in Owen's words, "almost everything there is to change about golf... professional golfers all over the world have begun lifting heavier weights, eating healthier food, and going to bed earlier, in the hope of becoming good enough to be considered second-best." Only 26 years old, Woods, whom his father describes, as the first "naturally born and bred black professional golfer," is already being regarded as the greatest golfer of all time. But probably more importantly, his success is being seen—accurately—as a combination of talent, desire, and dedication.

During the past three years, Venus and Serena Williams, the two top-ranked women's tennis players in the world, have between them won all six of the world's most important tournaments—the 2000, 2001, and 2002

Wimbledon and U.S. Open Championships—a feat not only unrivalled in sporting history, but one without close competition. During that period, the sisters, still just 22 and 20 respectively, also won the French, Australian, and Wimbledon Championships as well as numerous other majors. It may be premature, since longevity is a factor, for either of them to be described as the greatest female tennis player of all time. But it is certainly not too early to say that, at their best, either of the Williams sisters would defeat any other woman, at her best, who has ever played the game.

Female tennis has never before witnessed anything like the tremendous court coverage, overwhelming all-round power, and shot-making ability from both sides of the court that the Williams sisters have brought to this once sedate game. With first serves frequently topping 110 miles per hour, both women not only serve far harder than any previous female player but also routinely serve harder than many of the top male players. While other female players have had powerful and effective forehands, the Williams sisters generate unparalleled power with both backhand and forehand strokes. And while female tennis has previously produced great female players with both great court coverage and power, the Williams' extraordinary athletic ability allows them to combine these qualities to a degree previously unknown.

The remarkable and unlikely triumph of the sisters is even more improbable because of its utter unorthodoxy. Raised in the tough South Central Los Angeles neighborhood of Compton, the girls learned to play on weed-infested public courts. They were coached by their father, who had taught himself the game by watching instructional videos and who enraged the tennis establishment by removing his daughters from the junior tennis circuit, or the "freak show" as he called it. Nevertheless, his "Cinderella of the Ghetto" (as he named Venus) would be ready by the time she was 14 years old to take on the very best players in the world. In her professional debut, she easily won her first match against a former NCAA singles champion; in her second match, she led the second-ranked player in the world, Arantxa Sanchez-Vicario, 6-2, 3-1, before running out of steam and losing.

An additional shock was coming for those in the tennis world who had hoped that Richard Williams would be, as L. Jon Wertheim writes in *Venus Envy*, "exposed as a fraud" and that the "the profiteering management groups, shoe companies, and tournament directors that had been hot on the Williamses' trail would walk away disappointed." Richard soon announced,

Wertheim reveals, as "good as Venus was, she wasn't even going to be the best player in the family. His younger daughter Serena had the build of an Olympic swimmer and she was every bit as athletic as Venus. Plus, he said gleefully, she was meaner. One day soon, Richard predicted, his daughters would rally the top ranking back and forth and play each other in Grand Slam finals. The tennis world laughed. This wasn't a tennis father from hell. This was a tennis father from outer space."

Despite their enormous success, Venus's and Serena's horizons, as Wertheim points out, "extend far beyond the baseline. Their priorities are God, Family, and Education. If tennis is fourth, it's a distant fourth." It is hard to believe, listening to the extremely articulate, well-spoken, and poised young women, that they are not products of the same privileged background from which most of their white counterparts spring. "To them," Wertheim explains, "there's nothing cooler than being smart. In addition to their coursework in fashion school, they are voracious readers, and they try, with varying degrees of success, to teach themselves foreign languages. They love learning new words. In her 2000 WTA Tour media guide entry, Serena—the defending U.S. Open champion—lists her most memorable achievement as 'receiving an 'A' in geometry'. Venus lists her passions as Russian history, French furniture, and Chinese culture. 'If I'm not enhancing myself,' says Venus, 'I feel like I'm wasting my time.'"

But all of this has not been enough to inoculate the sisters against the racist preconceptions of intellectual inferiority that have been the bane of almost every gifted black athlete. Wertheim reports an incident where a reporter asked Serena to respond to the criticism that despite their "great bodies," she and her sister weren't as "strategically aware" as other players. "It's an observation rooted," Wertheim commented, "in the most pernicious of racial stereotypes. Venus and Serena may not have Hingis's intuition—who does?—but they play every bit as creatively as most players. Rarely has Anna Kournikova, Jennifer Capriati, or even Monica Seles been asked to defend their strategic awareness. In a sense, the sisters' go-for-broke mentality *is* a conscious strategy. Were they simply playing on instinct, they would likely push the ball back to the middle of the court and avoid making errors. And somehow it went unnoted that, in addition to singles, both Venus and Serena played six rounds of doubles and practiced every day. You'd be hard put to find two players who spent more time working on their games during the tournament."

For many years, white journalists failed to appreciate that long years of hard work had developed and honed whatever natural physical gifts these athletes were born with; this signal failure was most responsible for the tendency of black athletes to deny their undeniable talents. Understandably, given America's sad racial history, "natural," when used to describe a black athlete's talent, had almost become, at least to African Americans, a sly substitute for unintelligent or lazy. But, as the coverage of Woods and others like Barry Bonds and wide receiver Jerry Rice indicates, white reporters are beginning to recognize and acknowledge that the success of the greatest black athletes is due to a unique combination of talent and character. At the highest levels of success, even the most extraordinary physical gifts must be complemented by intelligence, commitment, and perseverance.

There is a general realization, all over the world, that an extraordinarily disproportionate number of the greatest athletes in the world are black. In fact, the term *great athlete* has almost become synonymous with black male. Perhaps nothing illustrates this more eloquently than the most recent list of the top product endorsers in sports. For many years not only did white male athletes dominate this list, but it was virtually impossible for even the most accomplished black athletes to get on it: this has changed, dramatically. In 2002, Tiger Woods was named the top product endorser for the fourth consecutive year, according to Burns Sports and Celebrities, a company that matches athletes with advertisers. Four other black males—Michael Jordan (who himself headed the list for years), Kobe Bryant, Shaquille O'Neal, and Barry Bonds—were ranked among the top nine endorsers, with Jordan and Bryant placing second and third behind Woods. Two black females, Venus and Serena Williams, placed seventh and eighth, to give seven of the top nine places to black athletes.

Over the next decade or two, as the liberalization of American society increases, the number of blacks participating in golf, tennis, hockey, cycling, and even swimming will continue to increase and the current white dominance of these athletic activities will be severely tested. Contrary to the contention that poverty and lack of opportunity is the fulcrum of African American athletic achievement, discrimination has been a hindrance. African American athletes are not as dominant as they are because of discrimination, but despite it. The record clearly shows, as Part 2 will document, that in every athletic activity whites have only been dominant when blacks were excluded. There is not one example of white athletes even holding their own in open competition with blacks.

The athletic dominance of African Americans is now so pronounced, widespread, and obvious that it is difficult, especially for those who are unaware of fairly recent history, to believe that this was not always so. Yesterday, in historical time, African Americans (or Negroes as they were then called) were widely regarded as inferior to whites in both mind and body. The concept that physical superiority could somehow be a symptom of intellectual inferiority only developed when physical superiority became associated with African Americans. That association did not begin until about 1936, which is where we will begin our historical review of baseball, football, basketball, track and field, and boxing. These are the athletic activities that have long been at the center of American life and, not coincidentally, the focus of the energies and talents of African Americans. But first, let us examine, in some detail, the political and scientific foundations of the various arguments that have been proposed to both explain and explain away the undeniable disproportionate athletic success of African Americans.

2

The Great Debate:
Nature or Nurture?

When Otto Freiderich Van Der Grobben first saw the little canoes, he was three miles out at sea. As he recorded in his memoirs: "I had to marvel that the blacks dared to come so far out to sea in their little canoes, which are nothing more than a small piece of wood about eight foot long and two foot wide. In these they travel very fast, sitting back on their heels and with small paddles in their hands. When the sea becomes too high and overturns their canoe, as often happens, they are very skillful in tipping out the water and swinging themselves back into the canoe. Our skipper wanted to try paddling a canoe himself but scarcely had to climb in on one side when he was in the water on the other."

The speed, grace, and agility of the Africans on land also astonished the German sea captain, who was describing his visit to the West African country of Sierra Leone in 1692. "I also wanted to know how they danced for joy," he wrote. "They therefore asked me to have the shacoms play to them; and I gave orders for a Polish dance to be played. To this music the blacks capered so adroitly that no dancing master could have imitated them. Indeed, they observed the cadence as properly as the best Pole—a capacity, which seems inborn to all Moors, of whom I have seen thousands. They ran towards us with their assegais so quickly and pulled up so instantly that I could not help being astonished."

The German then asked the Africans to show him how they fought their enemies. "They ran swiftly away from me," he wrote, then "turned around in an instant, as if they wanted to stab me, and then jumped away over me. I drew a broadsword and shouted to one of them that he should run up to me as before. He was not willing to do this, but instead replied that when they see a gun in their enemies' hands, they throw an assegai at it from ten paces away. I picked up a musket and told him to throw. He refused, however, saying that I would not hit him anyway; and he jumped skillfully from side to side, like a chamois. When I had observed all this and watched with pleasure, we took our leave and sailed away."

This account in Von Der Grobben's memoirs, which was published privately in 1694, filled as it was with superlatives, must have been one of the very first of millions of glowing reviews black athletes would receive from appreciative white reporters.

A far more recent review but similar in its awe of black athletic talent, appeared in the *Houston Chronicle* in June 1991. The reporter, Jonathan Feigen, began the first article in a series previewing the NBA draft this way: "Kenny Anderson slammed the ball from one hand to the other, bouncing it in a blur between his legs. He quickly, blindingly, slammed it back again. And again. And again. How many times did his legs do that tap dance? How many times had he shifted the ball in that impossible sleight of hand? Four? Five? Six? Finally, Anderson mercifully cut left and around a paralyzed Bobby Hurley, frozen in amazement and helplessness, and glided to the basket for an effortless layup. I saw that on a replay, Anderson said. People asked me, how did you do that. I said, I didn't know I did. He couldn't possibly. Some natural forces within allowed him to do something that just can't be done, never mind created and ordered up like a pitcher choosing a curveball. It's all too natural, too special, to be taught or developed or understood."

Discussing the unfortunate player who was the unwitting victim of Anderson's legerdemain, Feigen wrote, "Hurley can run the plays. He can even win a championship, playing point guard, as a coach would teach it to his son. He could never do the impossible. Anderson's gifts are not his ample quickness or jumping ability or anything else that could be measured and recorded. It's deeper than that." Perhaps, not surprisingly, Kenny Anderson is black and Bobby Hurley is white. The writer, Jonathan Feigen, also not surprisingly, is white.

The debate on whether the disproportionate success of black athletes is culturally or biologically driven has long been shaped by two powerful and related fears: those of racial biology and "the dark history of eugenics." Most black intellectuals and some white sympathizers, for very good reasons, have adamantly opposed the concept that black physical ability is "inborn" and "too natural to be taught and developed or understood." Given America's regrettable racial history and the fact that for a long time the theories that purported to explain black athletic success were based on prescientific and clearly ridiculous racial biology, the objection of many black intellectuals to biological explanations of black athletic success is certainly understandable. But it is impossible to comprehend the current wide acceptance of environmental explanations for black athletic success in the general intellectual community without understanding what Grant Steen described as "the dark history of eugenics."

One of the major goals of the campaign to justify slavery was to convince the world, including the enslaved Africans themselves, that they were a people without history—a race so naturally inferior that they contributed virtually nothing to the civilization of the world. Perhaps the clearest and most definitive statement by an American politician of the racial ideology used by whites to justify the evil of slavery was delivered on the floor of the United States Senate in 1858 by Henry James Hammond of South Carolina. A successful planter and one of the largest slaveholders in the country, Hammond told his colleagues that "in all social systems there must be a class to do the menial duties, to perform the drudgery of life. That is a class requiring but a low order of intellect and but little skill. Its requisites are vigor, docility, fidelity. Such a class you must have... It constitutes the very mudsill of society. Fortunately for the South we have found a race adapted to that purpose... We do not think that whites should be slaves either by choice or necessity. Our slaves are black, of another, inferior race. The status in which we have placed them is an elevation. They are elevated from the condition in which God first created them by being made our slaves."

Hammond's statement was just one chapter of an intensive, systematic, and decades-long campaign waged on both sides of the Atlantic. Seeking to reconcile the irreconcilable, Christian slaveholders struggled mightily to create a moral basis for excluding black Africans from the human family. That task had been made more difficult by the formation of the United States and its embrace of the concepts of equal justice and divinely endowed inalienable rights and more urgent by the success of the abolitionist movement in Britain and the United States. Founded as a shining city on a hill, as a rebuke to the aristocratic and corrupt governments of Europe, the fledgling nation had faced in slavery the first great test of its moral authority.

Abolitionists were having considerable success exposing the inescapable contradiction between slavery and the religious and ethical teachings at the very base of the country's moral foundations. Genuinely frightened by this, the defenders of slavery concluded that their position could only be justified if they could clearly demonstrate that God, in an unalterable act of nature, had made Africans inferior.

The formal development of this ideology was prompted by the discussion of emancipation in the Virginia Legislature, in the winter of 1831-32, after Nat Turner's uprising took the lives of more than sixty white citizens. The intensification of the American abolitionist movement after 1831 drove Southern leaders to summon the region's finest minds to defend slavery by methodically enumerating all possible reasons for human bondage. Southern intellectuals responded enthusiastically to this clarion call, and one result was the development of a Southern publishing industry focused primarily on the defense of their "peculiar institution." Pro-slavery writers who had earlier attracted very little attention were now acclaimed. George Frederick Holmes, a pro-slavery essayist, openly acknowledged his and his fellow writers' indebtedness to the controversy for the creation of a genuine Southern literature: "For out of this slavery agitation has sprung not merely essays on slavery, valuable and suggestive as these have been, but also the literary activity, and the literary movement which have lately characterized the intellect of the South."

Initially, much of the defense of slavery was based on Scripture. But, in the eloquent words of the writer and scholar Drew Gilpin Faust: "For an age increasingly enamored of the vocabulary and methods of natural science, biblical guidance was not enough. The accepted foundations for truth were changing in European and American thought, as intellectuals sought to apply the rigor of science to the study of society and morality, as well as the natural world." The result of this growing dependence on science was the development of a new ideological position, one that sought to establish its moral authority by creating a scientific rationale for slavery and postbellum racial oppression.

Even in the United States there had been very little effort, prior to 1830, to justify slavery on the basis of race or to argue, as Hammond did some three decades later, that black labor and unskilled labor were synonymous. In fact, it was only the failure to procure sufficient numbers of Indian or European laborers that prompted planters to turn to Africa for an alternative source. And it is clear that Africans brought to the New World considerable skills in tropical cultivation, cattle breeding, mining and smelting.

The quality and extent of African contributions to their new homes were dictated not by their abilities but by the requirements of their environments and the range of opportunities they were permitted to explore. In Brazil, Africans subdued the land, raised cattle, mined and smelted gold and other metals and founded towns and whole provinces. One of the most famous and important of the early Brazilian settlers was an African woman, Jacintha de Siqueira, who was the founding mother of Minas Gerais, the richest of all the Brazilian provinces. This remarkable woman, who is credited with the discovery of gold in the Quatro Vivens ravine and the founding of the settlement of Villa Novo de Principe in 1714 was, like so many other Africans in Brazil in the seventeenth and eighteenth centuries, one of the legendary bandierantes who fled slave plantation and helped to open up the wild, mineral-rich interior of the country. Like pioneers on other frontiers in other countries, these bold black men and women, once free of the tyranny of slavery, would forge frontier societies out of the wilderness and create their own laws.

In the Villa Nova de Principe they applied the skills and knowledge of cattle breeding developed on the African savannahs, and their old skills in mining for metal and in smelting ore and forging tools. Like pioneers everywhere, these Africans sought to build a life for themselves and their forebears, and to search for the gold, silver, diamonds and minerals that reputedly lay beneath the fabulous but completely unexplored sertao. Some were fortunate and enterprising enough to build their camps into towns, some of which became the cities of modern Brazil. And they married and took mistresses and produced children, of all shades, some of whom helped to create the Brazil we know today.

In North America opportunities were far more limited, particularly in the later years after the United States had evolved from a society with slaves to a slave society. However, despite tremendous limitations, African slaves made considerable contributions to the development of American agriculture.

African slaves were primarily responsible for rice becoming a major agricultural crop in South Carolina. Africans had grown rice along the entire West African coast for centuries and had extensive knowledge of the planting, cultivation and processing of the crop. In *Black Majority*, Peter H. Wood, relying exclusively on records, newspapers, church reports and letters and ledgers of colonial Carolinians, demonstrated that the early European planters prized the African's technological knowledge of rice production, something almost unknown to Englishmen. Woods also pointed out that while the early white settlers in South Carolina "felt uneasy about open grazing at first, numerous black newcomers understood this practice. People from along the Gambia River, a location for which South Carolina slave dealers came to hold a steady preference, were expert horsemen and herders." But new times and circumstances demanded a new approach, and the result of this new dependence on science was the rise of polygeny, which Europeans described as the "American School of Anthropology."

Polygeny claimed that human races were separate biological species, the descendants of different Adams. The claim was not a novel one. Several decades earlier, in 1799, the English physician and surgeon Charles White had decided, based on laughingly biased anatomical and physiological evidence, that blacks were a completely separate species, intermediate between apes and whites. White "concluded" that the feet, fingers, toes, "gibbous" legs, hair, cheekbones, chin, arms, the size of their skull and sex organs, and even their body odor placed blacks closer than Europeans to "brute creation." In a farcical display of hubris, White declared that his own racial group—the white European—was "the one most removed from brute creation...the most beautiful of the human race... the most superior... in intellectual powers."

White's "study" was part of a wider attempt by European scientists—as Europeans increasingly came into contact with darker-skinned people from newly discovered lands—to create a hierarchical ordering within humankind. The concept of vertical ordering, of a great chain of being allocating every form of life to its appropriate rank, was rooted in the Aristotelian notion that inequality was the foundation of the natural order. Alexander Pope's *Essay on Man*, which had famously declared that "Order is heaven's first law, and this confess, / Some are, and must be, greater than the rest," had given literary expression to the idea.

Despite his unquestioned influence, White was not the founding father of scientific racism. That distinction belongs to Thomas Malthus, the first professor of political economy in British university history. Ironically, unlike White and the Americans he inspired, Malthus' focus was not race but class. He bitterly opposed all governmental intervention to improve the lives of the poor—from sanitary reform to housing assistance—as immoral, unpatriotic, and an assault on the laws of God and Nature. In his famous book *Essay on the Principle of Population*, the coldly logical Malthus wrote, "The infant is, comparatively speaking, of little value to society, as others will immediately supply its place." And also: "All children born, beyond what would be required to keep up the population to this level, must necessarily perish, unless room be made for them by the death of grown persons."

With diabolical logic, Malthus concluded: "We should facilitate, instead of foolishly and vainly endeavoring to impede, the operations of nature in producing this mortality; and if we dread the too frequent visitation of the horrid form of famine, we should sedulously encourage the other forms of destruction, which we compel nature to use. Instead of recommending cleanliness to the poor, we should encourage contrary habits. In our towns we should make the streets narrower, crowd more people into the houses, and court the return of the plague. In the country we should build our villages near stagnant pools, and particularly encourage settlements in all marshy and unwholesome situations."

For the infants taking the place of the "grown persons" so removed, Malthus envisioned the bleakest existence. Poverty, he believed, was a social good because it was what he described as the "necessary stimulus to industry." Poverty guaranteed cheap child and adult labor to the homes and fields of the landed gentry, and to the shops, factories and mines of the new class of merchants and entrepreneurs created by the Industrial Revolution. To Malthus, and those for whom he spoke, the mere possession of white skin meant nothing. The poor, of all colors, were a race apart, "a definite race of chronic pauper stocks." Their woes—poverty, disease, illiteracy—were seen as hereditary endowments, scientifically ordained by nature, neither preventable nor reversible.

Despite the European roots of polygeny, it was Americans, who, as the biologist Stephen Gould has observed, "developed the data cited in its support and based a large body of research on its tenets." One of its leading spokespersons was a Swiss naturalist, Louis Agassiz, who migrated to the United States in the 1840s and was appointed a professor of zoology at

Harvard University. Agassiz argued that the Genesis story of Adam and Eve applied only to Caucasians because the bible did not address areas of the world unknown to the ancients. Ignoring his own academic discipline, Agassiz based his support of polygeny on a version of history which claimed, as he explained, that "there had never been a regulated society of black men developed" on the continent of Africa. "Does this not indicate in this race," he wrote, "a peculiar apathy, a peculiar indifference to the advantages afforded by civilized society."

But while Agassiz preferred to rely on abstract reasoning and soft evidence, scores of eager physicians were able and willing to find hard evidence of natural inferiority in the anatomy and physiology of African Americans. One such person was John H. van Evrie, who published a lengthy analysis after a detailed examination of the body parts of a number of slaves. To support his thesis that Negroes were an inferior race, van Evrie compiled a long list of what he regarded as their physical and intellectual shortcomings. Since emotions such as the "blush of modesty" and the "bloodless white" of grief could not be physically expressed on dark skin, he charged that the emotions did not exist in blacks. Blacks, he insisted, lacked both the brain and the vocal organism essential to music. Their hands, he concluded, were too coarse and blunt to function in areas such as the art or surgery.

This poorly developed sense of touch was apparently limited to the fingers, because he found an oversensitive tactile sense in the rest of the body, which is what, he judged, had caused a 50-year-old slave to howl like a schoolboy from a few lashes with an ordinary switch. In contrast to this oversensitivity of the skin, blacks, he noted, bore "hanging very well" because of "the obtuse sensibility of the brain and nervous system." And, in a closing warning to those who advocated the education of blacks, van Evrie predicted that the broader forehead that education produces would disturb the delicate harmony between their bodies and their "narrow and longitudinal heads" and render them "utterly incapable of locomotion or of an upright position at all."

While van Evrie wrote to influence lay opinion, particularly in the North, a number of Southern doctors targeted their peers. One of the most notable was Samuel Cartwright, the chairman of a committee appointed by the Medical Association of Louisiana to report on the "diseases and physical peculiarities of the Negro race." Although his conclusions were similar to van Evrie's, Cartwright's report, which was published in a southern medical journal, was somewhat more technically sophisticated and detailed. Black intellectual inferiority was caused, Cartwright explained, by their smaller brains and larger nerves. The sad result of this unfortunate combination was that any little intellectual power they had was diffused into "nervous" energy, appealing only to the senses.

But that was not all: an insufficient supply of red blood, caused by "defective atmospherization," allowed all the dark humors and bile in blacks to "predominate." Cartwright concluded that this lethal combination of insufficient red blood, a smaller brain, and excess nervous matter was the "true cause" of the "debasement of mind" that was, he believed, a defining characteristic of black Africans. Because of his greater experience with blacks and the abundant evidence all over the South to the contrary, Cartwright disagreed with van Evrie that African Americans were incapable of producing music. But it was not, he qualified, the kind that involved "understanding." It was merely music with "melody, but no harmony, mere sounds, without sense or meaning."

Nevertheless, despite these daunting inadequacies, the kindly physician held out hope that the condition of these wretched people could be improved. "Under the compulsive power of the white man, [blacks] are made to labor or exercise, which makes the lungs perform the duty of vitalizing the blood more perfectly than is done when they are left free to indulge in idleness. It is the red, vital blood, sent to the brain, that liberates their mind when under the white man's control; and it is the want of a sufficiency of red, vital blood, that chains their mind to ignorance and barbarism, when in freedom." Slavery, Cartwright concluded, improved blacks "in body, mind and morals."

Since the benefits of slavery to blacks were so clear and obvious to him, Cartwright found it difficult to believe that any sane slave would willingly flee his master's tender care. The inexplicable desire of slaves to seek freedom could therefore only be explained, he wrote, by mental disease. He labeled this malady "drapetomania." But, once again, the irrepressibly optimistic doctor proclaimed that all was not lost. "With the advantages of proper medical advice, strictly followed," he wrote, this malady could be almost entirely prevented. Blacks should be treated just like children. They should be shown "care, kindness... and humanity" if they were appropriately submissive. But should they dare to "raise their heads to a level with their master," it would be necessary to "whip... the devil out of them," until they returned to "that submissive state which it was intended for them to occupy."

It was not only obscure Southern medical journals that published racial propaganda disguised as scientific inquiry. One of the most prestigious medical publications in the country, the *Boston Medical and Surgical Journal*, which would become the *New England Journal of Medicine*, lent its prestige to the astonishing claim that slavery lowered the rate of mental illness in blacks. The claim was made by Edward Jarvis, a specialist in mental disorders, who would eventually become the president of the American Statistical Association. After allegedly analyzing the data on the incidence of insanity in the federal census of 1840, Jarvis found that, among blacks, the proportion of lunatics in the free states was ten times greater than in the slave states, although there was no geographic difference among whites. In the South, blacks were far less likely to suffer from insanity than the whites of that region, but in the North, they were six times more likely to suffer from insanity than their white counterparts. The obvious conclusion, the exquisitely rational Jarvis decided, was that "slavery has a wonderful influence upon the development of moral faculties and the intellectual powers."

For those misguided enough to believe that mental activity helped to develop mental power, Jarvis explained that by keeping the mental powers of blacks "comparatively dormant," their minds had been saved from "misdirection or overaction." Refusing them "many of the hopes and responsibilities which the free, self-thinking and self-acting enjoy and sustain" saves them "from some of the liabilities and dangers of active self-direction." It was clear, he concluded, that, among blacks, "in the highest state of mental activity there is the greatest danger of mental derangement; where there is the greatest mental torpor, we find the least insanity."

Two months later, writing in the same journal, a chastened and embarrassed Jarvis completely disavowed the statistics on insanity among free blacks. On reflection, he had become suspicious, he claimed, about the "extraordinary and unaccountable proportion" of insane blacks in the north, particularly in the New England states. After checking the original reports, Jarvis discovered that in many northern New England municipalities the number of blacks reported as insane exceeded the total number of black residents. As an example, in seven Maine towns without a single listed black resident, twenty-six blacks had been reported as insane. Similar inaccuracies were discovered throughout the northern states. Jarvis professed disappointment and mortification, and said that he hoped the original documents would be reviewed and corrected in Washington. Not only were the errors not corrected, but for years they were used by the defenders of slavery to conjure up hordes of insane black savages, converted, as an inevitable consequence of abolition, from faithful servants to rampaging killers.

Despite all the evidence compiled by the polygenists purporting to prove that black Africans were not just inferior but a completely different species, many religious Southerners found the claim unacceptable. Not only did it appear to contradict the biblical version of creation, but also it clearly did not meet a customary scientific criterion for distinguishing between two species: the inability to crossbreed or the infertility of their offspring. Southern fundamentalists of the mid-nineteenth century were not the first believers to reject polygenesis. The doctrine, which had been developed in the mid-seventeenth century by Isaac de La Peyrere as a theological attempt to explain the presence of man in the New World, had also been firmly rejected by the Catholic Church.

At the time, and through the eighteenth century, monogenesis—the view that all types of man originated from a single source—was the dominant theory in both natural history and theology. Theologically, monogenesis meant that all mankind had descended from Adam and Eve: Scientifically, that man descended from one pair, or a single mold or prototype. By this account, the different types of man were the result of complex interactions between peoples and their environments. But since all developed from a single source, the different types were regarded as varieties, with a degree of fluidity between the varieties. To distinguish their position that the different types of man came from distinct and separate biological origins, polygenists described the different types as different species of man.

It is easy, but it would also be incorrect, especially from a twenty-first century perspective, to overstate the differences in these two positions. Monogenists of the period certainly did not subscribe to the view that color is only skin-deep. Generally, they emphasized the differences between the varieties. Although originally created by differences in environmental influences and separate histories, they believed these varieties had become fixed and were perpetuated by hereditary. As an example, Buffon, a major proponent of monogenesis, fully accepted the concept of a hierarchy among the varieties and regarded the nonwhite races as degenerations of the most fully developed type—the white European. Monogenesis did however hold out the hope, however slim, that mankind could once again become one, that what had been caused by the environment could be altered by a change of environment.

Polygenesis offered no such hope. The different species of men were regarded as permanently different because of differences in their constitutions from the very beginning. And no amount of environmental change could alter that.

Beginning sometime just before the commencement of the third decade of the nineteenth century, monogenesis ceded its once dominant position in natural history to polygenesis. Charles White, as noted earlier, deeply influenced the newly ascendant doctrine, but perhaps no single figure was more responsible for the triumph of polygenesis than the third president of the United States, Thomas Jefferson. Although the author of the Declaration of Independence never overtly proclaimed his allegiance to any side of the debate, he was interpreted by White and other polygenesis theorists as favoring their side of the argument. While there is some disagreement with this version of Jefferson's views on race, there is no doubt, as the eminent historian John Hope Franklin has noted, that Jefferson had "pronounced views on the inferiority of blacks."

Jefferson also had enormous pride in his Anglo-Saxon heritage. The author of the Declaration of Independence, whose views on individual liberty seemed to have been inspired by Anglo-Saxon myths, was so proud of this heritage he wrote a simplified grammar to make the language more accessible and included the subject in the curriculum of the University of Virginia. The notion that Anglo-Saxons had a special affection for liberty was first advanced by Richard Verstegan in his book, *Restoration of Decayed Intelligence*, published in England in 1605. According to Verstegan, Englishmen descended from Germans who settled in England from A.D. 449, and that by tradition the authority of their kings was limited. That version of history was advanced, as Michael Banton explained in, *Racial Theories*, "to challenge the ambitions of the Stuart monarchs who wanted to weaken the power of parliament and to rule by divine right." In the world according to Verstegan, the conquest by the Normans in 1066 had interrupted centuries of golden rule by Anglo-Saxon monarchs. In this way an ancestral myth, that the chief English virtues were derived from their Anglo-Saxon forbears, was created. Sir Walter Scott then effectively propagated the myth in his massive best-seller, *Ivanhoe*, which introduced the Anglo-Saxon hero, Robin Hood— the champion of the Anglo-Saxon peasants in their struggle against their oppressive Norman rulers— to the world.

Because of his great eminence, Jefferson's views on Negroes were probably more avidly sought and more widely read than any other until the middle of the nineteenth century. Jefferson's real views on the nature of man were seen to be more honestly expressed in the *Notes of the State of Virginia* than in the Declaration of Independence. In the *Notes* Jefferson had professed himself an agnostic on the question of the origin of alleged black inferiority. "I advance it therefore as a suspicion only, that the blacks, whether originally a distinct race, or made distinct by time and circumstances, are inferior to the whites in the endowments both of body and mind. It is not against experience to suppose, that different species of the same genus, or varieties of the same species, may possess different qualifications."

But his open embrace of the concept of a racial hierarchy, and his support of the probability of separate and distinct origins for mankind, was used by White and other polygenists to support their position. Jefferson's views were particularly influential because they were thought to be based on direct and extensive observation. Jefferson had proclaimed his fidelity to the new scientific approach of empirical observation in the *Notes*: "A patient pursuit of facts, and cautious combination and comparison of them, is the drudgery to which man is subjected by his Maker, if he wishes to attain sure knowledge." Jefferson was also seen as giving support to polygenesis by an exhortation, near the end of the passage on racial hierarchy, which seemed to signal discontent with the prevailing orthodoxy of monogenesis: "To our reproach it must be said, that though for a century we have had under our eyes the races of black and red men, they have never yet been viewed by us as subjects of natural history."

For American opinion leaders of all political persuasions, slavery was an agonizing moral conundrum. If the nation was to survive with its self-esteem intact, the enshrinement of legal slavery in a nation, which had formally declared that "All men are created equal," had to be explained and justified. Despotic and decadent Europe had few moral pretensions to protect. The Spanish and the Portuguese could, without disturbing their consciences, accept both slavery and the full humanity of their slaves. To them, Roman law, which regarded slavery as an accidental state and not a fate that befell men because of inferiority, was still in effect. In England, from the very beginning, the legal attitude was ambivalent. As early as 1771, Lord Mansfield described slavery as "so odious, that nothing can be suffered to support it, but positive law." And as the abolitionist movement there proved, unlike in the United States, many influential men and women were adamantly opposed to both the slave trade and slavery itself.

In the Islamic states of North Africa and the Near East, slavery never became a social problem because it was multiracial and unapologetic. Since the enslavement of non-believers was considered just, no ideology of racial inferiority was developed to justify it. As a result, blacks never formed a separate ethnic group, and they assimilated into the indigenous population without difficulty after converting to Islam. Among the faithful, racial distinction is contrary to the letter and spirit of the Koran. Frequent marriage with mawali women, as the non-Arabs who embraced Islam were called, helped to hasten the pace of assimilation. Consequently, as Peter Mansfield pointed out in *A History of the Middle East*, "in the process the term Arab began to gradually change from the name of a Bedouin nomad of the Arabian Peninsula to its present meaning of anyone whose culture and language are Arabic."

But the idealistic Americans were incapable of either the Old World sophistication of the Europeans or the religious fraternalism of the Moslems. To maintain the high regard in which they held themselves, the virtuous Americans invented a racial ideology unique in its spite, malevolence, hypocrisy, longevity, and power. In the violent, bloody history of mankind genocide and attempted genocide have, unhappily, been far too common. Even in the twentieth century the elected and popular leader of a mighty and civilized democracy almost succeeded in his insane plan to destroy the Jewish people. But historicide—the planned, deliberate destruction and obliteration of a people's history, identity, and self-worth—committed to cover-up the blasphemous evils of slavery and segregation, is a crime without parallel in history. Slavery was a monstrous crime but as is so often the case the cover-up substantially exceeded the original offense in its destructiveness.

The data to support polygenesis were supplied by a peculiar, pseudo-scientific theory called craniometry. Craniometry was an attempt to rank the races by establishing, supposedly objectively, the physical characteristics of their brains, especially their size. The aforementioned Charles White, a pioneer of phrenology, had attempted to use anatomical features, particularly the cranium, to make a connection between cranium size and intelligence. In his book, *An Account of the Regular Gradation in Man*, White argued that the craniums of whites were larger and that this alleged greater size was proof that their brains and mental capacities were greater.

The crusade of the British physician to rank the races by measuring the size of their skulls would attract a host of American disciples and create one of the most influential scientific disciplines in the United States during the middle and the latter half of the nineteenth century. One measure of craniometry's esteem was the respect accorded its leading theoretician, Samuel George Morton, a Philadelphia physician with two medical degrees who had amassed more than a thousand human skulls before his death in 1851. Lamenting his passing and praising his life, *The New York Tribune* observed that "probably no scientific man in America enjoyed a higher reputation among scholars throughout the world, than Dr Morton."

Morton, like White, passionately believed that the races were separate species. The standard test of that theory was whether human races could interbreed naturally. Morton not only accepted the theory by repeating baseless reports that some human groups—particularly Caucasians and Australian Aborigines—rarely produced fertile offspring, he also rejected it by claiming that "hybridization was common in nature, even between species belonging to different genre." No fool, Morton was not about to allow the abundant proof, in the United States and elsewhere, of healthy and fertile mulattos and other racial mixtures, to dispose of the theory.

Given his strongly held views, it is not surprising that Morton's efforts to rank the races by the average size of their brains produced the results he expected. Not only did he find that whites had the largest brains and blacks had the smallest, but he found that among whites, Teutons and Anglo-Saxons came first, Jews next, and Hindus last. In recent years, noted biologist and author Stephen Gould spent several weeks re-analyzing Morton's data. At the completion of his study, Gould concluded that Morton's summaries were no more than "a patchwork of fudging and finagling," clearly designed to support prior convictions. While perhaps too generously exonerating Morton of conscious fraud, Gould accused him of honest self-delusion inspired by "prior prejudice."

Gould's painstaking examination of Morton's data exposed just how thoroughly the doctor's prejudices had influenced his conclusions about the cranial capacity of the races. Sizes of brains, Gould pointed out in his book *The Mismeasure of Man*, "are related to the sizes of bodies that carry them: big people tend to have larger brains than small people. This fact does not imply that big people are smarter—any more than elephants should be judged more intelligent than humans because their brains are larger. Appropriate corrections must be made for differences in body size. Men tend to be larger than women; consequently their brains are bigger. When corrections for body size are applied, men and women have brains of approximately equal size."

Again and again, in order to get the "facts" to support his prior prejudices, Morton failed to separate his skulls by either sex or stature—although his tables recorded these data—because, as Gould explained, "he wanted so much to read differences in brain size directly as differences in intelligence." Conclusions matching his prior prejudice could be reached by simply including a greater percentage of females in a particular sample (as he did with blacks), or not correcting for differences in body size (as he did with Incas). Although he completed his analysis of Morton's data by concluding that he detected "no sign of fraud or conscious manipulation," Gould also noted: "All miscalculations and omissions I have detected are in Morton's favor. Morton used an all-female sample of three Hottentots to support the stupidity of blacks, an all-male sample of Englishmen to assert the superiority of whites." But the state of pre-Darwinian science and the eagerness to find scientific support for slavery was such, Gould concluded, that "Morton was widely hailed as the objectivist of his age, the man who would rescue American science from the mire of unsupported speculation."

Before 1831 only a handful of pro-slavery writers claimed that blacks were inferior. To the contrary, most of them pointedly rejected such views, except to contend that only blacks could work in extreme heat. That contention highlights the real reason for black slavery in the New World. It was inspired neither by racial hatred nor by a desire to save black souls, but by a more common human emotion: greed. Slavery, as Eric Williams contended, has been too narrowly identified with black Africans. It was, as he insisted, "an economic institution of the first importance." Slavery was the basis of the Greek economy, and it helped to create the Roman Empire. When Europeans first landed on the western coast of Africa, the great city-states of medieval Italy were still trading Christian slaves despite the best efforts of the Vatican to restrict the trade to infidels and Jews.

Throughout the thirteenth century, despite Vatican disapproval, European slaves had been carried in European ships to the Sultanate of Egypt. The excesses were so great that Pope Clement V excommunicated the Genoese merchants of Caffa in a vain attempt to halt the buying and selling of Christians. In modern times slavery, as a base for modern capitalism, provided sugar for the tea and coffee cups of the Western world as well as cotton. It created the American South and the Caribbean islands. Seen in historical perspective, Williams argued, "it forms a part of that general picture of the harsh treatment of the underprivileged classes, the unsympathetic poor laws and severe feudal laws, and the indifference with which the rising capitalist class was beginning to reckon prosperity in terms of pound sterling, and becoming used to the idea of sacrificing human life to the deity of increased production."

In the beginning, unfree labor in the New World was colorblind and nondiscriminating—brown, white, black, and yellow, Catholic, Protestant, and pagan. In fact, it was the native Indians, not blacks, who were first enslaved in the New World. But the new conditions were too much for them; they died rapidly and in large numbers from excessive labor, poor diet, and, mostly, diseases brought from Europe and Africa. Indian slavery was so inefficient that the Spaniards considered that one Negro was worth four Indians. Williams quoted a prominent official in Hispaniola who, in 1518, insisted that "permission be given to bring Negroes, a race robust for labor, instead of natives so weak that they can only be employed in tasks requiring little endurance, such as taking care of maize fields or farms." The disparity in strength and endurance was reflected in the prices paid for Indian slaves, which were considerably lower than those paid for black ones.

But it was poor whites, not blacks, who initially replaced the Indians. Some were indentured servants who had signed a contract agreeing to serve for a stipulated time in return for their passage. Others were "redemptioners" who arranged with the ship's captain to pay for their passage on arrival or within a specified time of arrival; if they failed to pay they were sold to the highest bidder. Still others were convicts sent by the government to serve their sentences in the colonies. Many of these distressed souls were manorial tenants fleeing the restrictions of feudalism, Irishmen desperately trying to escape the oppression of landlords and bishops alike, and Germans fleeing the devastation of the Thirty Years War.

The harsh feudal laws of England, which recognized 300 capital crimes, also provided a steady source of white labor. Hanging was prescribed for offenses like "picking a pocket of more than a shilling; shoplifting to the value of five shillings; stealing a horse or a sheep; poaching rabbits on a gentleman's estate." Transportation to the colonies was the punishment for stealing cloth, burning stacks of corn, maiming and killing of cattle, hindering customs officers in the execution of their duty, corrupt legal practices, stealing a silver spoon, stealing a gold watch, and even trade union activity.

This "dumping upon the New World of the outcasts of the Old," as Benjamin Franklin described this traffic, ended when doubts about the course of internal development in Britain caused a complete reversal of mercantilist thought on the question of emigration. The fear of overpopulation, which was an essential feature of mercantilist thought at the beginning of the seventeenth century, was replaced by a fear of under population by the middle of the same century. Mercantilist policy shifted from accumulating precious metals to promoting industrial development, expanding employment and encouraging exports. The most effective way of making the country's goods competitive, mercantilists argued, was to lower costs by lowering wages. Allowing the population to increase was the best way of lowering wages.

The change in mercantilist philosophy was not the only reason for the increase in the Negro slave trade. While white servants were often treated as brutally as black slaves, their loss of liberty was for a limited period and their status could not be passed on to their children. Servants had rights, however limited, which were recognized by law and written into contracts. White servants enjoyed the right to property and could aspire, at the completion of their services, to a plot of land. Black children took the status of their mothers. Since the law regarded them not as persons, but as mere property, their masters had absolute control over their persons and liberty at all times.

White servants often exercised these rights in court and merchants frequently found themselves engaged in costly legal battles with people who, after accepting clothes and food in exchange for a promise to emigrate, sued for unlawful detention. Escape from the plantation was also easy for white servants who could easily blend into the general population. The supply of white labor, it was gradually realized, was both insufficient and expensive. The money that could procure a white man's service for ten years could buy a Negro for life. "Here then," Williams wrote, "is the origin of Negro slavery: the reason was economic, not racial; it had to do not with the color of the laborer, but the cheapness of the labor... The features of the man, his hair, color and dentifrice, his subhuman characteristics so widely pleaded, were only the later rationalizations to justify a simple economic fact: that the colonies needed labor and resorted to Negro labor because it was cheapest and best."

But such brutal honesty was, as we have seen, well beyond the capacity of white, Christian slaveholders and their numerous apologists. Highly preferable was a disinformation campaign that was to be as successful as it was scurrilous. The very humanity of Africans would be challenged in a campaign that, long before Hitler and Goebbels, demonstrated the power of the big lie. The more outrageous the assertion, the more likely it will, at least in part, be accepted. The propaganda campaign was so stunningly successful that the mythology of natural black inferiority is deeply ingrained, even today, in the psyche of the entire world. The lingering echoes of this campaign, the inevitable suppression of black intellectual ambition and achievement (which was the most brutal and enduring legacy of slavery), and the long decades of segregation and discrimination that followed have combined to seemingly validate the original propaganda of black intellectual inferiority.

Even the most recent non-black immigrants to America, regardless of country of origin and previous views on the subject of race, quickly adopt the prevailing national scorn of black intellectual capability. Even dark-skinned immigrants, especially those from ancient and intact cultures with strong family structures, arriving in an America newly cleansed and transformed by the civil rights struggles of black Americans, obliviously enjoy the fruits of that victory while disdaining the warriors who fought and won that long and bitter war.

Perhaps nobody better typifies this type of new American than the young conservative writer and commentator Dinesh D'Souza, who has been harshly critical of the "failure" of African Americans. In his book, *The End of Racism*, D'Souza, who is from India, airily proclaims that racism is no longer a problem in America and lectures that a "dysfunctional" group culture is the real source of African American problems. Although D'Souza does not, at least openly, attribute black intellectual underachievement to a lack of intellectual capacity created by fundamental biological differences, other Asians have embraced a theory that claims that East Asians are intellectually superior to all other racial and ethnic groups. First proposed by white psychologists in the late 1970s to explain the emergence of Japan as an economic power, the theory has gained influential converts all over the world: the most notable being the former ruler of Singapore, Lee Kuan Yew. During an interview with an Australian business magazine in 1993, Lee not only described the work ethic of Chinese in Singapore as superior to that of Indians in Singapore, but also wondered aloud about a genetic basis.

The following year Lee told an American publication that the genetic link between East Asians and fellow Mongoloid Native Americans had been severed by the mixture of East Asians with Central Asians and by the migration of Native Americans across the Bering Strait. The result of this genetic split, Lee explained, was that East Asians were now more neurologically and culturally developed than their newly distant cousins.

Lee was neither the only nor the first East Asian leader to enthusiastically endorse this theory. In 1986, at a time when the Japanese rise to world financial dominance seemed all but inevitable, Japanese Prime Minister Yasuhiro Nakasone was reported to have made the following boast to a meeting of his party: "So high is the level of education in our country that Japan's is an intelligent society. Our average IQ score is much higher than those of countries like the U.S. There are many blacks, Puerto Ricans, and Mexicans in America. In consequence, the average score over there is exceedingly low." When these remarks were greeted with a torrent of criticism from the United States, the diplomatic Nakasone explained that he had intended to praise the remarkable achievements of America, *despite* the presence of minorities.

It is not surprising, therefore, that in the face of such sustained onslaught from so many quarters, many black intellectuals are afflicted with what has been described as the fear of racial biology. Because they fear, understandably, that the flip side of black athletic superiority could be black intellectual inferiority, many black intellectuals contemptuously deride biological explanations and have attempted to ascribe black athletic success to a variety of sociological and psychological factors. A leading proponent of this viewpoint, Professor Harry Edwards, describes black athletic success as the result of "a complex of societal conditions" that steer disproportionate numbers of blacks into athletic careers. He argues that the paucity of role models in "high prestige, occupational positions outside the sports realm" results in the concentration of a disproportionate percentage of extremely gifted black males in that one area. Edwards fears that "by asserting that blacks are physically superior, whites at best reinforce some old stereotypes long held about Afro-Americans—to wit, that they are little removed from the apes in their evolutionary development."

Environmental explanations of black athletic success by the black intellectual community are not a recent phenomenon. In 1943, clinical psychiatrist Laynard Holloman theorized that "hatred and desire for revenge against whites was one reason for the supremacy of black athletes in certain American sports." He believed that black boxers dominated boxing because "it was an ideal way for them to express their hatred for the white man." But hatred, in Holloman's considered opinion, was not the only psychological factor driving the success of African Americans in athletics; compensation for feelings of inferiority was another powerful motivating factor.

Three decades later, another prominent black psychiatrist, Alvin Poussaint of Harvard University, in his own analysis of the black male psyche, would also attempt to explain black athletic success in psychological terms. Athletic prowess, Poussaint claimed, was a means for African Americans to express masculinity and power. Stripped of social power, African American males, he speculated, turned to displays of power for validation.

Thomas Sowell, a conservative black intellectual, has attempted to explain differences in all kinds of achievement between the various racial and ethnic groups in America in purely environmental terms. In his book, *Ethnic America,* Sowell examined the histories of nine ethnic groups from Europe, Asia, Africa, and Latin America before they arrived in America. He argued that their initial difficulties and successes in America were intimately linked to their original backgrounds. He tried to explain away the current success of black athletes by pointing to the earlier success of the Irish. "Many Irish Americans," Sowell wrote, "rose to prominence in sports and entertainment, a pattern to be repeated by later ethnic groups living in poverty and without an intellectual and entrepreneurial tradition."

To underline what he regards as similarities between the Irish and African American patterns, Sowell pointed out that the Irish "dominated some sports, such as boxing, baseball and track, but were not nearly as prominent in swimming and wrestling." What he failed to explain or perhaps understand, however, was that the dominance of American sports by white ethnic groups such as the Irish and the Italians took place in the absence of African Americans who were, until the second half of the twentieth century, deliberately and systematically excluded from competing against white men.

The great Irish and Italian athletes were generally better than athletes from other white ethnic groups, but failed utterly to compete successfully against African American athletes once they were allowed to compete.

The recent successes of Tiger Woods and the Williams sisters in two traditionally "white" sports—golf and tennis—have forcefully underlined that fact. Even today, relatively few blacks have either the means or the desire to become professional golf or tennis players, and whites still comprise the overwhelming majority of participants in those two sports. Given that, the fact that a 26-year-old black male golfer and a 20-year-old black female tennis player are the best in the world at their respective sports should be highly instructive.

Since the emotional resistance to the acceptance of racial biological differences is understandably powerful, denial has assumed a variety of guises. One very subtle method is to deny the very concept of race as a meaningful biological construct. Although there is considerable validity to this claim, as will be discussed in the final chapter of this book, there are also clear, athletically significant anatomical and physiological differences between the races. The denial is also attempted by claims that Africans and African Americans "do not come from some magical common gene pool," that "genetic literature is consistent with the fact that there are more differences within any one group as a whole than there are between two different groups," and that "the American individual to whom the term Negro is applied is almost always a biracial hybrid."

Public attempts of this nature, by prominent African Americans, to genetically distinguish at least some African Americans from the "pure" Negro type in Africa—in effect to try to separate lighter-skinned African Americans from their darker-skinned counterparts—has a long and distinguished pedigree. The African American social theorist and political leader, W.E.B. DuBois, made the first formal presentation of black Americans as a biologically and culturally distinct species at the beginning of the twentieth century. The light-skinned DuBois, who would in later years clash fiercely and repeatedly with the dark-skinned Marcus Garvey, was apparently obsessed with correcting what he described as "the first and usual assumption concerning this race…that it represents a pure Negro type." Since this was clearly intolerable, the indefatigable DuBois decided to write an entire book to correct the record.

In his pioneering work, *The Health and Physique of the Negro American*,

DuBois pointed out: "The Negro-American [type] represents a very wide and thorough blending of nearly all African people from north to south; and more than that, it is to a far larger extent than many realize, a blending of European and African blood. In America we have, on account of the widespread mixture of races of all kinds, one of the most interesting anthropological laboratories conceivable. This is true also so far as the mingling of the two most diverse races, the black and the white, is concerned as well as in other cases... We have had going on beneath our very eyes an experiment in race-blending such as the world has nowhere seen... and we have today living representatives of almost every possible degree of admixture of Teutonic and Negro blood."

As visual proof of the genetic diversity of African Americans, DuBois included plates of what he described as 48 prominent "Negro American" types, with detailed descriptions of their various degrees of admixture attached. His conclusion that one-third of the African American population was racially mixed, DuBois pointed out, was hardly casual or arbitrary, but the result of a series of some 40,000 classifications he had personally carried out.

While it is obviously true that so-called "black" Americans come in almost every skin hue, and that many are clearly and obviously of mixed racial descent, it does not follow, inevitably, that most African Americans are so different from each other that they do not share, generally, certain physiological characteristics which distinguish them from all other population groups. What can be argued, and what appears logically and on observed evidence to be true, is that the least racially-mixed black Americans are the most likely to possess the anatomical and physiological characteristics of their African ancestors. But it is also clear that some of the greatest black athletes—Muhammad Ali, Joe Louis, Tiger Woods, and Jesse Owens, among others—although obviously racially mixed, inherited the West African-developed genes that endowed them with their unique blend of speed and power.

Although it seems ludicrously unnecessary today, DuBois' primary motive in presenting Negro Americans as a population of extreme biological, cultural, and socioeconomic diversity was, probably in part, to debunk popular notions that the then-high rates of sickness and death among black Americans were more "proof" of black racial inferiority. By proving that black Americans were not a homogeneous group, DuBois hoped to demonstrate that no unequivocal causal relationship between race and fitness could be established. Most phenomena identified as "racial" or "pathological," he explained, "are in reality caused by the social relations within a given social formation." The Negro death rate and sickness, DuBois wrote, "are largely matters of conditions and not due to racial traits and tendencies. [What we have] is not racial disease but social disease."

Ironically, the same hybridity that DuBois labored so hard to establish would provide some twentieth century "scientific" racists with the ammunition to once again "prove" the racial inferiority of black Americans. Inspired by supposedly higher rates of sickle cell anemia in black Americans than in native Africans, despite higher rates of sickle cell trait among Africans, European and American medical scientists proposed a link between hybridization and biological and genetic degeneracy. The "fact" that the hybrid American Negro suffered from far higher rates of sickle cell anemia than his pure Negro counterpart in Africa was living proof, they claimed, of the inherently diseased nature of the American Negro and the dysgenic effects of race-mixing.

The separation of the black race into two groups, African and American, it was argued, had introduced genetic differences between the two that were important in the study of sickle cell disease. A. B. Raper, the author of this two-group explanation, also developed a theory of how this genetic differentiation had occurred. "In seeking an explanation for the different incidence of the trait," he wrote, "we must assume that the forebears of each group were indistinguishable in this particular respect two or three centuries ago, and that it is the less stable community, the American, that has suffered the change. The lower incidence of the trait in the New World may have resulted from intermarriage with non-Negroes, or, if we allow that fatal complications are for some reason commoner in America, it may be due to a higher mortality amongst sickling families there."

Since there was absolutely no evidence to support the latter conclusion—if anything the evidence pointed in the opposite direction—Raper, a senior pathologist at the Medical Laboratory in Kampala, Uganda, suggested the possibility that "some factor imported by marriage with white persons, is especially liable to bring out the hemolytic aspect of the disease, while the anomaly remains a harmless one in the communities in which it originated." Although this factor was never clearly identified, he became convinced that "the appearance of the sickle cell anemia depends not only on the extent to which the trait is present in a community, but also on the extent to which admixture with other genetic strains has occurred."

Raper's views were heavily influenced by the 1944 study of the Black Caribs of Honduras by the sickling researchers T. H. McGavack and W. M. German. The study was undertaken to determine whether it was justifiable to continue to regard sickling as a "hereditary racial trait" specific to the Negro population. The Black Caribs were selected, according to the researchers, because they had had very little opportunity to compromise their "racial essence." Although displaced to the New World, their close resemblance to the African prototype marked them as essentially different from most African Americans. Since it was reported that not a single case of sickle cell anemia had been identified among the "pure-blooded" Black Caribs, German and McGavack concluded that it was racial admixture, rather than displacement to the New World or African origins, that was responsible for the high rates of sickling among hybrid North American Negroes.

But Raper's conclusions were hardly shared by many of his colleagues. The problem, it seemed, was with the very basis of his thesis that sickle cell anemia did not occur in pure-blood African natives, despite a rate of sickling trait that was nearly three times higher than in African Americans. In fact, all but a few of his fellow colonial physicians ascribed the failure to find sickle cell anemia in Africa to insufficient clinical knowledge of the disease and inadequate observation techniques.

In a particularly scathing criticism of the Raper viewpoint, H. C. Trowel, a physician and lecturer at the Uganda Medical School in Kampala, indignantly rejected the notion that sickle cell anemia did not occur among native Africans. Although sickle cell anemia originated in West Africa and is still primarily found there, Trowel insisted, that there were "probably few diseases which are more common in East African natives, and yet less frequently diagnosed, than sickle cell anemia." He attributed the absence in the literature of any definite account of sickle cell anemia in Bantu Africans entirely to the fact that "the clinical picture is not clearly visualized, and that it is extremely easy to confuse the disease with malaria."

An editorial titled "Sickle Cell Anemia," published in the *East African Medical Journal* in 1945, introduced a paper of the same title by Trowel. The paper, the editorial proclaimed, documented for the first time, in a systematic way, that sickle cell anemia constituted a considerable medical problem in Africa, but had, in the words of the editorial, "passed unrecognized, because unknown, in many an African hospital and for many a long year." In the accompanying article, Trowel reported finding thirty-five cases of the anemia distributed among seven East African tribes.

Despite this kind of clear evidence of sickle cell disease in Africa, and despite the fact that the relationship between sickle cell trait and sickle cell anemia had been established, in 1949, Raper and his fellow travelers continued to cling tight to the dated and discredited theories of eugenic genetics and racialist anthropology. They insisted, in eloquent testimony to the continuing power of the propaganda that had been devised to justify slavery and the oppression of black Africans, that racial intermixture had, in some mysterious way, weakened the constitution of the American Negro and rendered him susceptible to disease and early death.

While black intellectuals have long labored to explain the disproportionate athletic success of African Americans in environmental terms, the white scientific-medical community has frequently taken the opposite view. For decades, white attempts to explain black physical prowess ranged (not surprisingly, given the poisonous history of African-European relationships) from the ridiculous to the sublime. The ability of Civil War era black soldiers to march long distances with what seemed to some white observers as remarkable ease, and later the ability of black athletes to outrun all competitors, was attributed to a variety of factors including double-jointedness, larger adrenal glands, a more primitive nervous system, more tendons, less muscle, and longer heel bones.

As recently as 1995, Sir Roger Bannister, the first man to run a mile in less than four minutes and a prominent neurologist, was still echoing that nineteenth century viewpoint. In a speech on the athletic limits of the human organism to the British Association for the Advancement of Science, Sir Roger decided to indulge in what he described as "political incorrectness," and speculate publicly on the reason(s) for black athletic success. "It is perfectly obvious," he claimed, "when you see an all-black sprint final that there must be something rather special about their anatomy or physiology which produces these outstanding successes, and indeed there may be—but we don't know quite what it is. It may be that their heel bone is a bit longer."

Although the theories that attempted to explain black physical aptitude were for years clearly ridiculous, they were also remarkably influential and enduring. One such was the so-called relaxation theory. This belief, that black athletes have a unique ability to maximize athletic performances by achieving a relaxed state during competition, appears to have been derived from old racist notions about the primitive nature of the black nervous system. This alleged special black capacity for relaxation even led to the incorrect and thoroughly discredited notion that blacks have lower blood pressure rates than whites. In fact, the available evidence strongly suggests the opposite is true.

Perhaps attempting to explain the success of Jesse Owens and the other great black athletes at the 1936 Berlin Olympics, the head coach of the U.S. team in those Olympics, offered his own version of the relaxation theory. Dean Cromwell, in his book *Championship Technique in Track and Field*, wrote, "The Negro excels in the events he does because he is closer to the primitive than the white man. It was not so long ago that his ability to sprint and jump was a life-and-death matter to him in the jungle. His muscles are pliable, and his easy going disposition is a valuable aid to the mental and physical relaxation that a runner and jumper must have."

More than three decades later, another white coach of black Olympic medallists also turned to the relaxation theory, if in slightly more modern and diplomatic language, to explain the success of the black athletes he coached. Lloyd "Bud" Winter, a former coach of Olympic medallists, Tommie Smith and John Carlos claimed that black athletes "are far ahead of the whites in that one factor—relaxation under pressure. It is their secret. What heritage or heredity brought the black athlete this ability to keep out tension no one knows. In white athletes the conscious mind takes over and the tensions mount."

From the very beginning of contact between modern Europeans and West Africans, it was evident to the Europeans that there were important biological differences not only between the Africans and themselves, but also between the Africans and the Indians of the New World. The differences, they quickly realized, were not limited to the obvious, like skin color and hair type. More important, as the Spaniards discovered, were the physical sturdiness and immunological hardiness of the Africans. In dramatic contrast to the Indians who died in huge heaps like bedbugs, the black slaves who accompanied the Spaniards remained strong and healthy—so healthy that, in twisted tribute, the Spaniards proclaimed, "If we do not hang a Negro, he would never die." In another dubious tribute to his biological uniqueness, the Spaniards came to believe that not only could the Negro do the work of four Indians, but also that Negroes were four times as valuable.

Although it is no longer politically correct to publicly attribute black athletic prowess to biological differences between racial groups, the accumulating evidence—supplied by the highly visible, disproportionate success of black athletes—is leading many Americans of all races to conclude that African Americans do, indeed, possess some kind of biological advantage over other racial groups. But the accumulating evidence—supplied by the expansion of science and an increasingly integrated society—has also significantly diminished the credibility of the old racial shibboleths, which held that Africans were not only intrinsically inferior, but were also so different that they constituted a different species.

Not surprisingly, therefore, an essentially non-racist but biological explanation for African American athletic success has gained converts among commentators of both races. Although it was less-than-elegantly phrased, the historical context less than accurate, and his grasp of the theory he was espousing less than complete, the best-known example of this viewpoint—that the eugenic effects of slavery and selected slave breeding was responsible for black athletic superiority—came from the white sports commentator Jimmy "The Greek" Synder. According to Snyder, "the black is a better athlete to begin with, because he's been bred to be that way. Because of his high thighs that go up into his back. And they can jump higher and run faster because of their big thighs...The Black is the better athlete and he practices to be the better athlete and he's bred to be the better athlete because this goes all the way to the Civil War, when, during the slave trading, the owner, the slave owner, would breed his big Black woman so that he would have a big Black kid."

Although Snyder was merely, inarticulately, echoing a viewpoint with widespread support in the general African American community, he quickly became a casualty of America's deepest psychosis—the fear of racial biology. Years earlier, two prominent African American professional athletes had explained African American athletic success in similar terms. To Lee Evans, the Olympic gold medallist, black physical superiority was a riddle without mystery. The answer was clear and simple: "We were bred for it...on the plantations, a strong black man was mated with a strong black woman. We were simply bred for physical qualities."

Although stated in more scientifically sophisticated and politically correct terms, Calvin Hill, the Yale graduate and Dallas Cowboys star, also enthusiastically embraced the slave selection hypothesis. "I have a theory about why so many pro stars are black," Hill said. "I think it boils down to survival of the fittest. Think of what African slaves were forced to endure in this country merely to survive. Well, black athletes are their descendants. They are the offspring of those who are physically and mentally tough enough to survive."

The mere fact that his viewpoint was neither racist nor completely without merit was not enough to protect the unfortunate Synder. His comments unleashed a firestorm of denunciations, sparked a national debate, and led to his swift dismissal from his television job as a sports commentator of sorts. Another white male in the world of professional sports, Al Campanis, probably made Synder's dismissal inevitable by an earlier comment. Campanis, a vice president of the Los Angeles Dodgers, vividly demonstrated why the continuing fear of racial biology is fully justified. Appearing on the ABC program *Nightline*, Campanis responded to a question from host Ted Koppel about the shortage of African Americans in management positions in baseball by declaring that many "lacked the necessities." He then attempted to justify that assertion by pointing out what he regarded as another example of their differentness, their reputed unsuitability for swimming, allegedly because they are less buoyant.

First used in 1883 by Charles Darwin's cousin, Francis Galton, to describe his ideas of improving the human race by controlled breeding, eugenics eventually provided the Nazis with the scientific rationale for the systematic slaughter of ten million European Jews, Gypsies and other undesirable elements. But eugenics was not just the province of the insane—far from it. For many years eugenics was part of the scientific mainstream in the United States and Europe. In fact, when the American scientific journal *Genetics* was founded in 1916, all five principals were advocates of eugenics, although they were also established scientists with outstanding reputations.

In ascribing to eugenics the power of positive good, these men were merely following a long-established and highly reputable scholarly tradition. The intellectual root of eugenics, after all, has an enormously impressive and ancient pedigree. Plato himself believed chronic invalids should not receive medical treatment and that "superior" men and women should be temporarily united for the specific purpose of breeding "superior" children.

With relentless logic, the eugenics movement in Germany focused its attention on racial purity. National fitness was linked to racial fitness, and

Jews, Eastern Europeans, and Blacks were categorized as members of inferior races. Eugenicists advocated the genetic screening of the entire German population, and by 1928, there were hundreds of marriage-advice clinics screening couples who were planning to marry to ensure hereditary health. So widely accepted were these ideas in Germany that by 1928 Adolph Hitler was publicly advocating killing German infants with physical defects. Hitler estimated that up to 700,000 of these children would have to be eliminated each year.

After assuming power, Hitler and his party established an Office of Racial Policy to promote the benefits of racial hygiene. Genetic health courts were opened all over the country and doctors were ordered to register all cases of genetic illness with the courts. Those with congenital feeble-mindedness, schizophrenia, or hereditary epilepsy were forcibly sterilized. Unsatisfied with these relatively mild measures, Hitler established The Committee for the Scientific Treatment of Severe Genetically Determined Illness. The mission of the committee, despite its deliberately misleading name, was to destroy retarded and deformed children. Children judged as having "lives unworthy to be lived" were sent to one of twenty-eight killing facilities. There, either basic care was withheld until the children died, or they were deliberately killed, either by morphine injection or cyanide poisoning.

While the United States escaped the worst of the German excesses, the American eugenics movement was responsible for its own share of racial terror and abuse. As in Germany, eugenic theory in the United States was built on an edifice of Anglo-Saxon racial superiority, and purifying and protecting that "great" race became the preoccupation of eugenic laws and policies. Calvin Coolidge reflected the prevailing view of white America when he declared, "biological laws show... that Nordics deteriorated when mixed with other races." As a result, Congress passed the Johnson Immigration Restriction Act of 1924, which severely restricted the immigration of Eastern and Southern Europeans, particularly those of Jewish descent.

In the backlash against eugenics, environmentalism became the fashion. Geneticists stopped insisting that racial mixing was harmful. In 1951, the United Nations issued a statement, signed by twenty-three prominent geneticists, which declared "available scientific knowledge provides no basis for believing that the groups of mankind differ in their innate capacity for intellectual and emotional development." In keeping with the times, the mission of the American Genetics Association was changed from improving human racial stocks to improving human welfare.

The explanation of human behavior became increasingly complex—the result, social scientists decreed, of stimulation, nervous structure, internal chemical states, past experiences, and learning. As the multiple causation of human behavior became increasingly accepted, the influence of heredity was significantly degraded to just one in a mosaic of development influences.

Particularly influential was the success of child psychologists, psychiatrists and psychoanalysts in establishing a new approach to human development. Theorists and researchers sharply downgraded the role of innate ability and elevated the importance of the child's adaptation to the external world, particularly its relationship with its parents. Researchers such as Anna Freud, Jean Piaget, John Bowlby and Margaret Maller regarded the mother's role as so important that most childhood problems were believed to be a direct result of a defect in the mother-child relationship. So sweeping was her influence thought to be that even conditions now known to have neurochemical bases, like schizophrenia and autism, were attributed to the inability of the mother to properly nurture her child.

The pendulum has swung again: this time perhaps permanently. The evidence in favor of nature's superior role is clear and overwhelming. The emerging science of molecular biology is proving that heredity is primarily responsible for determining individual appearance, personality, behavior, and performance. We have long known that our genes are responsible for our height; the color of our skin, hair, and eyes; and the texture of our hair. Now there is considerable evidence that our ability to lose or gain weight, our susceptibility to addictive substances, our ability to learn languages, our temperament, and perhaps even our sexual orientation are, primarily, genetically determined.

Behavioral genetics is decidedly back in favor. Molecular geneticist Dean Hamer has linked specific genes to behavioral traits, such as anxiety, thrill seeking and homosexuality. Hamer believes "many core personality traits are inherited at birth, and that many of the differences between individual personality styles are the result of genes." Scientists at the Institute for Behavior Genetics in Boulder, Colorado, have discovered that the boldness and shyness of the most bold and the most shy twin babies was 70 to 90 percent determined by their genetic inheritance. The old concept of the bad seed was largely correct, it seems.

It was long understood in places such as Jamaica that bad blood ran in certain families. It was widely believed that while stern and regular discipline could perhaps control and sometimes even expel the evil from such afflicted persons, the only real protection for decent society was to avoid genetic contamination by the infested and their known relatives. But it was also understood that bad seeds, unfortunately, were not the exclusive province of known infected families. Sometimes the very best families inexplicably produced a moral mutant. But whether predictable or not, "born bad" was then the common and widely accepted explanation of aberrant human behavior.

The new explanations are more subtle and sophisticated, but the conclusions are pretty much the same. While Hamer emphasizes that "there are important nongenetic factors, such as parenting style and schooling," he concludes that "no single influence is more profound than genetic makeup." Not only do genes predispose people to certain ways of being, genes also appear to have a role in what experiences we seek, pushing us towards certain environments that will shape our behavior. The primary role of nature has also been underlined by the discovery of the genes that are responsible for diseases such as Alzheimer's, manic-depressive disorder, certain types of breast cancer, and Huntingdon's.

The link between genetic inheritance and physical characteristics has always been easier to make and accept than the one between genetics and behavior. Given the weight of the evidence on the primacy of heredity in determining behavior, there should be little doubt that the anatomical and physiological traits that influence athletic performance—such as body shape and proportion, ability to gain lean muscle tissue, subcutaneous fat levels, skeletal muscle fiber type ratio, and bone and fiber density—are also, primarily, genetically determined.

There can be little doubt, as the evidence in Part Three will clearly establish, that not only are blacks of West African descent genetically favorably endowed with the physical characteristics that determine athletic ability, but that their superior athletic ability became evident as soon as they were allowed to compete on even terms against their white counterparts.

3

The Turning Point

Nothing he had seen—and he had seen a lot in his thirty years of experience—had quite prepared Chief Inspector John Seery for the extraordinary spectacle that confronted him on that final night of 1935. Surveying the great multitude from the relative safety of the police booth at Forty-sixth Street and Broadway, Inspector Seery proclaimed the million-plus gathering to be "the greatest crowd in the history of Broadway."

The crowd had gathered slowly at first but, according to the *New York Times*, after 11:45, as if answering some mysterious summons, tremendous crowds began to pour in from the side streets, "sweeping everything before them." By 11:45 p.m., "everything" included the police, who had lost control and were being pushed back relentlessly but good-naturedly by the frenzied revelers. Looking out from the police information booth on the traffic island in Times Square, Deputy Commissioner Harold Fowler echoed the Chief Inspector's awe at the size of the crowd. "It's a bigger, noisier and obviously happier crowd than last year's," he said, "and I thought that was the biggest crowd I'd ever seen. You can see real happiness in their faces."

But the celebrating was not all in the streets. Nightclubs, hotels, dance halls, theaters, and motion picture houses were packed with deliriously happy patrons. At the bars, men and women stood three feet deep hoarsely shouting orders. In the more upscale and expensive nightclubs and hotels, champagne, at prices ranging from $6 to $16 per bottle, flowed like water as men and

49

women drank with wild abandon. Although cover charges started at $5 and went as high as $15, every hotel in the city had to turn away late-arriving customers. Earlier that day, even the battered Stock Exchange had gotten into the spirit of things. Reviving a custom that had been reluctantly abandoned during the long and bitter five years of the Depression, some 1,000 brokers, telephone clerks, pageboys, and others, supported by two orchestras, had "bade the old year a tumultuous farewell."

Chief Inspector Seery, Deputy Commissioner Fowler, and the millions of other white men all over America had every reason to celebrate the arrival of the New Year. For them the end of the Depression brought real hope for a vastly better future. In 1936 to be born white, male, American, and of reasonably sound mind and limb was to enjoy a special status among the peoples of the world. Obviously, not all white American males were rich and powerful—far from it. In fact, wide income disparities among white men were facts of life. In 1935, General Motors paid its top 20 officials an average of $200,000 per year (an enormous sum for the period) and paid the rest of its quarter of a million employees each less than $1,000 per year. When workers attempted to organize, violent, bloody strikebreaking was often the response. When a Senate committee wanted to know why the Pittsburgh Coal Company kept machine guns at its coal pits, the chairman, Richard B. Mellon, replied, "You cannot run the mines without them."

But however poorly educated and financially deprived, white American men—even the most recent immigrants—had the psychological satisfaction of knowing they belonged to a legally and socially superior class of mankind. While it was true that all white men were not equal, it was also true that almost all white men were more privileged than almost all other Americans.

If white men in America had every reason to celebrate in 1936, the same was not true for black men and black women. In 1936, to be born black in America was to be condemned, almost inevitably, to an existence of almost unimaginable hardship, degradation and humiliation. While not every black American lived in poverty, in 1936 the future of every black American, however talented, was constricted by a poverty of opportunity. While the Depression was devastating to many white Americans, it was a catastrophe of enormous proportions to most black Americans. Not only were blacks the last to be hired and the first to be fired, but blacks who had jobs earned less than 50% of the average white income. And while the national unemployment level was less than 15%, more than 50% of urban blacks could not find jobs of any kind, and rural blacks were frequently forced to sell their crops at prices below their costs.

"Negro jobs" disappeared in the cities, as domestic service and garbage collection suddenly became white occupations. In the Southern states, where the majority of blacks lived, not only were unemployment benefits lower than in the rest of the nation, but white officials openly discriminated against blacks in administering them. As a result, during the Depression, blacks across the country were continually threatened, to a far greater extent than their white counterparts, by privation, malnutrition, and not infrequently even starvation.

But in 1936, crushing poverty was not the major problem facing blacks in America. Poverty was merely one symptom of their subhuman status. To the majority white population, blacks were not Americans or even fully human. White lives and black lives were judged as having very different values. In Louisiana, a black man was sentenced to death for wounding a white man during a robbery. The first of the defendants in the notorious Scottsboro case was sentenced to seventy-five years in prison on a clearly trumped-up charge of rape; in Kentucky, a crowd of 10,000 whites attended the hanging of a black man who had been convicted of murder and assault.

Blacks, however well educated and accomplished, were still "niggers." In 1936, the American Bar Association was still refusing to extend membership to black lawyers; black doctors and nurses were finding it difficult to get hired in their field, even at Harlem Hospital; and black artists charged discrimination when their murals were rejected by the same hospital. Little had changed in the status of blacks since the Chief Justice of the Supreme Court declared in the Dred Scott decision of 1857 that a "Negro had no rights which a white man need respect."

Perhaps the most dramatic illustration of the subhuman status of blacks was the frequency, impunity, and ferocity with which blacks were lynched and the obdurate refusal of Congress to pass anti-lynching bills. In the South, lynchings were a lot more than a rough form of frontier justice. It is no exaggeration to claim that in some areas lynchings were a form of community blood sport; it was not uncommon for howling mobs, sometimes literally dripping with blood, to mutilate the bodies of lynching victims while men, women, and even children screamed their approval.

Unquestionably, in 1936, America was a deeply racist and completely segregated society. Led by the Supreme Court, the nation had turned its back on the promises made by the North to black Americans during the Civil War and Reconstruction periods. By the end of the first decade of the twentieth century, white, Protestant America, while welcoming millions of culturally dissimilar Europeans, Jews and Catholics alike from Eastern and Southern Europe, had decided that the fixed separation of the races was the appropriate way of handling the "Negro problem."

This fixed separation was dramatically apparent in the field of sports. In 1936, the most famous and revered athletes were all white men. That ultimate symbol of manhood, the heavyweight championship of the world, was held by a white man, Jim Braddock. He was merely the most recent in a series of mediocre white fighters who had become heavyweight champion by scrupulously avoiding blacks. But Braddock, in avoiding black fighters, was simply following in the footsteps of other white heavyweight champions, including the greatest white fighter of all, Jack Dempsey. Dempsey, who was champion of the world from 1919 to 1927, never fought a black man during his professional career, although he was stalked and hounded for years by Harry Wills, the leading black fighter of the time.

Dempsey campaigned to keep the title in white control after losing his crown. However, he did not go to the extreme lengths to avoid black fighters that Jess Willard, the man he defeated to become champion, did. Although he avoided black fighters in actual combat, Dempsey used them as sparring partners to prepare for his toughest fights. Willard had defeated Jack Johnson, the first black heavyweight champion. However, he shunned blacks completely, both in and out of the ring, once he became the champion.

In 1936, baseball had no rival from other professional sports for the affections of the American people. The New York Yankees would begin that year an extraordinary domination of Major League Baseball that was to last until 1939. During that period, they won four straight pennants by an average of nearly fifteen games, and won four straight World Series. The Yankees had dominated Major League Baseball since acquiring Babe Ruth, and they were rightfully regarded as an outstanding team. Although the great Babe Ruth's career had ended two years earlier, his teammate on the 1927 Yankee team (probably the greatest white team of all time), the legendary Lou Gehrig, was a member of the 1936 team, and the center fielder was a sensational rookie named Joe DiMaggio.

But the Yankees, despite their dominance of the major leagues, were merely the best white baseball team in the nation. When given the opportunity, despite crushing poverty and smothering segregation, black baseball players more than held their own against the best white major leaguers. In his book *Voices from the Great Black Baseball League*, John Holway revealed that in 167 games against the white major leaguers from 1930 to 1939, blacks won 112, lost 52, and tied 3. In 1936, great black stars like Satchel Paige, Josh Gibson, and Cool Papa Bell were attracting hordes of fans of both races as well as the attention of those in the white establishment who were concerned about the plummeting attendance in the majors.

Sportswriters, rarely bastions of liberalism, openly advocated bringing blacks into the majors. The conservative columnist Westbrook Fegler of the *Chicago Daily News* wrote that he could not understand why Negroes were not playing in the majors. As the National League season moved into the stretch with the Giants in a hard fight for the pennant, Jimmy Powers of the *New York Daily News* fantasized in print that there were seven black players who could practically ensure a flag for the Giants. The President of the National League, Ford Frick, would have none of it however. The league, he said, had not used Negroes because the public "has not been educated to the point where they will accept them." Baseball, he added, "is biding its time and waiting for the social change, which is inevitable. Times are changing."

But the manager of the New York Giants, Bill Terry, who had once objected to "nigger cops" patrolling the executive entrances of the Polo Grounds, disagreed strongly. He predicted that "Negroes will never get into the big leagues." Will Harridge, the president of the American League, took a look at the 40,000 fans at the East-West game that August and made his own prediction that the bars would be down in five years or less. Harridge, events would prove, was far too optimistic. It would be a full decade before just one black man, Jackie Robinson, was allowed to play Major League Baseball.

But 1936 was more than just a time when white males were dominant socially and athletically, when black men were not even allowed to compete against white men. It was also a turning point, for after 1936 America's and the world's perception of the black athlete would be forever changed. In supreme irony, the primary agent of that change would be history's most notorious racist, Adolph Hitler. The 1936 Olympic Games—in some ways the most momentous in history—were held in Berlin and presided over by the German Chancellor. Hitler had hoped that the elaborately staged games would confirm, before the entire world, his insane racial theories.

But all the scientific training and extraordinary preparation of finely tuned German athletes would prove totally inadequate when faced with the inherited physical superiority of the sons of the deadly West African forests, led by Jesse Owens. In one of the greatest Olympic performances of all time, Owens would win four gold medals, frustrate the butcher of Berlin, entertain the German people, delight the American people (black and white alike), and begin the process of imprinting on the world's consciousness the image of the black American as a great athlete.

Jesse Owens was not alone that year in knocking white males off their perch atop the athletic world. Although he would not win the world heavyweight title until the following year, another poor son of the South, Joe Louis, would serve dramatic notice of his arrival on the world stage with a devastating knockout of the former world champion, Max Baer. For black athletes, 1936 was the start of a long, slow, but inevitable rise to the very pinnacle of the athletic world.

That rise would be accompanied almost inevitably, given the racist sentiments of the time, by an enormous wave of white anxiety and an explosion of pseudo-scientific explanations of black athletic dominance. Shaking off slave era theories of black anatomical and physiological inferiority, white commentators strained myth and imagination to concoct new theories to both accommodate the unshakable concept of white superiority and explain the hard reality of black athletic dominance. As extraordinary as it seems from today's perspective, such theories were not regarded at the time by white society as offensive. After all, the most popular radio program of the era, *Amos 'n' Andy*, was based on crude racial stereotypes. But so popular was the program that stores and movie theaters were obliged to broadcast it to prevent patrons from rushing home at airtime. It was so popular that reportedly even President Calvin Coolidge demanded that he not be disturbed during the fifteen minutes the program was aired every weekday at 7:00 p.m.

But America was changing. The world was changing. The year began with the death of George V of England in January and ended with the abdication of his son, Edward VIII, in December. The destruction of Victorian values that the Abdication dramatized was underlined by the burning of the Crystal Palace, that last relic of authentic Victorianism. In between, Germany occupied the Rhineland and started filling the concentration camps, the Spanish Civil War began, and Italy escalated its unchecked and barbarous assault on Ethiopia by deploying poison gas against the lightly armed Africans. In this country, Hitler's murderous excesses helped to sound the death knell of the old eugenics which had once argued in favor of sterilization and racial purification, and gradually relegated public assertions of black biological inferiority to the lunatic fringe of white society.

However, the silencing of the public debate would also leave unresolved the subject matter of this book: the reason or reasons for the unquestionable athletic superiority of black athletes, and the implications of the answer to that question.

Part Two

The Performance Evidence

4

In Baseball, Race Has
Always Been a Factor

To Curt Gowdy, it was the last moment of innocence in American life. The year was 1946, and the occasion was a Major League Baseball game at Yankee Stadium between two all-white teams in front of 63,000 cheering, jeering, mostly white fans. The teams playing that day, the Boston Red Sox and the New York Yankees, would resist integrating their teams for almost another decade, and America at large was almost as racist and as determined to deny African Americans the benefits of citizenship as it had been a decade earlier.

In Alabama, on the urging of the Executive Committee of the State Democratic Party, the state constitution was amended to restrict the right of Negroes to vote. In Arkansas, Governor Laney announced his intention of barring Negroes from voting in Democratic Party primaries, and the State Supreme Court upheld the constitutionality of legislation designed to prevent Negroes from voting for State officials in Democratic Party primaries. In California, the State Bar Association upheld the ban on Negro members. In Mississippi, Senator Bilbo urged whites to employ all means possible to prevent Negroes from voting. The rising tide of brutality against Negroes, epitomized by the lynching of nine of its members in the South that year, was protested in Harlem. Paul Robeson denounced racial inequality in the South;

and Dr. C. H. Foreman warned that the outbreak of violence against Negroes was due to a rise in fascism in the United States.

But to the young white sportscaster in his broadcasting tower, America would never again be as good or as pure as it was that magical day in Yankee Stadium.

More accurately than any other activity, sporting or otherwise, baseball has reflected the state of the American nation. In the introduction to the 1997 *Cooperstown Symposium on Baseball and American Culture,* Peter Rutkoff described the game as a "unique social and cultural mirror." Baseball, he explained, was a game that "provided the males of America with heroes aplenty... where fathers passed along skills and lore to their sons." Baseball's masculine ethos, he elaborated, "brought women to the ballpark to witness but not share the rituals. Even the innovation of Ladies Day...only opened the public spectacle of baseball to the distaff sex. The dugout, locker room, and road remained enclaves closed to all save the male participants who guarded the secrets of sweat, liniment, tobacco, and philandering."

David Halberstam has also eloquently described baseball's historic role in American life. Baseball, he wrote in the, *Summer of '49,* "was not so much the national sport as the binding national myth. It was also the embodiment of the melting pot theory, or at least the white melting pot theory of America."

It is not difficult to understand how a young white American male, with an enviable position with the most glamorous baseball organization in the world, could believe that all was right with the world. In 1946, blacks and white women were still quiescent, and with Europe exhausted and Africa and Asia still subjugated or destroyed, civil rights legislation and the global economy were still several decades away. For white American men, those years immediately following World War II were truly magical. They stood by dint of nationality, race, and gender, unchallenged as the pre-ordained masters of the universe. Wherever their glances fell, at home or abroad, submissive women and subjugated races affirmed their special status.

This special status was reaffirmed most satisfyingly on the baseball field. The best boxers and the fastest runners may have been black, but only white men played Major League Baseball. Baseball was different and special and very precious. It was, Halberstam has written, "rooted not just in the past but in the culture of the country; it was celebrated in the nations' literature and songs." Like nothing else, baseball defined how white men saw America and themselves, and defending that heritage against a black onslaught was for millions of them as sacred a responsibility as defending the shores of America.

Allowing black men to compete against and defeat white men on the baseball field was therefore simply intolerable. Adrian "Cap" Anson, the captain of the Chicago White Stockings and the greatest white player of his time, had set the example. By 1886 the Cuban Giants, the first great black team in history, was strong enough to beat the Cincinnati Red Stockings of the National League; a year later they almost beat the champions, the Detroit Tigers, losing 6-4 in the ninth on an error. Naively, but understandably, hope among blacks was high that because they had proven their ability to compete against the very best white players, the majors would soon open their doors.

But that hope, like so many others, was smashed one chilly April morning in 1887 in Newark, New Jersey. John Holway described the events: "The Chicago White Stockings were scheduled to play Newark of the Eastern League, whose pitching star, thirty-five game winner George Stovey, was a light-skinned Negro from Canada. Chicago captain Adrian Anson, the greatest player of his day, stomped off the field rather than face Stovey. His walk set a pattern that would last exactly sixty years. One by one blacks were eased out of organized baseball. The long blackball decades had begun"

Despite the ban, black baseball continued to flourish. In 1903, the Cuban X-Giants beat the Philadelphia Giants 2-1 in the century's first black World Series, a month before the Pittsburgh Pirates and Boston Red Sox played the first modern white World Series. But the next year, Sol White, the manager of the Philadelphia Giants (who Holway describes as the "first great black organizer") lured away the X-Giants' star pitcher, Andrew "Rube" Foster, who would himself become a great manager and the founder of the Negro National League. In the rematch, the Phils trounced the X-Giants and remained on top of the black baseball world for the next few years.

By 1906 the Phillies, who had won 108 and lost 31 games that year, were so good their white owner, sportswriter Walter Schleichter, sent a letter to the New York papers challenging the winner of the white World Series to meet his club "and thus decide who can play baseball the best, the white or the black American." But the White Sox, who had beaten the Cubs that year, refused the offer. To white men, including some of the game's greatest stars, being outplayed by blacks—who were then almost unanimously regarded as intellectually and physically inferior to whites—was a disgrace that could neither be risked nor tolerated.

The great Ty Cobb was one of those white men. The Detroit Tigers, Cobb's team, were then the champions of the American League. They had visited Cuba in 1909, minus Cobb himself and Sam Crawford, and had won only four games while losing eight. One of their losses was to a no-hitter by Eusaquio Pedroso. The Tigers returned for revenge the following year, this time with Cobb and Crawford. They won seven and lost four, though Cobb was thrown out every time he tried to steal, and three American blacks— John Henry Lloyd, Grant Johnson, and Bruce Petway—outhit him. Cobb stomped off the field and vowed never to play blacks again. And he never did on either American or foreign soil.

Until Jackie Robinson made his debut with the Dodgers at Ebbets Field in April of 1947, no black ballplayer had ever been allowed to play Major League Baseball. Baseball, as Bruce Chadwick pointed out in his book *When the Game Was Black and White*, "was a game as segregated as movie theaters in the North, bus depots in the Midwest, restaurants in the West, and restrooms in the South." But despite enormous difficulties, blacks continued to play wherever they could: on sandlots in city parks, at fair grounds, and even in mill yards. They played however they could: on factory teams and in summer leagues. They played for the love of the game: in South Carolina, South Domingo, and Mexico City. The very best of them played in the Negro National League, the Negro American League, and the Eastern Colored League, the major leagues of black America.

Blessed with enormous natural talent, the black stars played, to the delight of devoted fans of both races, a faster, less inhibited, more daring, and more entertaining brand of baseball than the white major leaguers. As Chadwick explained, "batters and pitchers followed no one form as they did in the majors, and styles of hitting varied greatly—Satchel Paige had his big windup, Max Manning used a high-kick windup, while Leon Day used no windup at all and threw from his shoulder. Batters were the same way." Since there were no coaches or instructors, the players did what came naturally. Some held their bats high, others on their shoulders; some had wide stances and others narrow stances. The great Josh Gibson had a very short, compact stroke and others had big, wide swings.

Black baseball produced great pitching duels and occasional 1-0 games, but it was, as Chadwick described, "a hitter's game, with many more bunts, hit-and-run plays, and stretched singles than turned up in white games." Cool Papa Bell would often go from first to third on a grounder to second. Bunts became a science. And since there were no illegal pitches, spitters, shine balls, emery balls, darkened "dirt" balls, and knockdown pitches were common. Nevertheless, it was not unusual for each team to get fifteen or more hits, and one game in 1936 included an amazing total of forty-six hits.

The names of the teams were almost as imaginative as the play. Teams had names like the Monarchs, Grays, Royal Giants, Crawfords, Barons and Buckeyes, and they barn-stormed all over the country in dilapidated old buses with stuttering engines, poor ventilation, uncomfortable seats and peeling paint. They took on all comers, from lower-level black professional teams to white semi-pro teams. They played clubs in the United States, in South America, Central America and Canada; some even went to Japan. They also, challenged white major league teams like the Philadelphia Phillies, the Detroit Tigers, and all-star teams led by such greats as Dizzy Dean, Babe Ruth, and Lou Gehrig; frequently, they beat them. Despite the barriers, black baseball produced giants of the game who are now enshrined in the Baseball Hall of Fame: Satchel Paige, Josh Gibson, Ray Dandridge, Monte Irvin, Cool Papa Bell, Judy Johnson, Pop Lloyd, Martin Dihigo, and Oscar Charleston.

Not surprisingly, the Depression was devastating to black baseball. By the spring of 1932, the Eastern Colored League and the Negro National League were both out of business, and the Southern Negro League was barely alive. But two innovations, night baseball and the East-West All-Star game, and President Roosevelt's job program, revived black baseball, which by the close of the thirties was so successful that Satchel Paige could credibly claim, "In the late Thirties, any Negro league club could have beaten any white major league team."

Black baseball teams pioneered the introduction of night baseball. The white major leagues did not have lights until 1935, but J. L. Wilkinson, the owner of the Kansas City Monarchs, developed a portable lighting system in 1929-30; the Pittsburgh Crawfords installed baseball's first permanent lights at Greenlee Field in 1933. The dramatic increase in attendance that followed allowed Pittsburgh to offer lavish salaries to some of the greatest black players in the game, including Josh Gibson behind the plate, Cool Papa Bell in center field, Sam Bankhead in left field, Jimmy Crutchfield in right field,

Judy Johnson at third base, and Satchel Paige on the mound. Nine Crawfords were selected on the fourteen-man East All-Star team in 1936, and some experts believe that the Crawfords were probably the strongest team in all of baseball in both 1935 and 1936.

Although largely ignored by the white press, the Negro leagues produced many of the greatest players in all of baseball during the thirties and forties. There were pitchers like the legendary Satchel Paige, described by the great white pitcher Dizzy Dean as the greatest pitcher in the country. Leon Day, who went 15-0 in a forty-game Negro league schedule in 1937, and Cannonball Dick Redding, who won twenty-two games in a row, were widely regarded by blacks and whites alike as being every bit as good or better than the very best white major leaguers. Cool Papa Bell was probably the greatest base stealer of all. Although no formal records were kept, Bell reportedly once stole 175 bases in 200 games, all in a single year. Bell, who twice hit. 400, was so fast that when Jesse Owens ran the bases in special pre-game exhibitions in 1936, he refused to race him.

Josh Gibson was probably the greatest hitter of the decade. More than six feet tall and powerfully built, with a broad chest and muscular arms, Gibson generated enormous power with a short, efficient swing. He led the Negro leagues in home runs ten times and was credited with eighty-four home runs in one season of barnstorming. In 1936, Gibson hit twenty official league home runs in a thirty-eight game schedule, the equivalent of eighty-five in a 154-game season. In 1942, Gibson hit twenty again, this time in forty-two league games.

During his first summer in the black major leagues, when he was only 18-years-old, Gibson became the first player to hit the roof-top facade at Yankee Stadium. But Gibson was not just a power hitter. He also hit for average, with a lifetime mark of .384. Although some skeptics have questioned the reliability of Negro league records, the highly-regarded Elias Baseball Bureau credited Gibson with a league leading .393 in the first season they kept records for the Negro leagues. Gibson's hitting was so extraordinary and legendary that fans would usually fill ballparks up to ninety minutes before a game to watch him take batting practice.

Gibson was not the only great black power hitter of the era. Buck Leonard and Mule Settles also had tremendous power. According to observers, Leonard once hit a home run so far off Bob Feller "it cleared the fence, the bleachers, a row of houses, and hit a big old water tower." He was a great fastball hitter who averaged .341 in the Negro National League over seventeen years and had a career high of .395 in 1948. Leonard, who was elected to the Hall of Fame in 1972, teamed up with Gibson to lead the Homestead Grays to nine straight pennants and World Series titles in 1943 and 1944. Like Gibson, Settles was extremely powerfully built, with thick arms and enormous hands. In one thirty-six game league season, Settles hit three homers, three times, in a single game. But his most remarkable statistic was that he hit eleven home runs in seventy-seven at-bats against major leaguers, a pace that would have resulted in more than eighty home runs in a full season.

In the forties, black major league baseball was at the height of its glory. In 1943, a Negro League East-West All-Star game in Chicago's Comiskey Park attracted 51,000 fans. In 1946, more than 46,000 packed Yankee Stadium to watch Satchel Paige duel Bob Feller in a black-versus-white All-Star game. As late as 1948, the East-West All-Star game drew 42,000 people to Comiskey Park. But by 1950, the era of the great black major leagues was over. The opening of the doors to the previously all-white major leagues doomed the black major leagues to extinction.

By 1947, changing racial attitudes in the white population, fair employment policies instituted by the federal government, a talent shortage aggravated by the manpower depletion of World War II, and the exploits of Joe Louis and Jesse Owens combined to convince major league baseball to end its sixty-year practice of racial segregation. It was achieved without the support of the owners of the Major League teams, who were more concerned that integration would cause them to lose the income they had been getting from renting their ballparks to the Negro Leagues. When they met in the winter of 1947 to consider Branch Rickey's plan to promote Robinson to the majors, they voted 15-1 against it. The lone supporter was the commissioner, "Happy" Chandler.

Nevertheless, the signing of Jackie Robinson by the Brooklyn Dodgers and his immediate success opened the door for other black stars. The standard excuse given to justify the exclusion of black players had been that they lacked the ability to perform in the clutch. Robinson's performance destroyed that old slur. Despite an extraordinary level of taunting and attempted intimidation from players and fans alike, the 28-year-old rookie hit .297 his first season, sparked a championship season for the Dodgers, and won Rookie of the Year honors.

In ten Major League seasons, this son of a Georgia sharecropper and a domestic servant would hit .311, including a career high of .342 in his 1949 MVP season. Fast, daring, and intensely competitive, Robinson played every position except catcher and center field. Never a great home run hitter—he never hit more than nineteen in a season—Robinson had a devastating line drive and was a master of the art of bunting. At his best, in the six years between 1949 and 1954, only Stan Musial was able to challenge Robinson's claim as the most dominant player in the National League. No other single player was more responsible for the Dodgers' rise to greatness as they won National League Championships in 1947, '49, '52, '53, '55 and '56, tied with the Giants in 1951, and took the World Series against the Yankees in 1955.

Although integration came too late for many of the established black stars, Robinson paved the way for future greats who had started their careers in the Negro leagues. Players such as Hank Aaron, Willie Mays, Roy Campanella, Ernie Banks, Monte Irwin, Larry Doby, Joe Black and Don Newcombe formed the vanguard of a black onslaught that would revolutionize major league baseball. In the decade from 1932 to 1941, the American League won seven of ten World Series encounters with the National League and six of the first nine All-Star games. During this period American League hitters topped their National League counterparts in batting average, homers, RBIs, and stolen bases, while National League pitchers posted lower ERAs. All this would change with the integration of the game.

The Japanese assault on Pearl Harbor in late 1941 plunged the country into full-scale war with the Axis powers, and the military drafts that followed sapped the strength of the teams. The Cardinals of the National League won three of the four World Series played during the war years. The Cardinals' dominance of Major League Baseball during this period was, many believe, largely due to the efficient farm system developed by Branch Rickey, the man who would sign Jackie Robinson in baseball's "great experiment." Inspired by Rickey's example and the success of the first black stars, National League owners were, for more than a decade, considerably more aggressive than their American League counterparts in signing black players.

As a result, the National League reversed the American League's previous dominance, and throughout the fifties it led the majors in both offensive performance and, to the surprise of many, attendance. In 1949, in just his third season in the majors, Robinson became the first black player to win a

Most Valuable Player Award. During the next decade, seven black stars, including sluggers Roy Campanella, Ernie Banks, and Willie Mays, would win National League MVP awards. The annual Cy Young Award, honoring the outstanding pitcher of the season, was instituted in 1956. The first recipient was Don Newcombe, the black pitching ace of the Brooklyn Dodgers.

If blacks had proven that they could more than hold their own with their white counterparts, Major League Baseball was still not ready for real integration. In 1956, ten years after Robinson's signing, there were only forty African American players on the rosters of Major League teams; the Philadelphia Phillies, the Detroit Tigers, and the Boston Red Sox had no black players. By the mid-1950s, according to historian Ben Rader, "many if not all clubs had unwritten understandings to restrict the total number of blacks. Driven in part by the profit motive, the owners tried to calculate whether increasing the number of black players would result in more wins and thereby increase attendance or whether it would adversely affect the identification of white fans with their teams and therefore reduce attendance and revenues."

Jules Tygiel, Robinson's biographer, has argued that "baseball's failure to integrate more rapidly reflected not only a persistent hostility to blacks, but prevailing racial attitudes and assumptions, and widely shared player development strategies. Many teams stalwartly resisted desegregation. Others moved haltingly, bypassing established Negro League stars in favor of young prospects and demanding higher standards of performance and behavior from black players than white." Curt Flood, the black star of the St. Louis Cardinals who would become best-known for challenging baseball's reserve clause, claimed that white owners were disturbed by interracial dating between black players and white women.

Commenting on baseball's unacknowledged racial quota system, Tygiel has written: "Many teams adopted a *de facto* quota system limiting black access and disproportionately relegating blacks to specific positions. While superstar African American athletes experienced minimal difficulty reaching the major leagues, those of average talent and even of above average talent often lost out to less talented whites. Racism and discrimination plagued black players in spring training, off-field accommodations, fan reactions, salaries, and endorsement opportunities. Most tellingly, major league organizations made no efforts, and apparently gave minimal thought, to bring blacks into coaching, managing, front office, or ownership roles."

In the sixties, although still a small minority of all players, blacks dominated Major League Baseball. That dominance was made possible by a gradual opening up of both leagues. In 1948, outfielder Larry Doby, who had been signed by the Cleveland Indians, became the first black player in the American League and hit .301 his rookie year. The Indians also signed the aging Satchel Paige that year, and although well past his prime, Paige contributed six wins and a save to the team's victory drive. But the American League's dominant team, the New York Yankees, did not add a black player to its roster until 1955, when catcher Elston Howard was summoned from the farm system.

George Weiss, the general manager of the Yankees, was quoted as saying in private, "I will never allow a black man to wear a Yankee uniform. Boxholders from Westchester don't want that sort of crowd. They would be offended to have to sit with niggers." In public, Weiss was more circumspect; in the spring of 1952 he claimed that the team had been looking for a long time for a black player who was "good enough to make the Yankees." What Weiss meant by "good enough" was clarified by an article on Howard written by the reporter Dan Daniel for the *Sporting News*. Daniel's article made it clear that factors other than a black player's baseball skills were used to evaluate his suitability for Major League Baseball. Howard was praised for being "quiet and well-behaved," and for not raising any objection when he was unable to stay with the team at the Emerson Hotel in Baltimore because of that city's segregation ordinances. Daniel concluded his article by claiming that "The Yankees would like to find another Negro player. But they insist that he be of the Howard stamp, and that is not going to be easy. In fact, at the moment, it's impossible."

As Ron Briley pointed out in his contribution to *The 1997 Cooperstown Symposium on Baseball and American Culture,* "In addition to indulging in racial stereotypes regarding character, the Yankee management seemed to accept a double standard based on race. While Howard was expected to always demonstrate exemplary behavior, and the Yankees refused to call up Afro-American Vic Power from the minor leagues, the 'party' antics of white stars such as Mickey Mantle, Billy Martin, and Whitey Ford were tolerated."

Nevertheless, despite these barriers, by 1958 approximately one hundred black Americans and some eighty Hispanics of African descent were playing in the major leagues; and throughout the sixties, black hitters dominated major league offenses. During that decade, blacks in the National League won seven home run titles, seven MVP awards, and six batting titles. In the American League, blacks won three batting titles and three MVP awards. But even those statistics did not do justice to the impact of the great black stars, who were beginning to transform the game by combining speed and power in ways previously unknown.

The sixties produced outstanding white players, such as Roger Maris, who hit a record sixty-one home runs in 162 games in 1961; Carl Yastrzemski, who won an American League Triple Crown; and Pete Rose, who would later break Ty Cobb's record of 4,191 hits. But it was a foursome of black players who were widely regarded as the most talented and exciting players of the decade: Willie Mays, who was voted "Player of the Decade" by the *Sporting News*; Hank Aaron, who would break Babe Ruth's home run record; Frank Robinson, who became the first player to win an MVP award in each league, and Roberto Clemente, who won three National League batting titles.

Although the great black trio of Aaron, Mays, and Frank Robinson had probably seen their best years in the previous decade, the seventies were, in many ways, the golden era of black participation in Major League Baseball. The number of black American players in the major leagues peaked at twenty-six percent in 1974. Additionally, Hispanic players, most of them of mixed African ancestry, constituted another ten percent of all major league players. By the end of the decade, blacks established themselves as the greatest homerun hitters of the modern era. Not only did Aaron break Ruth's all-time home run record with a new mark of 755, but Mays retired in 1973 with 660 homers to rank only behind Aaron in the modern era, and third all-time. Frank Robinson's total of 586 placed him third in the modern era, and fourth all-time.

During the decade, Aaron, Robinson, Mays, Lou Brock and Roberto Clemente all joined the 3,000-hit club, and Rod Carew captured seven American League batting titles, including four in a row from 1972 to 1975. Brock also set a seasonal stolen base record of 118 and shattered Ty Cobb's lifetime total of 892 bases. Twelve black and Hispanic stars won MVP awards during the decade, while pitchers Bob Gibson and Juan Marichal hurled their way into baseball's Hall of Fame. The leading player of the decade was arguably Reggie Jackson, who hit seven home runs in two World Series appearances with the Yankees finishing his career with 563 home runs.

Despite their impressive performances, black players still faced discrimination both on and off the field. In *The History of Major League Baseball*, author David Q. Voight expressed a familiar complaint when he pointed out that "studies showed that black players had to be better than average players to make it the majors. Thus there were few marginal black players on team rosters; moreover, teams were fearful of playing too many black players in a game lest it affect attendance. And retired black players seldom found jobs in baseball as field managers or in top administrative posts. However, Frank Robinson became the first black manager to be hired (and fired), and a few token black umpires debuted in this area."

During the seventies, baseball's special status was underlined by an extraordinary torrent of hate mail directed at Henry Aaron as he approached Babe Ruth's home run record. At the end of 1973, the U.S. Postal Service calculated that he had received 930,000 letters and gave him a plaque for receiving more mail than any other non-politician in the country. Dinah Shore was a distant second with a mere 60,000 pieces. While the overwhelming majority of the letters were supportive, tens of thousands were filled with vicious racial diatribes, menacing death threats, and fervent death wishes. Typical of the latter was a letter expressing the hope that "lightning strikes you for trying to blemish Ruth's record." The death threats were usually aimed at Aaron personally. One man wrote to warn that "I will be going to the rest of your games and if you hit one more home run it will be your last. My gun is watching your every black move. This is no joke."

Other letters also threatened his family. Although grammatically weak, one writer's intent was very clear: "I got orders to do a bad job on you if and when you get 10 from B. Ruth record. A guy in Atlanta and a few in Miami Fla don't seem to care if they have to take care of your family too." If the letter writers had intended to intimidate or deter Aaron, they were woefully unsuccessful. In *I Had a Hammer: The Hank Aaron Story*, co-written with Lonnie Wheeler, Aaron recalled that "as the mail piled up, I became more and more intent on breaking the record and shoving it in the ugly faces of those bigots. I'm sure it made me a better hitter."

All that hatred, Aaron acknowledged, "left a deep scar on me. I was just a man doing something that God had given me the power to do, and I was living like an outcast in my own country, I had nowhere to go except home and to the ballpark. I was a prisoner in my own apartment. That whole period, I lived like a guy in a fish bowl, swimming from side to side with nowhere to go, watching everybody watching me. I resented it, and I still resent it. It should have been the most enjoyable time in my life and instead it was hell. I'm proud of the home run record, but I don't talk about it because it brings back too many unpleasant memories."

Aaron's feat provoked not just death threats but also the inevitable comparisons between him and Ruth. Ruth's supporters pointed out that he had fewer at-bats, a higher lifetime batting average, and had been a pitcher for much of his career. They argued that travel was tougher and pitchers were better in Ruth's time, and that Aaron played with a livelier ball. In his book, Aaron decided to make a case for himself and for other modern players. He pointed out that he "had to fly all over the country and play night games in bigger ballparks while facing fresh relief pitchers who threw sliders, which is the nastiest pitch of all and hadn't even been invented in Ruth's day."

But Aaron's most important point was that Ruth played at a time when there were no black players in Major League Baseball. "To me," Aaron wrote, "that's the most relevant point of all, because it stands apart from the changes that reflect the natural evolution of the game—things like new facilities and better equipment and modern innovations. This goes deeper than the other changes because it has to do with the people who play the game. It goes right to the foundation of the Babe Ruth legend, which is the fact that he towered over all the other hitters of his time. He did that, and there's no denying it. There has never been a more dominant hitter. But it should be understood that he dominated a very weak field. If black players had been allowed to play in the major leagues at the time, it is highly unlikely that Ruth would have dominated in the manner that he did. Think about it. What would the National League have been like in my time without black players? Who would have been the greatest home run hitter if I had not been in the league, or Mays or Banks or Frank Robinson or Willie McCovey or Orlando Cepeda or Willie Stargell or Billy Williams or Richie Allen? I'll tell you. The white player who hit the most home runs in the National League in the 1960s was Ron Santo, who was almost fifty ahead of the next white player, Eddie Mathews. With no black players Ron Santo—who is not in the Hall of Fame—would have stood well above all the other home run hitters in the league during his time. By the same token, if I had played with only whites, as Ruth did, I would have outhomered every other player in the National League in the Sixties by more than 120....In addition, it would have been significantly easier to hit in the National League if there hadn't been black pitchers like Bob Gibson, Juan Marichal, Ferguson Jenkins and Bob Veale."

Despite their dominance of major league baseball in the modern era, the percentage of blacks in the major leagues continued to decline throughout the final two decades of the century. But even dwindling numbers and the rise or maturing of white superstars, such as Mike Schmidt, Dale Murphy, George Brett, Wade Boggs, and Mark McGwire, failed to prevent blacks from dominating major league offensive statistics during the eighties and nineties. During these decades, four players joined the 500 home run club; two of them (Reggie Jackson and Eddie Murphy) were black, and two others (Mike Schmidt and Mark McGwire) were white.

Home runs hardly told the entire story. Tony Gwynn was the dominant hitter of the period, winning eight batting titles in the National League and ending the century with the highest batting average of the modern era (.339). Black stars won eighteen of the twenty National League batting titles, and despite McGwire's prodigious home run hitting, blacks also dominated the power statistics. Ken Griffey Jr. won four home run titles and one RBI title in the '90s; Cecil Fielder won two home run titles and three RBI titles; Albert Belle won three RBI titles and one home run title; Juan Gonzales won two home run titles and one RBI title. Perhaps the clearest expression of black offensive dominance in the '90s was in the Most Valuable Player Awards. Not only did blacks win fourteen of the twenty awards, but they were also the only multiple winners, with Barry Bonds claiming three awards in the National League and Frank Thomas and Juan Gonzalez claiming two each in the American League.

During the '90s, the two best players, Barry Bonds and Ken Griffey Jr., were black. Not only did Bonds end the decade as the only major leaguer with 400 home runs and 400 stolen bases, but in the 2001 season he broke Mark McGwire's single-season home run record with an astounding total of 73. Bonds, who also won the Most Valuable Player awards in 2001 and 2002 for an unprecedented fourth and fifth time, turned in what must have been the greatest single season performance of all time in 2001. In addition to the home run record, Bonds surpassed Babe Ruth's slugging percentage record of .847 set in 1920 with his own .863 mark; his 177 walks also broke a Babe Ruth single season record. If he remains healthy, Bonds, who should surpass the 500 steals mark in 2003 and become the sole member of the 500 home runs and 500 steals club, is now the favorite to break Aaron's home run record.

The now 33-year-old Griffey, who hit 382 home runs during the decade—

more than anybody except the now-retired Mark McGwire—reached the 400 home run mark faster than anybody in history. He was once the favorite to break Aaron's record, but injuries during the past three seasons have raised questions about his desire and off-season training habits. Nevertheless, Griffey is still a formidable talent and he could yet return to his old form. Griffey and Bonds also ranked second and third in runs batted in during the '90s, with another black player, Albert Belle, coming in first.

Perhaps the clearest example of the superior athletic skills of black baseball players is their dominance of a rarely published statistic: 30 home runs and 30 stolen bases in a single season. Of the seven players who have managed this feat more than once, only two—Howard Johnson, who did it three times, and Jeff Bagwell, who did it twice,—are white. The top performers, the father-son combination of Bobby and Barry Bonds, have done it five times each. The other multiple winners, with two apiece, are Willie Mays, Ron Gant and Sammy Sosa.

Not even the impressive statistics piled up by black ballplayers over the past fifty years tell the full story of black dominance of baseball. Despite all the unquestioned civil rights advances, hiring in baseball—on and off the field—is not yet colorblind. Even today, the environment in baseball is truly hospitable only to black superstars who are willing and able to function effectively in a white world—a world often very different from the ones in which they were born and raised. It is still true that average black players, unlike even mediocre white ones, are rarely kept on rosters for their intangible qualities. Black players are expected to produce tangible results, measurable in hits and runs. Consequently, a far greater percentage of the stars in baseball are black than their representation in the league would suggest. In fact, despite being a tiny percentage of the players on Major League rosters since their admittance in 1947, blacks have been a clear majority of the greatest ballplayers in the game during the modern era.

If the relative abilities of black and white players are to be fairly and accurately compared, then 1950—a mere three years after the color barrier was finally broken and a time when only a handful of blacks were playing in the major leagues—should be regarded as the beginning of the modern baseball era. Since the statistics from the Negro Baseball League are not considered, the statistics of white players from the segregated era of Major League Baseball should also be disregarded. Certainly it is not unfair to white players to judge them by the same standards that are applied to blacks. The home runs, hits, and stolen bases of Babe Ruth, Joe DiMaggio, and Ty Cobb should be no more relevant to a fair and accurate comparison of black and white baseball players than the home runs, hits, and stolen bases of Josh Gibson, Oscar Charleston, and James "Cool Papa" Bell. This is especially true since the average percentage of blacks in the major leagues, from 1947 to the present, is miniscule. Major League Baseball's statistics are dominated by men who played before the start of the modern era of integrated baseball. When the statistics of black and white players of the modern era are compared, black players clearly dominate. The only men to exceed 600 home runs in the modern era—Hank Aaron with 755, Willie Mays with 660, and Barry Bonds with 613 and counting—are black.

Among players of the modern era whose careers were over before 1990, all of the top five leaders in hitting average are black. Rod Carew, with a career average of. 328, is easily, the best contact hitter. Roberto Clemente is second with. 317; Jackie Robinson is third with .311; Hank Aaron and Bill Matlock are tied with .305. Pete Rose with .303 is the highest ranked white player. Willie Mays, with .302, also completed his career with a batting average in excess of the magical .300 barrier.

Others, perhaps less inclined than me to recognize the dominance of black athletes, have also noted and commented on the achievements of black baseball players. The white, conservative political columnist and baseball super fan George F. Will, in his book *Men at Work*, several years ago, before Barry Bonds' extraordinary rise, wrote that "although the first black players did not make it to the major leagues until 1947 and baseball was not really fully open to blacks until the mid-1950s, it is possible to select an all-black team that could hold its own with a team drawn from all the other players during the first nine decades of this century."

Catcher	Roy Campanella
First base	Willie McCovey
Second.base	Rod Carew
Third base	Jackie Robinson (256 games at third)
Shortstop	Ernie Banks
Outfield	Willie Mays, Henry Aaron, Frank Robinson
Pitcher	Bob Gibson

Despite this extraordinary record of achievement, the proportion of American-born black players in Major League Baseball has continued to decline from approximately one in four in the late 1960s to only one in six in the late 1980s. The low and declining percentages of African Americans in Major League Baseball, even as commentators complain about a decline of talent in the league, clearly has nothing to do with the ability of black players. Or perhaps it does in an extremely regrettable way. To many baseball aficionados, baseball is still much more than a sport. It appears that, in some ways, baseball remains firmly entrenched in its ugly, racist past. It retains just enough of a veneer of black and Latin players to disguise its real purpose: providing a refuge for white athletes, many insufficiently talented to survive in fair competition with black players.

Joe Morgan, the Hall of Fame second baseman who starred with the Cincinnati Reds in the 1970s, addressed this topic in a recent book. In *Long Balls, No Strikes*, Morgan wrote: "Throughout my career…I have noticed that African Americans had to be vastly superior to their white counterparts if they were to hold their places on a major league roster. Hank Aaron, Willie Mays, Lou Brock, Billy Williams, and Ernie Banks had no trouble finding playing time. But there were few jobs available if you were a black, middle-tier talent." To support his allegations, Morgan pointed to a 1967 study by Aaron Rosenblatt, author of *Negroes in Baseball: The Failure of Success*. Rosenblatt found that among players with batting averages below .250, the proportion of black players steadily declined. He concluded that "the undistinguished Negro player is less likely to play in the major leagues than the equally undistinguished white player." This meant, Morgan noted, "that we didn't have any black versions of players like Ducky Schofield, who sat on the bench for most of his 19-year career, or Phil Gagliano, who played a dozen years in the majors without once holding a regular position."

Evaluating the current climate, Morgan pointed out that nothing had changed. "You could compile a long list of utility ball players who spent five years or more in the big leagues: I guarantee you won't find many African Americans among them. The only current black utility player I can think of is Lenny Harris, who hits around .270 every season, can play six different positions, and has to fight for a spot on someone's roster nearly every spring. (I don't count guys like Tony Phillips or Bip Roberts, who are really semi-regulars.) For every Lenny Harris, there are twenty Tim Bogars. Houston recently gave Bogars, a white utility infielder, who hit about a buck-fifty last year, a two-year, $1.5 million contract. I'm happy for Tim and his family. But you don't see teams making deals like that with Lenny Harris, and Lenny's a better ballplayer."

Bogars' treatment, Morgan said, was in sharp contrast to the typical fate of talented but non-superstar black players. "A few years back, the Yankee starting shortstop was Bobby Meacham. Though not a star, Meacham had displayed excellent range at short, second and third. He was a switch-hitter who could produce some runs despite his mediocre batting average. Bobby had some occasional pop in his bat, knew how to work a pitcher for a walk, ran the bases well, and was an excellent base stealer. In other words, he had all the talents you look for in a bench player. As soon as it became apparent, however, that Bobby could not start for New York, he was not only off the team, but out of baseball."

It is difficult not to conclude that the gatekeepers of baseball, fully aware of the special gifts of black athletes, have established a new informal quota to prevent blacks from taking over the national pastime as they have the National Football League and the National Basketball Association. The quota is maintained in a variety of ways—some subtle, and others less so. One of the more obvious ways is to severely limit the number of blacks, particularly American-born blacks, in the so-called thinking positions like pitcher and catcher. "When I joined professional baseball," Morgan has written, "most coaches, managers, and execs were Southerners, many of whom helped perpetuate racial biases and stereotypes. They considered African American players to be physically gifted but mentally deficient. Few teams had black second basemen, shortstops, catchers, or pitchers, a trend that continues to this day; it's no coincidence that baseball people consider these spots thinking man's positions. No matter what position you played when you signed, clubs would try to fit an outfielder's glove on you if you were black."

Since pitchers and catchers usually make up at least 50 percent of a team's roster, this is an extremely effective tactic. According to *Sports Illustrated*, there were only twelve black pitchers, or less than five percent of the approximately 260 total, on major league rosters when the 1991 season began. Black catchers are an even rarer species; all four in the major leagues in 1991 were born outside the United States. Tellingly, not much has changed in the decade since those statistics were published.

Another less obvious but just as effective method of enforcing the quota is by establishing very different and much tougher entry standards for young black players. They are expected to succeed almost immediately. Those who need support and nurture, however talented, invariably fail to find it and inevitably join the extraordinarily long list of talented young black athletes who failed to make the cut in Major League Baseball. But even those who are instant hits are often treated harshly if they stumble. The career of Gerald Young, the former centerfielder of the Houston Astros, vividly illustrates how difficult it is for even highly talented blacks to make it in Major League Baseball.

Young, a minor league roommate of Dwight Gooden, was obtained from the New York Mets along with Manny Lee and Mitch Cooke for Ray Knight, who would become the MVP of the 1986 World Series. After almost three years in the minor league system, Young joined the Astros on July 8, 1987, to replace the disabled Billy Hatcher. He was immediately installed in centerfield as the starter. After hitting just over. .200 in his first thirteen games, Young hit .350 the rest of the way and ended the season with a .321 average, the highest for National League rookies with 150 or more at-bats.

Young, who also stole twenty-six bases in seventy-one games, finished fifth in National League Rookie of the Year balloting. In his first full year, Young's sixty-five stolen bases set a single-season club record, placing him second in the National League behind Vince Coleman and third in both leagues, behind Coleman and Rickey Henderson, the American League leader. Young also led the team in walks (66), tied Billy Hatcher for the team lead in runs (79), and ended the season with a .257 batting average. In his second full season, despite leading all National League outfielders in fielding percentage (. 998), putouts (412), assists (15), total chances (428), and double plays (5), Young's once bright star was already growing dim. His thirty-four stolen bases ranked eighth in the National League, but was below his record of the previous year and his batting average that year (.233) was also down.

It mattered little to his critics, the harshest of whom was his hometown press, that knee problems after the All-Star break—when he had thirty-one stolen bases—limited his productivity for the rest of the year. Young began the 1990 season, his fourth in the majors, engulfed in trade rumors and under intense press and fan scrutiny. There was a widespread feeling in the Houston baseball community, frequently expressed by journalists and fans, that Young was a terrible disappointment. In the cruelest of ironies, the 24-

year-old Young was being written off because his career batting average had fallen to .260, exactly the same as the lifetime averages of manager Art Howe and third base coach Phil Garner, both of them former Astros players.

Howe, who was primarily responsible for Young's demotion to the minor leagues after his slow start in 1990, is typical of the modestly talented white players who flourish in the major leagues. In his first three years in the majors, Howe played in 113 games and had 47 hits, 15 RBIs and a batting average of .189. Howe was then 29 years old, but the following season he became the Astros' regular second baseman. In dramatic contrast, Young, a brilliant defensive player who in 366 games had 194 hits, 90 RBIs, scored 194 runs, stole 125 bases, and compiled a batting average of. .260, was demoted to the minor leagues by a team with one of the weakest outfields in the major leagues. Like many other talented young black players who either got out of the blocks too slowly or stumbled after a fast start, Young was soon out of Major League Baseball.

Major League Baseball has generally been hostile to black athletes, but some teams have been more hostile than others. The Astros, historically one of the whitest and least talented teams in the National League, were for many years particularly hostile. Only a handful of black players, such as Joe Morgan, Bob Watson, Cesar Cedeno, J. R. Richards, and Enos Cabell, have started for the Astros for more than five years. The team has not been much less hostile to Hispanic players. Despite its longtime antipathy to minorities, the club's all-time batting records were, for many years, dominated by them. Richards, the only black pitcher to have a productive career in Houston, ranks among the top three or four in almost every pitching category.

The Joe Morgan story is particularly instructive. Morgan, generally regarded as one of the greatest second basemen to ever play the game, made his big league debut with the Astros (then called the Texas Colt 45s) in 1965. According to Morgan, the Astros wanted him to switch to the outfield "even though it was obvious I didn't have a strong enough arm to play there… they only dropped the idea when I threatened to go home." The Houston team was never happy with Morgan and his outspoken ways. Despite winning the *Sporting News* Rookie of the Year Award and twice being named to the All-Star team, Morgan was traded to Cincinnati in 1971. In Cincinnati, Morgan would blossom under the deft handling of Sparky Anderson, his new manager, who so respected the player's high intelligence that he never gave him a "take" sign in all their years together. Morgan was named the National

League's Most Valuable Player in both 1975 and 1976, the first such player since Ernie Banks in 1958 and 1959. When Cincinnati swept the New York Yankees in the 1976 World Series, Morgan homered in the first inning of the first game; tripled, singled and stole a base in game two; doubled in a run in game three; and walked, stole a base, and scored the first run of game four.

The single most effective method of enforcing the quota is the one that Major League Baseball has followed the most assiduously. They have made it increasingly difficult for African Americans to enter baseball. While the participation of American-born blacks in basketball and football—the other two major sports—has increased by approximately ten percent during the last decade, it has decreased in baseball over that same period by about a third. Bob Watson, the black former general manager of the Astros and the New York Yankees, and himself a highly successful major league player, has repeatedly pointed out that baseball is no longer getting the "stud players coming out of the inner city anymore. Eric Davis and Darryl Strawberry were the last of that stud group. If Darryl Strawberry were coming up today, it would be as a basketball player." According to Morgan's own testimony: "I am a Hall of Famer, but if I were 18 years old today, I probably wouldn't get the chance to play pro ball."

Baseball, Morgan explains, is no longer scouring America's inner cities for talent. "The African American bird dogs" who first touted players like Dusty Baker, Curt Flood, Vada Pinson, Tommy Harper, and Morgan himself to white scouts were eliminated by a decision of the owners to cut expenses by slashing their scouting staffs and replacing them with a scouting combine. Since the combine, that prepares reports on prospects for all major league teams began operating, the signing of African Americans has sharply declined. Combine scouts, Morgan has charged, "rarely venture into the inner-city neighborhoods where the preponderance of minority athletic talent resides. College has become the primary showcase for young baseball players; over 80 percent of the draftees signed in the last decade came up through the collegiate ranks. For a variety of sociological and economic reasons, college attendees make up a smaller percentage of the African American population than the white. Those African Americans who do attend college often can't afford to go to those big-name schools that regularly attract baseball scouts to their games. Therefore, many potential star players never get seen."

A study conducted some years ago by John Young, a former scouting director for the Detroit Tigers, vividly illustrated how difficult it has become for young African Americans to enter professional baseball. Young found that more than forty percent of all the drafted players came from one region of the country, Southern California, and that barely two percent of those players were black. In 1998, according to Morgan, "there wasn't a single African American on the U.S. National Baseball Team. I cover the College World Series for ESPN every year. The overwhelming majority of the players I watch are Caucasian. Out of every 100 players drafted only five or six have a legitimate chance to make it to the big leagues. But the other 95 at least get the opportunity to fail. That's not the case for African Americans. The only ones who get signed are the absolutely can't miss prospects."

It is not surprising therefore that a majority of the most talented and exciting young players in baseball, a significant majority of them black, are from Latin America. Alfonso Soriano and Vladimir Guerrero both finished the 2002 season with thirty-nine homers and more than forty steals. Alex Rodriguez hit fifty-seven home runs to lead the American League in that category for the second straight season. Manny Ramirez won the American League batting title with a .349 mark. Francisco Rodriguez, the baby-faced 20-year-old from Venezuela, won five games for the Anaheim Angels in the 2002 postseason to equal the previous record. And Miguel Tejada finished among the American League leaders in home runs (34), batting average (308), RBI (131), and hits (204); he beat out fellow black Latinos Alex Rodriguez and Alfonso Soriano for the Most Valuable Player Award in the American League for the 2002 season.

The television ratings during the 2002 World Series reached historically low levels for the Fox network, declining by about 25 percent from the ratings of the previous year. While some of this was due to the regional nature of the contest that pitted two California teams against each other, baseball's appeal has been slipping for some time. Judged purely on the basis of fan appeal, football is now the real national pastime and basketball is on the verge of overtaking baseball. As the enormous popularity of Tiger Woods, Michael Jordan, and the Williams sisters indicates, American sports fans are becoming increasingly colorblind. The failure of baseball to grasp this new reality will ensure that baseball's appeal will continue to shrink. In this new century, young Americans, black and white alike, will be far more interested in the quality of the athlete's ability than in his or her race or color. Baseball's white quota, unless repealed, will guarantee that baseball in the not-too-distant future will become like hockey, a minor sport with limited appeal.

5

Basketball: A Showcase
for Black Athletic Talent

Amerca in 1956 was prosperous, smug, and very, very white. The
suburbs were white. The fronts of buses were white. Pop stars were
white. Sports heroes were white. Even the National Basketball
Association was white. Adlai Stevenson, the standard-bearer of the
Democratic Party, explained that he was in favor of "gradual" integration and
lectured the North to end its own segregation before criticizing the South.
President Eisenhower proposed the establishment of a commission to study
alleged civil rights violations. Senator Jack Kennedy warned that segregation
in the North was sanctioned not by law but by a silent understanding. Led by
General Secretary Ralph Bunche, the United Nations denounced "bigoted"
whites for seeking to "smear" supporters of Negro rights as communists.

But beneath the placid white surface, America was roiling with change.
On the streets of the South, a remarkable 27-year-old Baptist minister with
the unforgettable and propitious name of Martin Luther King was just
beginning a career that would transform his nation and enshrine him as one
of history's seminal figures. But unlike his namesake, the German leader of
the Reformation who angrily denounced the sale of papal indulgences and
was excommunicated by the church, the young black American, in emulation
of the martyred Indian nationalist leader Gandhi, began his crusade by urging

passive resistance and love.

On the basketball courts, another young black man was launching another revolution that would also help to transform America and the world's view of black ability and potential. Martin Luther King's civil rights revolution would, of course, smooth the way, particularly off the court, for Bill Russell and the other great pioneering black athletes. Without King, America would, unquestionably, be a very different and far lesser place. So, too, basketball would be unrecognizably different, and far less exciting, without the changes initiated by Russell and the other great black athletes who followed.

Before Russell, the NBA was white, slow, and earthbound. The first black players—Chuck Cooper, Sweetwater Clifton, and Earl Lloyd—had been signed in 1950. But before Russell, blacks were mere role players assigned to play defense, rebound, and set picks. In baseball, blacks were already stars. Hank Aaron won the batting title in the National League and Don Newcombe won twenty-seven games and the MVP title in the National League. When Russell arrived, the Mikan era had been over for a few years, but the style of play he pioneered had lingered. George Mikan was the game's first dominant big man and the hottest basketball property of his time. He led the Minneapolis Lakers to five NBA titles in six seasons, from 1949 through 1954, and established the foundation of the NBA.

The 6-10 Mikan was sturdily built and his game was based on power, not speed or agility. His favorite move was to plant himself in the low post and use the hook shot to score from close in. Russell's game was custom-designed to destroy the careers of that kind of center, to render them obsolete. What he did to Neil Johnston of the Philadelphia Warriors was a perfect example of that lethal talent. Johnston had led the NBA in scoring for three straight seasons and was only 26 years old when Russell entered the league. His favorite shot was a sidearm hook that had been considered virtually unblockable until he met Russell, who effortlessly and repeatedly blocked it when they first met during Russell's rookie year. Johnston continued to play well against other teams, but against the Celtics he was virtually useless. His abject and repeated failures against Russell were too much for Johnston's psyche, and within two years he was out of the league, his confidence destroyed.

White-dominated basketball was horizontal; Russell made it vertical. In 1956 basketball was still slow, plodding, and predictable. The two-handed and one-hand set shots were still major offensive weapons. Many guards and forwards had not mastered the art of the jump shot, and centers relied on hook shots and inside power moves. Russell's phenomenal leaping ability and unparalleled quickness changed all that. Shot blocking was a rare event before he arrived. He made it a fundamental part of his game.

But it was not just centers whose games he disrupted. His tremendous rebounding and outlet passing unleashed the Celtic fast break, and a whole new type of game was born. Never before and never again would a rookie have such a profound impact on an established sports league. Russell's rookie season marked the beginning of sports' greatest dynasty, a reign that would produce eleven championships in thirteen years. More importantly, Russell began the transformation of the NBA into what it is today, the world's premier showcase for the unique and extraordinary talents of black athletes of West African origin.

Russell played in the air, but the next great black superstar seemed capable of defying gravity itself. Elgin Baylor's ability to apparently hang in the air foreshadowed the gravity-defying feats of Connie Hawkins, Julius Ervin, Michael Jordan, and Vince Carter. Baylor was only 6-5, not tall for a forward, even in 1959. But his strength, athleticism, and scoring ability made him more than a match for his taller rivals. Baylor was a star from the day he arrived in the NBA. He had spent thousands of hours honing his skills on the public playgrounds of the nation's capital, but he regarded his amazing body as a gift from God. His team, the Minneapolis Lakers, had been 19-53 the year before he arrived, but he led them to the playoffs in his rookie season by averaging 24.9 points and 15 rebounds per game. And he was even better in the playoffs.

The St. Louis Hawks and the Boston Celtics had easily won their respective conferences, and the general expectation was that they would meet in the NBA finals. After a tremendous struggle with Syracuse, the Celtics won the Eastern Conference, but St. Louis failed to get past Baylor and the Lakers. After falling behind 2-1, the Lakers won three straight games to oust the Hawks and gain the dubious distinction of meeting the Celtics in the final. Three of the four games in the final were close, but Russell and the Celtics swept the series 4-0. Baylor, who made the All-NBA team in his rookie year, would eventually be named captain of the Lakers and become one of the game's most popular players; he also became a moving force in the development of the Players Association. But because of the dominance of the Celtics, Baylor played on only one championship team in his fourteen-year career. While his impact was not as great as Russell's, his extraordinary physical gifts established athletic benchmarks that only the most supremely gifted black players have been able to meet. By the time his career was over, the very definition of "athlete" had changed forever.

When Wilt Chamberlain entered the NBA in the 1959-60 season, a 50-point game was, as it is today, highly unusual. In fact, Elgin Baylor's 55-point eruption in his rookie season only one year earlier had been, at the time, the third-highest score in NBA history. Incredibly, in just his rookie season with the Philadelphia Warriors, Chamberlain scored more than 50 points, seven times, and won both Rookie of the Year and Most Valuable Player by leading the league in both scoring and rebounding. Russell's extraordinary defensive prowess, and his ability to make his teammates better, revolutionized professional basketball and made the Celtics almost unbeatable for more than a decade. However, the towering Chamberlain brought a new level of individual dominance to the NBA. Nobody had ever seen anybody quite like him before. At 7-foot-1 and 275 pounds, he towered over the 6-9 Russell and the other centers of the time. Chamberlain was not just enormous, he was also an outstanding athlete and tremendously strong. A native of Philadelphia, he had won shot putt titles at that city's famed Overbrook High School and later at the University of Kansas.

Chamberlain's rookie season was unprecedented, but his accomplishments in his third season are the stuff of which legends are made. He not only played all but eight minutes of the entire season, but he averaged more than 50 points per game, shattering by twelve points the NBA record he had set in his rookie season. Perhaps most incredibly, on March 2, 1962, Chamberlain scored 100 points against the New York Knicks to become the first and only man to break the century mark in an NBA game.

The game had been played in Hershey, Pennsylvania, and only 4,124 people were in attendance, but in the following decades tens of thousands would claim to have personally witnessed the single greatest offensive performance in the history of the National Basketball Association. The Warriors had gone only 32-40 the season before Chamberlain arrived, but improved to 49-26 in his rookie season and attracted capacity crowds most nights. The Celtics remained the NBA's dominant team and Chamberlain was even unfairly tagged with a "loser" image early in his career, despite his accumulation of NBA individual honors. Chamberlain, who played with three different teams, eventually won his first NBA title seven years after his rookie season and cemented his status as perhaps the greatest big man to ever play in the NBA.

The first great black players in the NBA were big men: two centers and a forward. In 1960, Oscar Robertson, the first great black guard, entered the league after winning a gold medal in the 1960 Olympics in Rome. Entering the league the same year was Robertson's white Olympic teammate, Jerry West. Both men would have outstanding NBA careers, but Robertson had a more immediate impact, averaging 30.5 points per game and leading the league with 9.7 assists per contest in his rookie season.

In 1960, only twenty-six percent of the league was black, but the three leading scorers, Chamberlain, Baylor, and Robertson, were black. Their achievements marked the first time in NBA history that three players had exceeded 30 points per game in the same season. By the 1961-62 season, although there were still only two or three blacks on most rosters, seven of the top ten rebounders were black and Robertson averaged an astonishing triple-double of 30.8 points, 12.5 rebounds, and 11.4 assists per game. Robertson, at 6-foot-5 and 210 pounds, was the first great, big guard to play in the NBA. He could, as his triple-double average indicated, do everything. A native of Tennessee, he attended Crispus Attucks High School, where he led his team to two state titles in three years. In that basketball-crazy state, the victorious high school team had traditionally been feted with a parade through its hometown; but because Crispus Attucks had defeated a white school, the celebrations were directed to a remote part of town by police to avoid racial incidents.

It was a slight that Robertson would never forget. At the University of Cincinnati, he became the first college player to lead the NCAA in scoring for three consecutive seasons, but he was so disillusioned with life there that he could not wait to leave. "All I want," he said, "is to get out of school. When I'm through I don't want to have anything to do with this place." Nevertheless, Robertson signed with the Cincinnati Royals, and his brilliant play helped the team to attract more fans in his rookie season than during the team's previous three seasons. He spoke out openly against the NBA's unwritten but very real quota system for blacks, which he said kept "a lot of good Negro ballplayers" out of the league because "generally only four or five spots are open on a team."

Eleven years after entering the league, Robertson, one of the most complete players of all time, finally won an NBA title when he teamed up with Lew Alcindor (Kareem Abdul-Jabbar) to lead the Milwaukee Bucks to victory in 1971.

As late as 1947, the very same year Major League Baseball was integrated, John Gunther had publicly declared that he doubted blacks would ever compete against whites in basketball. "This is an indoor sport," he had written, "and taboos are strong (though not so strong as in the South) against any contact between half-clad, perspiring bodies, even on the floor of a gym." But by the end of the sixties, a little more than twenty years later, fifty-eight percent of the players in the league would be black, despite the best efforts of all the teams to limit the number of blacks on each team.

The problem was simple but frustratingly confounding. Black players were not only better, they were also unquestionably more exciting to watch. The statistics were clear and eloquent. Blacks accounted for fourteen of the top twenty scorers, five of the top ten in field goal percentage, seven of the top ten in free throw accuracy, seven of the top ten assists leaders, and seven of the top ten rebounders. Blacks didn't just dominate the statistics; the statistics were also more impressive than in earlier, whiter eras. As an example, in field goal percentage, the average of the ten leaders in this category was an impressive .527 compared with .432 in 1951 and .449 in 1952.

The end of the sixties also brought an end to the Russell-Chamberlain era. Russell's retirement after the 1969 Championship marked the end of the Celtic dynasty, and Chamberlain's exit three years later brought the curtain down on an era that had been marked by unprecedented growth in the league. Driven by dramatically improved quality of play, television coverage expanded enormously and salaries rose significantly.

The seventies produced several great players, black and white, but the greatest, unquestionably, was Kareem Abdul-Jabbar. An enormously graceful seven-footer, his sky hook became the single most devastating weapon in the game. Drafted by Milwaukee, Abdul-Jabbar entered the league in the 1969-70 season and, like the great black players before him, immediately had a major impact on the league. In only his second season, Abdul-Jabbar led the league in scoring with an average of 31.7 points per game, won the first of his many Most Valuable Player Awards, and led his team to the ultimate prize: an NBA championship.

The decade was also marked by a tremendous increase in the percentage of black players in the league and by the emergence of black point guards. Point guards are the quarterbacks of basketball and, not surprisingly, that position was the final bastion of white dominance on the basketball court. The improvement in public school facilities, particularly in the South, triggered by civil rights legislation in the sixties, had resulted in a tremendous increase in the number of black athletes going to college and, consequently, playing professional sports.

In basketball, black big men had long established their dominance, and now was the time for black guards to demonstrate their superior speed and quickness and their leadership ability. Russell and Robertson had helped to dispel the myth that blacks, although superb natural athletes, lacked courage under fire and the ability to think and make quick decisions in the heat of battle. In this new decade, outstanding guards such as Nate "Tiny" Archibald, Earl "The Pearl" Monroe, and Walt "Clyde" Frazier would bring the moves of the black playgrounds to the league, help to widen the differences in playing styles between black and white players, and make white guards a rarity by the end of the decade.

At the end of the 1979-80 season, the leaders in assists and steals (the two categories most associated with guards) were all black for the first time. The NBA's merger with the rival American Basketball Association in 1975 also brought black players with flashy playground styles, such as Julius Erving, into the NBA. As the eighties began, blacks made up almost eighty percent of the league. A white backlash was almost inevitable. Not only were blacks a significant majority of the players in the NBA, but many were clearly unprepared for their new affluence and celebrity. Many of the new black stars were, inevitably, from poor and culturally impoverished backgrounds, and increasingly the sports pages were filled with stories of profligacy and run-ins with the law. White basketball players such as Pete Maravich, with skills approaching those of the best black players, had long been prized commodities. Joe Jares of *Sports Illustrated* tellingly described Jerry West and John Havlicek as "collector's items." Every team in the league was doing its best to find as many white players as possible while remaining competitive.

Black players understood and resented this practice. When a clearly less talented white was retained instead of a more talented black, the black players would say among themselves, "he's stealing, just stealing it." Another, subtler but no less effective method of limiting the number of blacks was psychological testing. White players with clearly inferior physical skills were often given a boost by psychological exams that purported to measure psychological coherence. Blacks of enormous physical ability, on the other hand, were not infrequently identified by the same tests as psychologically fragile head cases with disabling emotional problems.

Despite these efforts to restrict the percentage of blacks in the league, for many white fans the NBA was simply too black. The seventies ended with attendance all over the league plunging, and by 1982 almost a half of the teams in the league were in desperate financial shape. Critics of the league typically camouflaged their racial animus by complaining about salary squabbles, drug use, lethargic play and even the number of games. But the real problem was hardly a secret. One team official put it bluntly, "it's race, pure and simple. No major sport comes up against it the way we do. It's just difficult to get a lot of people to watch huge, intelligent, millionaire black people on television." Perhaps the most vivid illustration of the NBA's plight came on May 16, 1980, the night a brilliant rookie nicknamed Magic guided the Los Angeles Lakers to an extraordinary victory over the Philadelphia 76ers, and America saw it on tape delay.

What America wanted and the NBA needed—a great white hope—was on his way. In fact, he was already there. Larry Bird, a white kid from Indiana, and Magic Johnson, a black kid from Michigan, had entered the league together in 1979. The two had first met on the court on March 26, 1979, in what remains one of the highest-rated TV finals in NCAA history. Magic's Michigan State had won that first matchup 75-64, but both men were coronated as future NBA stars. Bird was the perfect antidote for what ailed the NBA. He was white and a genuinely great player—perhaps the greatest white player of all time—and a perfect counterpoint for the effervescent Magic Johnson. Bird was dour, plainspoken, and hard-working, a white everyman. His foil, Magic Johnson, combined the flash of the playground with an infectious smile and palpable enthusiasm. Together they would be responsible for the most successful turnaround by any league in the history of sports.

But it was left to a black player to lift the NBA to its current level of global popularity. Magic and Bird saved the NBA, but led by Michael Jordan, the league now challenges baseball and football at home and soccer around the world. Instantly recognizable worldwide, Jordan was, until his second retirement at the end of the 1998 season, by far the most popular active athlete in the world. His appeal appears to transcend both race and nationality. Frank Deford declared him a creature beyond color; Chinese students voted him, in a tie with Chou En-Lai, "the world's greatest man;" Louis Gates Jr. declared him to be "the greatest corporate pitchman of all time." Considering the difficulty other black athletes have had attracting corporate endorsements, the latter title is perhaps a greater acknowledgment of his skills than even Larry Bird's remarkable "God disguised as Michael Jordan" tribute.

The gravity-defying skills of Elgin Baylor and Julius Erving should have prepared the world for Michael Jordan, but in truth, nothing could have. The completeness of his game was unlike anything previously seen. His extraordinary natural athletic ability, high intelligence, and mental toughness set him apart from even other great players. Today, he is universally regarded as the greatest player of all time, but it was not always so. Early in his career Jordan had been regarded by some as just another phenomenally physically gifted black athlete, without the necessities to win an NBA title.

White sportswriters, searching for the soft underbelly of great black athletes as is their wont, thought they had found Jordan's. He didn't make his teammates better, they opined. Unstated but implied was that Jordan lacked the leadership skills and perhaps the raw intelligence to win at the highest level. David Halberstam described it as the myth of black incapability. Michael Jordan has won six NBA titles, but his utter destruction of this myth is perhaps his greatest accomplishment.

6

In Football, Quotas Kept Blacks off College and Professional Teams

After a triumphant senior college season, Rosey Grier was looking forward to his first postseason game. Penn State had finished with a 7-2 record, its best in four years, and the future All-Pro defensive tackle had made third-team All-American and first-team All-East. So when Coach Engle invited him to his office at the end of the season, Grier had every reason to expect good news. In reality, Coach Engle had anything but good news. He began, in tones that Grier later described as "strangely foreboding," by congratulating the man who would become famous around the world for capturing Sirhan Sirhan—the man who assassinated Robert Kennedy—for helping to "put Penn State on the map ever since you got here."

The somber-faced coach then assured the suddenly apprehensive Grier that the season had confirmed his place as "one of the finest football players to have attended the school." He had earned the right, the coach said, "to participate in at least one of the postseason games." Clearly uncomfortable, the coach paused before adding, "But I have to tell you you're not going to get an invitation to any of them." When asked for an explanation by his bewildered player, Coach Engle blamed the college quota system. "Rosey," he said, "it's a shame on college football, but the powers that be have ordained a quota system. Only a certain percentage of the students selected for the special games can be colored. The rest have to be white."

The year was 1954, and the National Football League had been integrated eight years earlier with the signing of Kenny Washington and Woody Strode by the Los Angeles Rams in 1946. That year, Willie Mays won the batting title in the National Baseball League and was named Most Valuable Player in the league, and an Associated Press poll named him Athlete of the Year. But in football, highly restrictive racial quotas and other methods of limiting the involvement of black athletes were still commonplace on both college and professional teams. In fact, it would be another eight years before the Washington Redskins, under intense pressure from the Kennedy administration, would sign Bobby Mitchell in 1962 and become the last team in the NFL to sign a black player. In those early years, professional teams typically not only restricted the number of blacks to six or eight, but also frequently stacked several of them at just one position.

Jim Brown, the great running back who entered the NFL in 1957, explained how the system worked in his book *Out of Bounds:* "When I entered the NFL—1957—there was a quota for blacks. I doubt it was written, you probably couldn't prove it in court, every owner would deny it, but it was there. We always knew each team would have six, perhaps eight, blacks on a roster. Never seven though: it was always an even number, so none of the white guys would have to share a room with a black. Once we went on the road, had an odd number of black guys and an odd number of white guys; one of the black players was back in Cleveland with an injury. Rather than pair off the extra black with an extra white, management bought each player a separate room. They were willing to pay for an additional room in order to preserve the color line.

I never had to worry about making the team, but I still hated final cuts. The last few days of cuts I'd walk around the locker room, silently counting the remaining brothers. I knew they'd get pared down to six or eight. I knew some great black ballplayers would lose their jobs. There were even restrictions within the quotas. Some teams would stack up three or four of their black guys at the same position. If a team had three black receivers, they'd stack them at one particular spot—typically flanker—so blacks wouldn't occupy all the receiver spots. We'd see guys who were second and third string, running back punts and kickoffs, and know they should be starting across the board."

Gradually, as the civil rights revolution changed America, the NFL was forced to shed its more odious and blatant racial practices and adopt more subtle forms of discrimination. To maintain the morale of white players and the allegiance of white fans, teams decided to reserve certain positions exclusively for white players. The theory of "centrality" was used to determine which positions would be preserved for whites and which would be opened for blacks. Positions that required interaction among two or more players were deemed "central" slots and were largely reserved for whites. Quarterbacks, centers, offensive guards, and linebackers had to communicate with their teammates and were therefore regarded as white positions. Safeties, wide receivers, cornerbacks, tackles, and running backs operated largely on their own and were therefore regarded as suitable positions for blacks.

White coaches and administrators in both professional and college football had also been long aware of the superior speed of black athletes. Responding to a question about why his school had decided to sign black players, a Kentucky sports information director explained, "the blacks have given us something we haven't had—speed. And speed is the name of the game." Today, not only do blacks comprise more than sixty-five percent of all the players in the National Football League, they also hold a virtual monopoly on the most athletically demanding positions. By the end of the 1997 season there were only a handful of whites starting at the positions requiring the most speed and quickness—running back, wide receiver, defensive back, outside linebacker, and defensive end.

Blacks dominate the NFL's lifetime rushing and receiving records. At the end of the 1996 season, thirty-six of the forty players listed among the twenty leading lifetime rushers and the twenty leading lifetime receivers were black. Running backs John Riggins and Larry Csonka and receivers Steve Largeant and Fred Biletnikoff were the only white players to make the grade. Although no player from a black college has ever won a Heisman Trophy, the leading lifetime receiver, Jerry Rice, and (until the 2002 season) the leading lifetime rusher, Walter Payton, were products of the varsity sports programs of black colleges. That is a remarkable achievement, considering that the vast majority of the best black players have attended white schools since 1971.

In total contrast, nineteen of the twenty leading lifetime passers are white.

Only one black quarterback, Warren Moon, was listed among the leaders in this category at the end of the 1996 season. Although he spent the first five years of his professional career in the Canadian Football League, leading his team to five consecutive Grey Cup titles, Moon's 43,787 yards in the NFL ranked second only to Dan Marino's 51,636 yards. Since he has averaged more than 3,000 yards per season during his career in the NFL, it is not unreasonable to assume that if he had spent his entire career there Moon would be the NFL's lifetime leader in passing yardage.

Moon capped an outstanding college career by leading his team Washington University team to a victory in the Rose Bowl, but with NFL teams uninterested in drafting him as a quarterback, Moon was forced to begin his career in Canada. When the Houston Oilers signed him as a free agent in 1984, Moon was the only black starting quarterback in the National Football League. Six years earlier, in 1978, Tampa Bay had made Doug Williams the first black quarterback ever chosen in the first round of the NFL draft for the purpose of playing that position. Despite leading them to the playoffs in three of the five seasons he spent there, including to the NFC championship game in his second season, Williams was out of the league by 1984.

In his final season in Tampa Bay, Williams' salary was only $125,000, an amount less than forty-five other quarterbacks were paid that season. Since there were only twenty-eight teams in the league at the time, Williams was not only paid less than any other starting quarterback but also less than the majority of the backups. When Williams and his agent asked for a multi-year deal similar to other established quarterbacks, Tampa Bay refused even to negotiate. Disappointed and hurt, Williams decided to sit out the season. True to form, no other NFL team made him an offer. So when the Oklahoma Outlaws of the upstart United States Football League offered three million dollars over five years, Williams signed with the spring league.

Compared to the earliest black quarterbacks in the NFL, Williams and Moon were relatively fortunate. Williams would return to the NFL in 1986 as a backup with the Washington Redskins. Injuries to starter Jay Schroeder in the 1987 season made it possible for Williams to claim the starting job; on the final day of January, 1988, he become the first and still only the second black quarterback to make a Super Bowl appearance.

Despite the success of Williams and Moon, the second black quarterback to play in the Super Bowl, Steve McNair, also had to overcome the doubts of pro scouts and sportswriters that he was smart enough to mentally master a pro offense. And although, unlike Williams, the 26-year-old McNair did not win his first Super Bowl start, he was, according to the *New York Times,* "brilliant" in defeat in one of the closest and most exciting games in Super Bowl history. McNair's performance throughout the 1999-2000 season, when he was 11-2 as a starter, was particularly courageous. He had missed several games earlier in the season because of a devastating back injury, which had required surgery, and he had played in the American Football Conference with an extremely painful turf-toe injury.

A quarterback occupies a unique place in team sports. At his best he is expected to be part great athlete, part battlefield general, and an inspiring leader of men. It is a role that, even today, many white Americans apparently believe is best performed by white men. In 1986, the opposing quarterback was John Elway of the Denver Broncos, and the men and women covering the Super Bowl seemed to have had little doubt about which quarterback possessed the requisite qualities to lead his team to victory. The blonde, blue-eyed Elway had long been a fan and media favorite. In the first quarter the conventional wisdom seemed to be absolutely justified. Elway uncorked a fifty-six yard bomb to Ricky Nattiel on the very first play from scrimmage to put Denver ahead. On the next series, a trick play ended with Elway catching a pass from his halfback for a twenty-three yard gain. With the game just five minutes old, Elway and Denver were up 10-0. Things were to get worse. Late in the first quarter Williams was sacked and limped off the field with a twisted knee. Denver sacked backup Schroeder on the very next play.

The second quarter was totally different, however, and became one of the most momentous in Super Bowl history. It is difficult to overstate the importance of what happened when Williams re-entered the game in the second quarter. He had heard, all his life, all the reasons why blacks would not make great quarterbacks. It had nothing, obviously, to do with his athletic ability or the strength of his arm. The questions were about his intelligence, his mental toughness, and the size of his heart. Now with hundreds of millions around the world watching, he knew the questions would be answered negatively if he failed.

Elway had to face no such test. Failure for him would not reflect negatively on the very quality of his humanity or the worthiness of his manhood. For Elway, failure would be just one bad day in a life of good days. But for Williams, the stakes were higher than those who had always enjoyed the esteem of authority could even imagine.

Given the circumstances, quivering nerves and faltering confidence could perhaps have been excused. Williams responded, however, like a man who had absolutely no doubt about his ability to do what had to be done. On the very first down he found Ricky Saunders, who was streaking down the sidelines, for an eighty-yard touchdown. On the next possession he connected with Gary Clark for a twenty-seven yard touchdown to take the lead 14-10.

In the meantime, the Redskins' defense was keeping Elway in the pocket, preventing him from scrambling and forcing him to decipher the intricacies of the defensive formations. In supreme irony, it was the white quarterback whose athletic ability was most feared and whose ability to read defenses was being questioned. The Redskins would score three more times that quarter to lead 35-10 at halftime. Four of the touchdowns were on passes from Williams, and the thirty-five points were the most ever scored in one quarter of the Super Bowl. Playing conservatively, Washington scored only once in the second half to win in a 42-10 rout.

Fittingly, Williams, who had thrown for 340 yards and four touchdowns, was voted the Most Valuable Player. As he walked off the field in triumph, he was hugged and congratulated by an emotional Eddie Robinson, his legendary college coach. Choking back tears, Coach Robinson told his former player that he had never expected to "live to see the day that one of my quarterbacks could win the Super Bowl." Then the old man tried to place Williams' accomplishment in a historical context. "Doug," he said, "you don't realize the impact you made. You are Jackie Robinson today. You're the Jackie Robinson of football. You don't understand what I'm talking about. You had to live in Jackie Robinson's era to understand it. Then you would know what Jackie had to go through, and then you would understand what this means."

Two years earlier, in the Super Bowl between the Chicago Bears and the New England Patriots, another less heralded breakthrough had perhaps helped to prepare the way for Williams. The quarterback calls the offensive plays and the middle linebacker does the same for the defense. For a long time, black middle linebackers were as rare as black quarterbacks. Then, in 1981, the Chicago Bears drafted a linebacker, Mike Singletary, who would help to change all that. The following year, Mike Ditka, a former all-pro tight end and an assistant with Dallas, was named head coach and quarterback Jim

McMahon was drafted. By 1984 Chicago's famed "46" defense, devised by defensive coordinator Buddy Ryan and led by middle linebacker Mike Singletary, was the best defensive team in the league, and Singletary was the defensive player of the year.

In 1985, the Bears, with Walter Payton breaking the rushing record, paired the league's best defense with the most potent rushing attack to cruise through the playoffs. The smothering, Singletary-led defense shut out the New York Giants and the Los Angeles Rams and in the Super Bowl routed New England 46-10.

In the National Football League, any debate regarding the respective athletic abilities of the races has long been settled in favor of blacks. Today, a white running back, wide receiver, defensive back, outside linebacker, or defensive end is more rare than a black quarterback. The very decision to recruit blacks was, in the first place, recognition of the unique athletic skills of black Americans. Being debated now are the intellectual abilities and leadership skills of black football players. Judging by the number of black head coaches and starting black quarterbacks in the league, the answer still is a lot less of these necessities than whites.

When the 2002 season began there were thirty-one teams in the NFL and only two black head coaches—fewer than anytime in the past five years, despite the addition of an additional team during the period, the Houston Texans. Finally, though, progress is being made in the area of starting quarterbacks. In 2001, at least ten teams had black quarterbacks who started at least one game, and in 2002 there was only a slight fall-off from this number. Although racial bias continues to account for the under-representation of black athletes at this position, it is encouraging that a majority of the best young quarterbacks in the league are black.

Two decades earlier, in 1977, only two of the 1,379 players in the league, James Harris and Vince Evans, were black quarterbacks. In the final draft of the twentieth century, three black quarterbacks—Dante Culpepper, Donovan McNabb, and Akili Smith—were selected in the first round; a fourth, Shaun King, who almost guided his team to victory in the National Football Conference championship game, was selected in the second round. Until that draft, only four black quarterbacks had been selected in the first round. Perhaps, finally, at the dawn of the twenty-first century, race is becoming less of a factor in professional football. Maybe.

7

An Extraordinary Dominance
of Sprinting, Jumping, and Hurdling

He was only 5-foot-7, and today very few Americans would recognize his name, but in some ways Eddie Tolan was a giant. He certainly was the first great black sprinter. Largely unhindered by the organized discrimination that kept them out of baseball, basketball, football, and even boxing, black Americans had competed successfully in the Olympic Games as early as 1904 when George Poage won a bronze medal in the 400-meter hurdles in St. Louis. In the 1924 Paris Games a pair of black Americans, William Dehart Hubbard and Edward Gourdin, took the gold and silver medals in the long jump. Hubbard, a student at the University of Michigan, became the first black athlete to win an Olympic gold medal. Gourdin, who was then the world record holder, became the first black American to sit on the Massachusetts Supreme Court.

But Tolan was the first great black track and field athlete, and he began what would become an extraordinary dominance of international sprinting by black males of West African origin. Like Hubbard, Tolan was a student at the University of Michigan when he was selected to represent his nation in the Olympics. He had dominated U. S. sprinting from 1929 to 1931 but was dethroned by Ralph Metcalfe in 1932. Metcalfe, another of America's great black sprinters, breezed through the 1932 season undefeated and beat Tolan in the 100 and 200 meters at the U. S. Olympic Trials, and went to Los Angeles as the prohibitive favorite. But Tolan recaptured his form at the Olympics and set an Olympic record of 10.4 seconds in the second round; in one of the closest finishes in Olympic history, Tolan edged out Metcalfe by two inches in the final.

Metcalfe and Tolan renewed their rivalry in the 200 meters, with both men breaking the existing Olympic record in the heats. In the final, the little American was at his best, winning by almost six feet and setting a new Olympic record of 21.2 seconds. Metcalfe, who inadvertently dug his starting hole three or four feet behind where it should have been, had to settle for the bronze. Four years later, at the 1936 Berlin Olympics, Metcalfe was still one of America's greatest sprinters. But the man who was to finally become a winner, when he was elected to the U. S. Congress thirty-four years later, was destined to once again play second fiddle in the Olympics, this time to one of the greatest track and field athletes of all time. Jesse Owens had announced his arrival on the international track scene on May 25, 1935, with what is even today the greatest single day performance of all time.

While competing at the Big Ten Championships at Ann Arbor, Michigan, Owens broke five world records and equaled a sixth, all in a mere forty-five minutes. He began his epic day at 3:15 p.m. by equaling the world record of 9.4 seconds in the 100-yard dash. Ten minutes later he broke the world record in the long jump by six inches with a leap of 26 feet 8¼ inches. It was his only jump of the day, but the new record was not broken for a quarter of a century. At 3:45, Owens won the 220-yard sprint by ten yards in 20.3 seconds and chipped three-tenths of a second off the existing world record. He was also given credit for lowering the world record in the shorter 200-meter dash. At 4:00, he capped his incredible day by becoming the first man to break 23 seconds in the 220-yard low hurdles with a time of 22.6 seconds. Along the way, Owens also established a world record for the 200-meter hurdles.

The 1936 Olympic Games in Berlin was perhaps the most memorable in history. The German Chancellor, Adolph Hitler, had hoped the elaborately staged games would confirm his theories of Aryan superiority. Aryans, he believed, were the Promethean bearers of light. Only they were capable, he claimed, of establishing states and founding cultures. Mingling with subject peoples had caused decline and downfall, but all that would change in the

Third Reich. Hitler's National Socialist revolution was designed to do more than merely create new institutions.

Hitler's goal was also to develop a new type of man, a pure Aryan type that could be recovered by eugenic measures, including special laws regulating marriage and programs of sterilization and euthanasia. While he spoke of the "superiority of the mind over the flesh," Hitler expected his new man to combine Spartan hardiness with "the instinct to annihilate others." The ability of Aryan supermen to dominate others physically, on the athletic field and on the battleground, was an essential part of Hitler's preparation for world conquest.

In Hitler's Germany, blacks were regarded as an inferior species and the United States was taunted for relying on "black auxiliaries." But in stunning performances that presaged their current dominance, black American male athletes, led by Jesse Owens, won gold medals in the 100-meter, 200-meter, 400-meter and 800-meter runs, and the 110-meter hurdles, the long jump, and the high jump. Black men also won silver medals in the 100-meter and 200-meter runs, and the high jump, and competed in the 400-meter relay team, which won the gold medal.

Owens won the 100, 200, and long jump at the U. S. Olympic Trials and arrived in Berlin as the favorite in all three events. The 23-year-old son of sharecroppers and grandson of slaves was unfazed by the heavy glare of the international spotlight. Handling himself with remarkable aplomb, Owens tied the Olympic record of 10.3 seconds in the first round and easily won his semifinal heat in 10.4 seconds, while Metcalfe won the other in 10.5 seconds. In the final, Owens blazed into the lead from the first stride and held-off a fast-finishing Metcalfe to win by a full yard. The final of the 200 meters was run in a light rain, but Owens overwhelmed the field and won by four yards in an Olympic record time of 20.7 seconds to win his third gold medal of the Games. Mark Robinson, the older brother of baseball immortal Jackie Robinson, was a surprise winner of the silver medal.

The long jump was the only event in Berlin in which the anticipated showdown between black American and white German athletes actually materialized. Although he was the world record holder and gold medal favorite, Owens was almost eliminated in the qualifying round. Still in his sweat suit, Owens took a practice run down the runway and into the pit. To his dismay, the officials declared it his first attempt. Understandably upset and rattled, Owens fouled his second attempt and found himself one foul away from elimination in his best event.

At that moment, fatefully, as the story has been told and retold again and again, Germany's greatest long jumper and Owens' toughest opponent, Luz Long, introduced himself to Owens and made a suggestion that would change the course of athletic history. After making it clear that he did not share Hitler's racial theories, the tall, blonde, blue-eyed Long, almost a caricature of Hitler's Aryan warrior ideal, suggested that Owens move his mark back to several inches in front of the take-off board and jump from there. He also reminded Owens that the qualifying mark was only 23-5½, a distance he reassured the anxious Owens "you should be able to make with your eyes closed." Owens took his new friend's advice, jumped from eighteen inches in front of the board, and just qualified.

The final was held that very afternoon. Shaking off the doldrums of the morning, Owens began by breaking the Olympic record with a leap of 25-5½ in the first round, and followed with another Olympic record of 25-10 in the second round. In round five, Long brought Hitler and the rest of the huge German crowd to their feet by equaling Owens' Olympic record. Inspired by the challenge, Owens responded with another Olympic record of 26-3¾. Then in the sixth and final round, the young American underlined his superiority by setting yet another Olympic record, this time of 26-5½.

Long, the silver medallist who would have won the gold medal if Owens had not qualified, was the first to congratulate the great black athlete—and he did so in full view of Adolph Hitler. Tragically, Long was killed in the battle of St. Pietro on July 14, 1943, but Owens continued to correspond with his family for most of his life.

Although legend has it that Hitler snubbed Owens, two other black Americans were the unfortunate subjects of this distinction. Cornelius Johnson, a black American, won the gold medal in the high jump with a leap of 6 feet 8 inches, without a miss, but places two through four were decided by a jump-off. Hitler had personally congratulated winners of the first two events of the day, a German and a Finn. But the Fuehrer left the stadium before the ceremony was held honoring the three Americans, who placed first, second and third. Johnson and David Albritton, the silver medallist, were both black. Delos Thurber, the bronze medallist was white.

If Owens was not snubbed by Hitler, he certainly was by American leaders and officials. Although he received ticker tape parades in New York City and Cleveland, President Roosevelt not only failed to invite him to the White

House, he never even sent a letter of congratulations. Owens had no more luck with the Amateur Athletic Union that he had with FDR. The AAU suspended him for refusing to compete in a Swedish meet, which he had not agreed to enter. His problems with the AAU were not new. In 1935, the year he set six world records, the AAU had presented the Sullivan award for the best amateur athlete in the U. S. to a golfer named Lawson Little. The following year, when he won four gold medals in the Olympics, the award went to Glen Morris, the Olympic decathlon champion. Not surprisingly, both Morris and Little were white.

The German masses, despite Nazi propaganda, considered Owens the hero of Berlin. Not only was he mobbed everywhere he went by fans seeking his autograph or photograph, but he also received several proposals of marriage. Back at home, however, the hero of Berlin was reduced to working as a playground instructor for $130 per month and racing horses, dogs, and motorcycles to make a living. Owens did not achieve financial security until the 1950s, when he became a public speaker on behalf of various corporate sponsors.

The performances of Tolan and Owens and the other great black track and field athletes of the 1930s were a harbinger of things to come. But it would be twelve long years before the athletes of the world would gather again in competition. For on September 1, 1939, the host of the 1936 Olympics would launch World War II by attacking Poland. It was the final provocation for even the supremely reluctant Western powers. After Hitler's troops crossed the border into Poland, Prime Minister Neville Chamberlain, who had already sacrificed Czechoslovakia, was confronted with the realization that he and his nation could no longer avoid what he had described as "the awful arbitrament of war."

In 1948, when Olympic competition resumed in the shattered capital of a victorious but depleted Great Britain, the world had utterly changed. The United States had become the preeminent power in the world, and the Axis powers, Germany and Japan, were broken and occupied. India had gained its independence. Pakistan had become a separate country, and Gandhi, the nationalist leader, had been shot to death by assassins of his own Hindu faith while on his way to a prayer meeting. Premier Ben Gurion proclaimed the establishment of the State of Israel, which had been immediately recognized by President Truman. Premier Nokrashy Pasha of Egypt demanded an unconditional withdrawal of British troops, and thousands of students rioted in support of Egyptian independence. In Libya, the Khutla party demanded independence from Britain and anti-British riots broke out across the country. In the West Indies, Jamaica held its second national election and assumed greater responsibility over its internal affairs.

But in the United States, on matters of race, very little had changed. Despite the urging of President Truman, anti-lynching legislation in the Senate was shelved indefinitely. Seventy-four House Democrats pledged opposition, and Southern leaders threatened secession from the Democratic Party over the issue. The American Medical Association rejected a constitutional amendment aimed at overturning the exclusion of Negroes from local medical associations. At their July convention, states rights Democrats reaffirmed white supremacy tenets. The War Hawk Aviation Club reported that few Negro Air Force veterans had been able to find jobs with commercial airlines.

Nevertheless, in spite of their second-class status in everyday life, black athletes would resume their extraordinary domination of international sprinting and jumping. No single athlete would dominate the London Games the away Owens had in 1936. But one, Harrison Dillard, who had received his first pair of running shoes from Jesse Owens, would by 1952 match his mentor's haul of four Olympic gold medals. Another, the Jamaican Herbert McKinley, who would later coach my high school track team, would become the first and only man in Olympic history to qualify for the finals in the 100, 200, and 400 meters.

Dillard had been a 13-year-old schoolboy in Cleveland when he attended the huge parade the city had organized to welcome its famous adopted son upon his return from Berlin. Inspired by Owens' exploits, Dillard won an unprecedented string of eighty-two consecutive victories, primarily in the 110-meter hurdles, from May 31, 1947, to June 27, 1948. Although his string of victories was finally broken just a week before the Olympic trials when he attempted to run four races in sixty-seven minutes, Dillard entered the trials as the world record holder and prohibitive gold medal favorite in the 110-meter hurdles. But in the final Dillard hit the first hurdle, lost his stride, hit two other hurdles, and failed to finish or qualify for the Olympic team in his favorite event. Fortunately, he had qualified for the Olympic team a day earlier by placing third in the final of the 100 meters.

In London, all three Americans—Mel Patton, the pre-race favorite, Barney

Ewell, who had won the U.S. trials while equaling the world record of 10.2 seconds, and Dillard—qualified for the 100-meter final. Also qualifying for the final were two West Indian-born sprinters of West African background, Mac Bailey and Lloyd Labeach, who had also run a 10.2 in the 100 meters. Labeach, whose parents were Jamaicans, represented Panama; Bailey, who was born in Trinidad, represented Great Britain. After one false start, Dillard got out ahead of the field and just held off Ewell, who almost caught him at the tape. His 10.3 timing equaled Owens' Olympic record. Labeach, who took the bronze in both the 100 and 200 meters, is the only Panamanian to ever win an Olympic medal.

Perhaps the most important development in 1948 was the dramatic rise of black athletes of West African descent who were born outside the United States. Nowhere was this more evident than in the 400 meters, where Jamaicans Arthur Wint and Herb McKinley took the gold and silver medals. McKinley, who had placed a very close fourth in the 200 meters, a mere tenth of a second behind the gold medallist Melvin Patton of the United States, had been described by Jesse Abramson of the *New York Herald Tribune* as "the surest sure thing of the Games." But it was his older teammate, 6 foot 4½ inch Arthur Wint, the silver medallist in the 800 meters to the great Mal Whitfield, who took the gold and equaled the Olympic record of 46. 2 seconds.

Wint, a 28-year-old medical student at the University of London at the time of the Games, was the son of a black Jamaican father and a Scottish mother. He was also quite a local favorite with London sports fans. Wint was also determined not to allow Whitfield, an African American, to beat him in the 400 meters. His teammate, McKinley, as was his custom, sped out of his blocks; he ran the first two-thirds of the race as fast as he could and came out of the final curve four yards ahead of Whitfield. Noticing that McKinley was struggling uncharacteristically early, Wint lengthened his stride, went past the American and, with about twenty yards to go, caught McKinley and won by a half yard. But 1948 was just a prelude for the Jamaicans, who were to achieve even greater success four years later in Helsinki.

On the night of June 25, 1950, ten elite North Korean divisions crossed the 38th parallel and smashed into South Korea. Led by commanders who had fought with Mao during the Long March, and equipped with heavily plated Russian T-34 tanks, the highly disciplined troops drove through the relatively frail South Korean defenses. By June 28, Seoul had fallen. In Washington, the invasion was viewed in almost apocalyptic terms. President Truman noted in his diary, "it looks like World War III is here," and Lieutenant General Matthew Ridgeway wondered to himself if this might be the "beginning of World War III... Armageddon, the last great battle between East and West." While it was certainly less than Armageddon, the Korean War would last for thirty-seven months and involve more than two million troops, including 350,000 from the United States. Of these Americans, 33,647 would be killed and 103,259 wounded.

The Korean War was an obvious drain on the manpower resources of the country during the first half of the decade, and it must have diverted tens of thousands of young men from the tracks and the playing fields to the battlefield. But the Korean War was not the only rival for the physical skills of young black men during the decade. Professional baseball, football, and basketball not only gradually opened their doors to blacks during the 1950s but also expanded considerably, driven by the booming postwar economy and the arrival of television. Television allowed professional sports to have a far greater impact on the national psyche than ever before. As author David Halberstam explained, "what had once happened before relatively small crowds now happened simultaneously in millions of American homes, in effect, it was going from the periphery to the very center of the culture."

The effects were profound. The showcasing of superbly gifted black athletes like Willie Mays and Jim Brown who, unlike most white superstars of the past combined speed with power, arguably had a greater social impact than the civil rights revolution being fought in the streets and in the courts. At a time when track and field was still a purely amateur activity, the kind of poor but supremely gifted young black athlete who had made black American track and field athletes virtually unbeatable in international competition in the 1936 and 1948 Olympics now opted for glory and dollars, playing professional baseball, football, and basketball.

One result of this black talent dilution—before the civil rights revolution eventually dramatically increased the size of the black college-going population and, consequently, the black talent pool—was that white males won the 100 meter sprint in the 1952, 1956, and 1968 Olympic Games. In 1952, Lindy Remigino, a white student from Connecticut, just edged Jamaica's Herb McKinley, the silver medallist in the 400 meters in 1948 and 1952, in what has been described as the closest finish in Olympic history.

Remigino's time of 10.4 seconds was slower than the winners in 1928, 1932, and 1936.

Four years later, in Melbourne, the top black American sprinter was an athlete too short for professional football, basketball, or baseball, the 5 foot 4½ inch Ira Murchison. Bobby Joe Murrow, a devout Christian and cotton and carrot farmer from Texas, won both the 100 and 200 meters. Morrow, the greatest white American sprinter of the century, won the 100-meter final in 10.5 seconds, even slower than Remigino's 10.4. Running with a bandaged left thigh, Morrow beat defending champion Andrew Stanfield decisively to set an Olympic record of 20.6 seconds in the 200-meter final.

By 1960, with the civil rights revolution nearing its turbulent peak and professional team sports attracting an increasing percentage of America's best black athletes, black males, for the first and only time since 1932, were shut out of the medals in the 100 meters. The race was won by Germany's Armin Hary in an Olympic record of 10.2 seconds. Silver medallist Dave Sime, a white medical student from New Jersey, was also timed at 10. 2 seconds. Hometown favorite Livio Berruti of Italy tied the Olympic record of 20.5 seconds and became the first non-North American to win the 200 meters.

Despite their defeat in the 100 and 200 meters, black men during this period continued their dominance of the 400 meters, 110-meter hurdles, and long jump. In 1952, Jamaica had repeated its 1948 gold and silver medal haul in the 400 meters. George Rhoden and Herb McKenley took the gold and silver medals, with Rhoden equaling the Olympic record of 45.9 seconds. Charley Jenkins of Massachusetts, who had only finished third in the U.S. trials, won in 1956 with a relatively slow 46.7. But in 1960, Alabama's Otis Davis, a basketball player who did not start running until just two years before the Olympics at age 26, won the gold medal and set a new world record of 44.9 seconds.

The great Harrison Dillard established a new Olympic record by winning the 110-meter hurdles in 1952, and Lee Calhoun won in both 1952 and 1960. Despite running into a 1.9 meters-per-second wind, Calhoun set a new Olympic record of 13.5 seconds at the 1956 Melbourne Games. The best performance in the long jump during the period came from Ralph Boston, who set a new Olympic record of 26-7¾ at the Rome Games in 1960. Boston, who would also win the silver medal in 1964 and the bronze in 1968, had broken Jesse Owens' 25-year-old world record just before the Olympics with a leap of 26-11½.

Walter Davis, who had been stricken by polio and had been unable to walk for three years, won the high jump in 1952 with an Olympic record of 6-8½. Nineteen-year-old Charley Dumas became the first person to break the seven-foot barrier at the U.S. Olympic trials in 1956 and easily, won the gold medal in Melbourne with a new Olympic record of 6-11½. With Dumas and new world record holder John Thomas on the U.S. team, American sportswriters boasted that the high jump gold medal was "in the bag." But Dumas could only manage a sixth place finish and Thomas finished third to two jumpers from the Soviet Union.

Black males regained their leadership of world sprinting at the Tokyo Games in 1964 with the decisive seven-yard victory of Bob Hayes in the 100 meters. The powerfully built Hayes, who would become the first Olympic champion to make a successful transition to professional football, equaled the 10.0-second world record in his overwhelming victory. Black American men also won the 200-meter dash and the 110-meter hurdles, but Michael Larabee of the United States and Britain's Lynn Davies became the first white males in thirty-two years to win either the 400 meters or the long jump.

Black males fared a great deal better at Mexico City four years later. Jim Hines, Tommie Smith, Lee Evans, and Bob Beamon not only won the 100, 200, 400, and long jump, but established world records in each event. Hines had become the first person to break the 10-second barrier in recognized competition—something that to this day only black males have ever accomplished—at the AAU championships earlier that year. But his electronically timed 9.95 seconds in Mexico was considered faster than his hand-timed world record of 9.9 seconds.

John Carlos, the 200-meter bronze medallist, had won the U.S. Olympic trials in 19.7 seconds. However, the time was never recognized as a world record because Carlos was wearing multi-pronged "brush spike" shoes, which were considered illegal at the time. And although he was also the world record holder, he was only a co-favorite for the gold medal, along with teammate Tommie Smith. Both men were students at San Jose State College and were members of the Olympic Project for Human Rights, a group of athletes organized to protest the treatment of blacks in the United States. Smith, who held eleven world indoor and outdoor records at distances up to 440 yards, equaled the Olympic record in the first round; in a stunning display of speed, he won the final decisively in 19.83 seconds, shattering

Carlos' world record of 19.92 seconds.

What the two men did during the victory ceremony was even more sensational than the race. Mounting the dais barefoot and wearing civil rights buttons, they each raised one black-gloved fist in the black power salute as "The Star-Spangled Banner" was played. Peter Norman of Australia, who had nipped Carlos at the tape to win the silver medal, made his sentiments clear by also donning a civil rights button. Predictably, Olympic officials were outraged and the two Americans were suspended and ordered to leave the Olympic Village. While international response was generally sympathetic, sportscaster Brent Musburger probably reflected the majority of white opinion in the United States when he described Smith and Carlos as "black-skinned storm troopers." When asked why he supported the American athletes, Norman replied that he supported human rights and opposed the "white Australia" immigration policy in his own country.

After his friends John Carlos and Tommie Smith were expelled from the village, Lee Evans, the world record holder and gold medal favorite in the 400 meters, announced he was withdrawing from the race. However, Smith and Carlos convinced him to run and win instead. And he did, spectacularly, lowering his own world record from 44.0 seconds, to 43.86 seconds in the process.

In 1948, Caribbean-born athletes of West African origin had first demonstrated that the sprinting talent of black Americans was not a result of unique cultural pressures or incentives operating in the United States. Twenty years later, it was the Africans' turn to do the same. Black Americans took the first three places in the Olympic 400 meters final, but in fourth position was an African from West Africa, Amadou Gakou, of Senegal. Gakou not only lowered his personal record from 46.7 to 45.0, a time which would have won the 400 meters in Tokyo four years earlier, but became the first black to hold the African 400 meters record. Also making the final and placing sixth and eighth were two Africans from outside West Africa: Tegeque Bezabeh of Ethiopia and Amos Amolo of Uganda.

Hines, Smith, and Evans were spectacular, but the greatest performance of the 1968 Olympic Games was by a 22-year-old from South Jamaica, New York. Although the three medallists from Tokyo were back and in excellent shape, it was the 22-year-old newcomer, Bob Beamon, who was widely regarded as the gold medal favorite in the long jump. Beamon had had a tremendous year, winning twenty-two of the twenty-three meets he entered in

1968. But his prospects for winning were clouded by his unusual propensity, especially for an athlete of his accomplishments, for fouling. Beamon had also been without a regular coach for several months, after being suspended from the track team of the University Of Texas at El Paso for protesting the racial policies of the Mormon Church by refusing to compete against Brigham Young University.

The night before the event, Beamon violated what he and many athletes of the time regarded as a major taboo: having sexual intercourse the night before a major competition. As reported by the late Dick Schaap in *The Perfect Jump*, at the very moment of orgasm, Beamon was suddenly overcome with the sickening feeling that he had blown away his opportunity to win a gold medal, and set the world record he had so audaciously predicted.

The next day was gloomy, with occasional showers. The conditions appeared to favor Great Britain's Lynn Davis, the defending champion. There were seventeen finalists and Beamon was slated to jump fourth. The first three jumpers fouled, and then it was Beamon's turn. Ralph Boston, the gold medallist from Rome, eight years earlier, had been coaching Beamon informally. As the young American gathered himself, Boston yelled, "Come on, make it a good one." Reminding himself not to foul, Beamon sprinted down the runway, hit the take-off board perfectly, and sailed through the air at an elevation that observers estimated to be between five and a half and six feet.

Boston knew immediately that it was over 28 feet, but Davis refused to believe that such a leap was possible on the first jump. Both former champions trotted over to the pit to get a better look and watched intently as the officials slid the sophisticated optical measuring device to the point where Beamon's feet had hit the sand. But the marker fell off the end of the rail before it got to Beamon's mark. One amazed official turned to Beamon and murmured, "fantastic, fantastic." Then an old-fashioned steel tape was used, and after repeated measurements the result was flashed on the electronic scoreboard: 8.90 meters. Beamon, being unfamiliar with the metric system, ran to Boston to find out how far he had jumped. Boston told him, "Bob you jumped 29 feet." After his jump had been officially converted to 29 feet 2 ½ inches, Beamon finally realized what he had done. His legs grew weak and he collapsed to the ground, experiencing what doctors later described as a "cataleptic seizure," a "catatonic state of the somatic muscles which develops suddenly on the heels of emotional excitement."

The other medal contenders were as stunned as Beamon. Russia's Igor Ter-Ovanesyan told Davis, "compared to this jump, we are as children;" Davis in despair muttered to Boston, "I can't go on. What is the point? We'll all look silly." Turning to Beamon, the defending champion accusingly exclaimed, "you have destroyed this event." Beamon's extraordinary leap broke both the 28-foot and 29-foot barriers, and was hailed by many as the greatest athletic achievement of all time.

Beamon's world record would not be broken until the 1991 World Track and Field Championships in Tokyo, during the greatest long jump competition in history. Carl Lewis, the reigning Olympic champion in the event, produced four of the seven longest jumps of all time (three over 29 feet and the fourth at 28-4½), but his arch rival, Mike Powell, won the gold medal and set a new world record of 29-4½.

Nineteen sixty-eight was an extraordinary year in an epochal era. The year began badly when the Tet offensive in January destroyed America's hope of a quick military victory in Vietnam. Disaster followed disaster with astonishing regularity and persistence. In March, Lyndon Johnson told the country that he would not seek re-election, and in April, Martin Luther King was assassinated, igniting massive rioting in 125 cities that took forty-six lives. That same month Columbus University was shut down by student radicals, and Robert Kennedy was assassinated in June. During the Democratic convention in August, blood flowed in the streets of Chicago, and in November, Richard Nixon was elected by a majority of just 50,000 votes.

Despite the passage four years earlier of the Civil Rights Act, racial tensions mounted as young, militant blacks proclaiming "black power" served notice that the moderate approach of the older black leadership was no longer satisfactory. The tenor of the times was captured by an article in *Ebony* magazine, which claimed that Lincoln believed in racial separation, and called on Negroes to abandon their view of Lincoln as the Great Liberator. The Citizens Councils of America responded by urging the separation of the white and black races, and cited President Lincoln's 1858 statement in support of racial separation. *New York Times* columnist Tom Wicker wrote that "black power" excludes white liberalism, because almost all of the civil rights struggles waged by white liberals to advance racial integration were being rejected by black militants in favor of "black power."

A pamphlet from the American Council of Judaism urged the Jewish community to do considerably more to help American Negroes, and compared the large amount of funds American Jews had sent to Israel with what they had given to various civil rights programs. Some Jewish leaders denounced the pamphlet. The leader of the Black Muslims, Elijah Muhammad, declared that the white man's world is "falling to pieces" and that Muslims would rule the world. Black militants demanded that the word "Negro" be replaced by "Afro-American" or "black," and in Harlem, New York, the *Amsterdam News* barred the word "Negro" from its columns. The *New York Times* ran a series on the concerns of Negro troops in Vietnam about the pace of racial progress in the United States. Vice President Hubert Humphrey, campaigning for the Democratic Party's presidential nomination, said that equal rights were among the central issues of the time. In a speech to the American Psychiatric Association, Dr. C. Pinderhuges compared the "black power" movement to an adolescent's attempt to achieve autonomy from resistant parents and proclaimed the movement's prognosis as guarded. Dr. W. Schockley's planned lecture calling for a scientific probe of the intellectual deficiency of Negroes was canceled by the Polytechnic Institute of Brooklyn. In a speech to the American Jewish Congress, Professor L. Fein charged that liberals, by relying on policy of escalating rhetoric and trivial investment instead of real equality, had failed to aid Negroes. And the Reverend Andy Young noted that millions of Negroes had been locked out of the American way of life.

By 1968, the undeclared war in Vietnam was costing the country about $30 billion annually, and American troop strength had reached 540,000. Heavy television coverage brought the war to the living rooms of America, and the country became only too aware of the enormous toll the conflict was having on America's young men. From 1961 to 1967, American casualties were relatively light: almost 16,000 killed and 100,000 wounded. But between, 1968 and 1972, 35,000 Americans were killed and approximately 200,000 were injured.

All this social upheaval led, inevitably, to a sharp decline in the quality of America's representation at the 1972 Olympics in Munich and to the rise of Valery Barzov of the Soviet Union as the leading sprinter in the world. In 1972, Barzov became the last white male to win an Olympic sprint title while black Americans were competing. Guy Drut of France, who won the 110 meters in the 1976 Montreal Games, was the only white male between 1932 and 2000, again with the exception of 1980 when America did not compete, to win a gold medal in the 110-meter hurdles.

Borzov's victory was facilitated by the failure of the Americans, Eddie Hart and Ray Robinson, who had both been timed at 9.9 seconds at the U.S. trials, to show up on time for the second round of the 100 meters, and by a training program that was prepared by an entire team of scientists. His coach, Valentin Petrovsky, explained that Borzov's program began "with a search for the most up-to-date model of sprinting. We studied slow-motion films of leading world sprinters of past and present, figured out the push-off angle and the body incline at the breakaway, and went deeply into a whole number of minor details." Although Barzov was unable to match the 9.95 or the 19.83 by Jim Hines and Tommie Smith in Mexico, his times of 10.14 and 20.0 were very commendable and, apparently, very close to the outer limits of white male capability.

In 1976, with Americans still not at full strength, it was the turn, once again, for Caribbean-born athletes of West African origin to grab the spotlight and the sprint titles. Donald Quarrie of Jamaica, Silvo Leonard of Cuba, and defending champion Barzov were the pre-Olympic favorites in the 100 meters. But the accident-prone Cuban stepped on a cologne bottle ten days before the Games and was eliminated in the quarterfinals. Meanwhile, Trinidadian Hasley Crawford, who had been a finalist in Munich four years earlier, was breezing through his heats, beating Barzov in the quarterfinals and beating Quarrie in the semi-finals.

In the final, Quarrie took the lead at 75 meters, but Crawford nipped the lunging Jamaican to win in 10.06. Quarrie was second in 10.07, and Barzov third in 10.14, the identical time that had given him the gold medal in Munich. In the 200 meters, Quarrie, whose Olympic career had begun when he was 17 years old, was not to be denied. Running strongly from the gun he had the lead coming out of the turn and won in 20.22, two feet ahead of the fast-finishing Millar Hampton of the United States.

Another Caribbean-born runner of West African background, the light-skinned Cuban Alberto Juantorena, became the first person to win both the 400 and 800 meters in official Olympic competition. Juantorena went to the Montreal Olympics as the clear favorite in the 400, but as an unknown quantity in the longer race although he had run the second fastest time of the year that April. The 800 final was run first, and Juantorena took the lead before the end of the first lap and won decisively in 1:43.50, a new world record. The big Cuban waltzed through the first two rounds of the 400; in the semi-finals, he started slowly, but quickly accelerated into first place and then jogged home in 45.10. In the final, Fred Newhouse of the United States, who had won the other semi-final in 44.89, sprinted into the lead and was ahead with only 20 meters to go. But he was caught by the long-striding Cuban, who broke the tape in 44.26, a full half-second faster than his previous best.

Guy Drut of France broke the Caribbean monopoly by winning the 110-meter hurdles. But Edwin Moses of the United States set a new world record of 47.63 in the 400-meter hurdles and continued a new dominance of this event by black males, which John Aku-Bua of Uganda began in 1972. With the exception of 1980, when America boycotted the Olympics, black men have won the 400-meter hurdles at every Olympic since Aku-Bua's victory. And when Arnie Robinson won the long jump in Montreal, it was the tenth time in twelve Olympics it had been won by a black American.

Prompted by the Soviet Union's invasion of Afghanistan, the United States boycotted the 1980 Olympics in Moscow. But since the 1984 Los Angeles Games, black males have been extraordinarily dominant in the 100, 200, 400 and 800 sprints, the 110 and 400 hurdles and long jump. They have won every gold medal awarded in the 100, 200 and 400 sprints, the 110 and 400 hurdles and long jump. They also won every medal—gold, silver and bronze—in the 400 meters, 110 hurdles, and long jump from 1984 to 1996. Incredibly, every finalist in the 100 meters since 1984 has been black.

The huge outpouring of black athletic talent, fueled by gains in educational opportunities made possible by the civil rights revolution, is making it increasingly difficult for athletes of other races to compete, on anything approaching an equal basis, in events requiring speed and power. Before 1984, only one winner of the 100 meters—Jim Hines, in the high, helpful altitude of Mexico City—had broken 10 seconds in a final. Since 1984, all five winning times have been below that magical barrier, a barrier only black males have ever broken in official competition.

The winner of two of those sub-ten-second races, Carl Lewis, is also the greatest track and field athlete of all time. From 1984 to 1996, Lewis won two gold medals in the 100 meters, one gold and one silver in the 200 meters, four golds in the long jump, and two golds in the 400-meter relay. But not even these amazing statistics do full justice to the extraordinary dimensions of Lewis' athletic achievements. In 1984, he won four gold medals to match Jesse Owens' legendary feat. When he won the 100 meters in 1988 and set an Olympic record of 9.92 seconds, he became the first male to retain his Olympic 100 meters title. His victory in the long jump also made him the first repeat winner in the history of that event.

When Lewis won the long jump in 1996, he joined Al Oerter as one of only two athletes to ever win the same Olympic track and field event four straight times. Lewis' total of nine Olympic track and field gold medals equaled the haul of the legendary Finnish distance runner Poavo Nurmi, who won nine gold and three silver medals between 1920 and 1928, a time when white males had the field to themselves. Lewis' three individual Olympic sprint gold medals, two relay Olympic sprint gold medals, and one Olympic sprint individual silver make him, indisputably, the greatest sprinter of all time. His unmatched 8.94 anchor leg in the 1984 Los Angeles Games gave the United States the gold medal in the 400 meters and the only track and field world record set during those Games. The heavily favored U.S. team was disqualified in 1988, but in 1992 Lewis again anchored the U.S. team to achieve a gold medal and a world record.

But as great of a sprinter as he was, Lewis was most dominating as a long jumper. The career span of athletes in explosive events like sprinting and jumping is notoriously brief. In fact, Lewis is the only male athlete to successfully defend an Olympic sprint or long jump title. But for an astonishing fifteen years, from 1981 to 1996, Lewis was the greatest long jumper in the world, winning almost every competition he entered. Lewis went to the 1988 Seoul Olympics riding a winning streak of fifty-five meets over seven and a half years. Not only did he win with a leap of 28-7¼, the best ever at sea level in the Olympics, but despite competing in both the 100 and 200, his four best jumps were the four longest in the competition.

Ironically, Lewis' only loss in major long jump competition came on a day when he produced the greatest long jump series of all time. It happened on the evening of August 30, 1991, at the World Championships in Tokyo during what has been described as the greatest duel in long jump history. By then, Bob Beamon's world record had stood for twenty-two years and 316 days, and Lewis had recorded sixty-one straight victories over a period of ten years and 170 days. In the third round, Lewis uncorked a wind-aided 28-11¾ leap, and in the fourth round he surpassed Beamon's world record distance by one half inch, with a 29-2¾ leap, also wind-aided. Then Mike Powell, who had lost fifteen straight times to Lewis over eight years, unleashed the greatest long jump of all time, a legal 29-4½. Stunned but undaunted, Lewis responded with a leap of 29-1¼, his longest legal jump ever.

In the final round, Lewis managed a mere 29 feet, a distance almost a foot beyond what any white or Asian male had ever achieved in official competition. The following year, Lewis would turn the tables on Powell at the 1992 Olympics, and then crown his Olympic career by winning his favorite event for the fourth straight time at Atlanta in 1996.

8

Other Africans: Champions
of Distance Running

When the British runner Roger Bannister became, to worldwide acclaim, the first human to run a mile in less than four minutes some four decades ago, Europeans were unquestionably the greatest middle and distance runners in the world. Kenyans were still lowly British subjects, for whom running was still a primary means of transportation.

So highly regarded was Bannister's breakthrough that the fateful day, May 6, 1954, has been described by white commentators as "probably the greatest day in track and field." Yet in 1997, when 21-year-old Kenyan David Komen became the first person to run two miles in less than eight minutes, the world took little note of this extraordinary feat, except as the latest example of black African dominance of middle and distance running—a dominance that has created both awe and consternation among white runners and commentators. Having long ago ceded superiority in sprinting and jumping to blacks of West African origin, whites are understandably disturbed at this new African onslaught and its implications.

During one astonishing eleven-day period in August of 1997, Africans launched an unprecedented attack on world distance-running records, setting seven records in the 800 meters, 3000-meter steeplechase, and the 5,000 and

10,000 meters. As each record brought what the *New York Times* described as "breathless wonder at what seemed to be astonishing breakthroughs," experts struggled to explain what was happening. Frank Shorter, a marathon gold medallist in the 1972 Munich Olympics, appeared to cede inherent superiority to the Africans. Shorter pointed out that "the record-holders used to be athletes from industrialized nations, who had access to technology and financial incentives," but that as more Kenyans and Ethiopians could go to Europe and achieve the same access to agents, money, and a lucrative running career, the balance of power changed. "The Africans finally got a level playing field. Then the game was over."

While Algeria, Burundi, Morocco, Ethiopia, and South Africa have all contributed to the growing African dominance of distance running, the Kenyans have been particularly impressive. Although not quite as dominant in distance running as their cousins from the opposite side of the continent are in sprinting and jumping, the Kenyans are clearly the greatest distance runners in the world. Kenya did not win its first Olympic medal until 1968 in Mexico City, when Kip Keino, a 28-year-old uncoached Naudi tribesman, defeated Jim Ryun of the United States in the 1500 meters. Although Ryun was the world record holder at 880 yards and 1500 meters, and although Keino had expended tremendous amounts of energy to place second in the 5000 meters four days earlier, the result was not even close. Throwing caution to the wind, the little-known Kenyan set a torrid pace from the start and held on to win by twenty meters, the largest victory margin in Olympic 1500 meters history, setting a new Olympic record of 3:34.9.

Keino's example must have inspired his countrymen. Although as late as the early 1970s there was only one regulation-size running track in the entire country, Kenya continued to produce world-class runners at a prolific rate. The most notable in the 1970s was, Henry Rono, who not only won a National Collegiate Athletic Association title as a student at Washington State, but also set four world distance records. During that incredible eleven-day period in August of 1997, Kenyans set world records in the 800 meters, 5000 meters, 10,000 meters, and 3,000 meters steeplechase. One of the Kenyans, Paul Tergat, set records in both the 5,000, and 10,000 meters, and his 10,000 meters record of 26: 27. 85,' was more than seventy seconds faster than the world mark of 27:38.4, set by the great Finnish runner, Lasse Viren, at the Munich Olympics.

Shorter, whose best time was 27:45, said that no one dreamed of running under 27 minutes at that time. "We thought the ultimate was in the low-27s," he said. The impact of the Africans on distance running can probably be best measured by the rate of decline of the world 10,000 meters record time. While it took seventeen years for the record to drop thirty seconds after Lasse Viren's record at the Munich Olympics, it declined by forty seconds in the four years from 1993 to 1997.

But if the African dominance of the track has evoked awe and admiration, its impact on U.S. road racing has generated waves of anxiety and consternation, as well as outbursts of jingoism and thinly disguised racism. In a column headlined "Kenyan Question," Joe Henderson of *Runner's World* magazine wrote that "the role of Kenyans on the U.S. race scene has grown too dominant and must change if the pro sport is to continue to prosper." Henderson acknowledged that his proposal could be regarded as "racist or isolationist," but insisted that continuing Kenyan dominance would reduce sponsorship dollars because "most event sponsors want something in return for their dollars—usually in the form of media attention paid to the race" and because "one American winner would grab more headlines for the race than any Kenyan combination." Tony Reavis, a TV commentator, in an article published by the *Boston Globe,* publicly supported Henderson's position. Reavis claimed that "sponsors are going to see there's nothing in it for them, and they'll pull out. Road racing in the form of Kenyan domination doesn't do it for them."

It is hard to imagine a greater tribute to the runners of this tiny, underdeveloped East African nation of only thirty million people than this open acknowledgment from the mighty United States that its distance runners cannot compete with theirs on an equal basis. But other Africans are not far behind. In fact, some would argue that the greatest distance runner in the world during the past decade was not a Kenyan but an Ethiopian, Haile Gebrselassie.

After defeating archrival Paul Tergat of Kenya in the 10,000 meters in the 1997 World Championships in Athens, *Runner's World* magazine described Gebrselassie as "the greatest distance runner of all time." In support of their contention, *Runner's World* pointed out that "In the last five years, Gebrselassie has won every notable world track race he's entered, beginning with a 5,000/10,000 double in the 1992 World Junior Championships. When not winning championships, he's setting world records. In late August,

Gebrselassie lost his 5,000 world record as well as the 10,000 record, but he cannot be beaten in head-to-head competition."

That judgment was richly vindicated at the 2000 Olympics in Sydney, Australia. Despite surgery to repair a torn left Achilles and a difficult recovery, the 27-year-old Ethiopian successfully defended his 10,000-meter title after a titanic battle with his old foe, Paul Tergat of Kenya. Tergat, who had also finished second in 1996, had turned into the homestretch in the lead and with 20 meters to go was still ahead. But the tiny warrior—5-foot-3 and less than 120 pounds—with his teeth bared and his arms and legs pumping furiously, caught the Kenyan four steps from the finish to become only the third man in Olympic history to win consecutive gold medals in the longest track event of the Games.

Gebrselassie is not the only great runner upholding the Ethiopian distance running tradition established by the legendary two-time Olympic champion Abebe Bikila. At the 1996 Olympics in Atlanta, Fatuma Roba became the first African woman to win the Olympic marathon. The 20-year-old policewoman on the Addis Ababa force won by the largest margin in the history of the women's Olympic marathon. In Sydney in 2000, 22-year-old Gezahgne Abera became the first Ethiopian male, since Mamo Wolde in Mexico City in 1968, to win a gold medal in the Olympic marathon. Abera, who began running as a child while tending cattle on his family's farm, overcame wind gusts of up to 30 miles per hour and a fall to defeat Eric Wainaina of Kenya, the bronze medallist from Atlanta. In Sydney, another Ethiopian, Millon Wolde, also won the 5000 meters, giving Ethiopian men a clean sweep of the three longest races at the Games.

Roba was not the only African woman to rise to international prominence in distance running in recent years. A Kenyan woman, Sally Barsosia, won the gold medal in the 10,000 meters at the 1997 World Championship in Athens. In 1997, seven of the top eleven women in the U.S. Road Racing Rankings were Kenyan. In Sydney, two Ethiopian women, Derartu Tulu and Geta Wami, won gold and silver medals in the 10,000 meters; Wami also won a bronze medal in the 5000 meters. Joyce Chemchumba of Kenya also won a bronze medal in the marathon. Handicapped for decades by national poverty and stifling social conventions, African women are just beginning to demonstrate that they are no less talented than their male counterparts.

9

Boxing: White Champions Avoided Fighting Blacks

In 1913, the first black man to become heavyweight champion of the world was arrested by the United States Government for white slave trafficking. Jack Johnson's real crime was humiliating white men in the ring and taking their women to bed in celebration, but he was indicted for eleven violations of the Mann Act.

Named for its sponsor, James Robert Mann, a conservative Republican Congressman, the Mann or White Slave Traffic Act of 1910 was worded in such a way that any man who crossed a state line with a white woman other than his wife and had sex with her could be prosecuted. After his conviction by an all-white jury, Johnson escaped while on bond and fled to Europe. Although embarrassing, Johnson's flight was a major victory for white America, which had long sought "to remove the golden smile" from Johnson's face.

After the retirement of the legendary James J Jeffries in 1905, the vacant title was captured by a mediocre fighter named Marvin Hart. In his first defense of the title, Hart was beaten by the little-known Tommy Burns, a German-Canadian whose real name was Noah Brusso. Burns was an active but uninspiring champion, and public interest in the heavyweight division deteriorated sharply during his tenure. Poor gates and popular fascination with the flamboyant Johnson helped to weaken boxing's color barrier.

Burns was white but he was an unpopular foreigner, and certain boxing interests came to believe that a black champion would bring interest and money back to the game. Serene in their belief in white supremacy, these people were convinced that the reign of any black champion would be very temporary and that Johnson's certain defeat would reaffirm white racial supremacy. For his part, Burns declared himself ready to fight Johnson anytime, anywhere—if guaranteed $30,000, an enormous sum at the time. An attempt by Johnson's white manager, Sam Fitzpatrick, to arrange a bout with Burns at the prestigious National Sporting Club in London came close, but it fell through because the proposed purse was not enough for either party.

Burns, who had always avoided black fighters, defeated a string of white challengers across Europe while continuing to demand a huge purse to meet Johnson. Finally, in Australia, Burns got the huge payday he had been demanding. Hugh "Huge Deal" McIntosh offered him the unprecedented sum of $25,000, to defend his title against the first black man to fight for the heavyweight title. Johnson had to settle for $5,000. Burns had knocked out eight challengers in a row and was installed as a 3 to 1 favorite.

The Australian press, which was as racist and even less restrained than its American counterparts, portrayed Johnson as a threatening black menace. Despite or because of the hostile environment, Johnson handled the world champion easily and contemptuously. He had waited a very long time for the opportunity, had endured numerous insults, and was determined to make the hapless Burns pay for every insult he had ever received from every white man. He knocked him down in the very first round and taunted him throughout the fight. Johnson made Burns look like a pitiful amateur. He spoke to him constantly, making insulting references about his wife and mother, even chatting with ringside spectators during the clinches.

By the thirteenth round Burns was badly beaten, his jaw broken, his eyes cut and bruised, and his body covered in blood. The police entered the ring but Burns refused to concede. In the fourteenth, Johnson dropped Burns for a count of eight. Spectators shouted for the slaughter to be stopped, and the police again entered the ring. This time they stopped it and Jack Johnson was declared, by promoter and referee Hugh McIntosh, the first black heavyweight champion of the world.

Perhaps because the fight had taken place halfway across the world, Americans, black and white, initially paid relatively little attention to the bout. But that began to change when the unapologetically racist novelist Jack London sounded the call for Jim Jeffries to come out of retirement and defend the white man's honor. London, the author of bestsellers such as *Call of the Wild, White Fang*, and *The Star Rover*, had written of the fight: "There was no fight. No Armenian massacre could compare with the hopeless slaughter that took place in the Sydney Stadium today. But one thing now remains; Jim Jeffries must now emerge from his alfalfa farm and remove that golden smile from Jack Johnson's face. Jeff, it's up to you. The White Man must be rescued."

Jeffries was a reluctant savior. He was not, he made it clear, interested in rescuing the white race. But Johnson's behavior as champion soon made the pressure on the former champion to come out of retirement virtually irresistible. Johnson was not content with just defeating the flower of white American manhood; he needed, it seemed, to humiliate and degrade them. He forced the popular lightweight heavyweight champion Philadelphia Jack O'Brien to sign for their fight in the back room of a sleazy saloon in a black ghetto. After knocking down Victor Mchagden in the first round, he spent the rest of the fight telling jokes to the spectators.

More provocatively to white Americans, the black champion flaunted his liaisons with white women and his surprisingly dissolute lifestyle. His superiority was so great, he seemed to be saying, that he could defeat the best white fighters without even bothering to train and get in shape. As Johnson defeated one Great White Hope after another, the clamor from white America grew increasingly louder. Finally, Jim Jeffries acceded to those entreaties and "The Fight of the Century" was scheduled for the most sacred of American holidays, July 4, 1910, in Reno, Nevada. Jeffries explained that he was responding to "that portion of the white race that has been looking to me to defend its athletic superiority."

Into this racial cauldron stepped the fight promoter, Tex Richard. The conditions were perfect, he realized, to make a great deal of money. Others may have flinched at fanning the flames of racial hatred, but Richard employed a highly professional publicity campaign that played on the deeply entrenched racial fears and animosities of the American people. Inflamed by Richard's campaign, white newspapers filled their pages with crude, racist insults. In a typical comment, one newspaper described Johnson as a coward who would be defeated as soon as he looked the champion in the eye, "for Jeffries had Runnymede and Agincourt behind him while Johnson had nothing but the jungle." Black newspapers reacted to these racist statements with defiant support of the black champion. The *Chicago Defender* editorialized that Johnson would be fighting "race hatred, prejudice" and "Negro persecution."

The fight itself, after the tremendous buildup, was an anticlimax. Jeffries had been a great champion, but he had never faced an opponent with the size, speed, power, and skill of the first black champion. Sensing their hero's inability to respond to the cruel beating being administered by Johnson and fearing a humiliating defeat, the spectators demanded official intervention—but none came. Jeffries' only relief from the relentless pounding was a merciful knockout in the fifteenth round. Johnson's victory sparked race riots throughout the United States. Jubilant blacks were beaten and several were killed by angry and resentful white mobs. According to Randy Roberts, "never before had a single event caused such widespread rioting. Not until the assassination of Martin Luther King, Jr., would another event elicit a similar reaction."

While Johnson's flamboyant lifestyle—particularly his fondness for white women—enraged white America and embarrassed the black elite, he became a hero to the burgeoning and increasingly assertive black urban masses. In an insightful explanation of Johnson's enormous popularity with ordinary blacks, historian Lawrence Levin pointed out that "Johnson ruptured role after role set aside for Negroes in American society," and that "the very extent of white anger and frustration made Johnson's victory sweeter." For them, Johnson was much more than a great heavyweight champion. He was, at a time when baseball and boxing held the unrivaled attention of the American sporting public, the first great symbol of black power, ability, and promise.

It was precisely this status as a swaggering symbol of black manhood that made Johnson so dangerous to the existing social order. If he could not be defeated in the ring, other ways had to be found to remove him. The first round in the campaign was the decision to ban the film of the Johnson-Jeffries fight. Not only was the film banned all over the country, but England and South Africa agreed not to show it. Encouraged by this victory, two known racist members of Congress—Representative Seaborn A. Roddenberry of Georgia and Senator Furnifold Simmons of North

Carolina—introduced bills in Congress between late May and early June, 1910, prohibiting the interstate transportation of fight films. White America was going to make sure that very few Americans would ever be polluted by the sight of a white man being beaten by a black man.

Roddenberry's next step was to press for national legislation prohibiting interracial marriage. Despite his predictions that miscegenation would lead to a race war even bloodier than the Civil War, his bill failed to gain sufficient support to become law. But, another less obviously racist piece of legislation, The White Slave Traffic Act, was passed that year. It was this piece of legislation that would drive Johnson out of the country and, ultimately, remove the heavyweight crown from his head. After wandering through Europe for two years, a flabby and dispirited Johnson lost his title to big Jess Willard in Cuba in 1915. It would be twenty-two years before white America allowed another black man to fight for the heavyweight championship of the world.

In the twenty-two years between Jack Johnson and Joe Louis, there were eight white heavyweight champions, none of whom fought a black challenger. Even the best of these white heavyweight champions, Jack Dempsey, actively avoided fighting blacks. It took unusual circumstances, a special black fighter, and a unique period in American and world history for a second black man to fight for the heavyweight title. By every measure, Joe Louis was a great fighter, one of the greatest of all time. Louis, the son of an Alabama sharecropper, ruled the heavyweight division for twelve years, the longest in history, and his twenty-six title defenses were also the most of all time. In his seventy fights, Louis lost only three times and only once in his prime.

But it was not his great physical talents that were most responsible for the opportunity he received to fight for the heavyweight championship. There had been other great black fighters before—such as Harry Wills, whom Dempsey adamantly refused to meet—who had not received the title shots they deserved. Far more important was Louis' personality and the rise of Adolph Hitler and his philosophy of Teutonic superiority.

It would be difficult to imagine two great fighters more unalike than Johnson and Louis. While Johnson was a flamboyant loudmouth who enjoyed flouting white America's conventions, Louis quietly and respectfully observed them. Johnson dated and married white women almost exclusively;

Louis limited his amorous interests, at least publicly, exclusively to black women. Johnson was a trash-talker inside the ring and a libertine outside; Louis was an efficient assassin in the ring and a dignified gentleman outside. Outraged by his behavior, white Americans drove Johnson out of the country; white commentators described Louis as "a credit to his race."

Louis' reticence and humility made it possible for him to be cast as an American hero by white Americans, who were alarmed at or enraged by Hitler's persecution of his country's Jewish citizens. Mike Jacobs, a prominent Jewish American who had succeeded Tex Richard as the country's leading boxing promoter, recognized that America was ready to accept the right kind of black heavyweight champion. Jacobs signed Louis after negotiating a contract with his original managers and began a campaign to make the black fighter acceptable to white America. His efforts were greatly assisted by the extraordinary performances of Jesse Owens and the other great black track and field athletes at the 1936 Olympic Games in Berlin.

Despite the careful preparation, not every segment of white society was prepared to accept another black heavyweight champion. The South grew understandably anxious about the impact of a black champion on the region as Louis moved closer to a title bout. No amount of humility, Lawrence Levine pointed out, could alter the fact that "Joe Louis, like Jack Johnson before him, stood as a black man in the midst of a white society and beat representatives of the dominant group to their knees."

Nevertheless, on June 22, 1937, Joe Louis, became the second black man to fight for the heavyweight championship of the world and the second black man to win it. The champion, the game but outclassed Jim Braddock, had beaten Max Baer in 1935 to win the title, but he was no match for the powerful young black man. After being knocked out in the eighth round, Braddock described Louis' punches. Louis' left jab, he said, "was like someone jammed an electric bulb in your face and busted it;" the right was even worse, "like someone nailed you with a crowbar. I thought half my head was blowed off. I figure he caved it in. I felt it after he hit me and I couldn't even feel it was there."

Louis' defeat of Braddock made him the heavyweight champion, but his destruction of the Nazi symbol and former world champion Max Schmelling elevated him to the status of American icon. The German had defeated Louis in 1936 by knocking him out in the twelfth round. The rematch transfixed the American public, capturing more attention than any fight since the bout between Jack Johnson and Jim Jeffries. The promotion of Schmelling as the symbol of Aryan racial supremacy by Joseph Goebels, Hitler's Minister of Propaganda, united the country behind the black champion.

The fight was billed as a battle between democracy and fascism, pacifism against militarism, and ultimately between good and evil. Even the Southern press described it as a symbolic confrontation between the United States and Nazi Germany. Buoyed by the embrace of white America, the normally taciturn Louis promised that he was "backing up America against Germany, so you know I am going to win."

And he did so spectacularly. The fight was brief and brutal. Louis fought like a man possessed, firing a volley of fifty punches that was answered by a single right from Schmelling. A right to the jaw drove Schmelling to the ropes and another right, to the body, drew a scream of agony from the German. Louis followed with a combination that dropped Schmelling, who arose at three, only to be sent sprawling by a vicious left hook. Demonstrating his toughness and courage, Schmelling struggled to his feet again, but a brutal right to the jaw dropped him for the third knockdown of the round. This time he was too badly hurt to respond and the referee stopped the fight with Schmelling still lying on the canvas.

Louis would meet and defeat all-comers for the next eleven years and retire undefeated on March 1, 1949. But in need of money to pay the Internal Revenue Service, Louis returned to the ring a year later. Although he was still good enough to defeat a number of top challengers, he was outpointed by Ezzard Charles and knocked out by Rocky Marciano before retiring for the second and final time.

In the sixty-six years since the open era of boxing began in 1937, there have been only two white heavyweight champions of the world, and between them they had exactly four successful title defenses. Rocky Marciano, the man who inspired the Sylvester Stallone movies of the same name, made all four of them. Marciano is often mentioned by white commentators as one of the greatest heavyweight champions of all time; on examination, the truth appears to be, at least, a little different.

Marciano won the title on September 23, 1952, by knocking out the champion, Jersey Joe Walcott, who was then thirty-seven years old. Despite his advanced years, Walcott knocked down Marciano in the first round and then completely outboxed him for the first twelve rounds. Eventually the tough, determined, and superbly conditioned Marciano caught up with Walcott and knocked him out in the thirteenth with a short, vicious right hand. The following May, Marciano again knocked out Walcott, now a mere shadow of his former self, this time in the very first round. His second defense was against Roland La Starza, a white fighter he had beaten in a close decision a few years earlier. Again, Marciano was outboxed in the early rounds, but his relentless attack finally pounded the challenger into submission in the eleventh round. For his third defense, Marciano selected another white fighter, Englishman Don Cockell. The fight was an extremely ugly one. Marciano repeatedly fouled the challenger, hitting him below the belt and when he was down, thumbing him and butting him. Finally, the referee stopped it in the ninth.

For his fourth and what would prove to be his final defense, Marciano selected another old black man, light heavyweight champion Archie Moore, who was approximately forty years old at the time. The older, smaller Moore almost won the fight in the first round. He knocked Marciano down with a short, sneaky right hand, but the champion jumped up at the count of two. As Moore moved in to finish the groggy champion, referee Harry Kessler inexplicably, moved between the two fighters and in violation of pre-fight agreements gave the champion a standing eight count. The resilient Marciano recovered, and by the seventh his furious assault paid off with a knockdown of Moore. By the ninth, Moore was unable to defend himself and was knocked down several times in the round before Kessler stopped the fight.

After this fight Marciano finally gave in to the entreaties of his wife and retired as the undefeated champion of the world. For years, Mrs. Marciano had wanted her husband to stop fighting. His rise to the top had been made possible by a grueling training regimen that required him to spend nine months of every year in training camp, and his fights were often wars of attrition, during which he often took as much punishment as he dished out. Unlike Joe Louis, Marciano did not return to the ring. Unfortunately, he was killed on August 31, 1969, when the small, private plane on which he was a passenger crashed in Newton, Iowa, killing all aboard.

The only other white heavyweight champion of the open era was Ingemar Johansson of Sweden. Johansson, who was the European champion, possessed a formidable right cross he called the "Hammer of Thor," and he used it to win the heavyweight title. Promoted as the best European fighter since Max Schmelling, Johansson earned his shot at the title held by Floyd

Patterson with a fifth round knockout of Henry Cooper, the British champion, and a round one demolition of Eddie Machen, the formidable American.

The fight took place on June 26, 1959, in New York, and in the third round Johansson struck suddenly and ferociously with the "Hammer of Thor." Patterson was knocked down seven times and was helpless when the referee stopped the fight. The return took place almost exactly one year later on June 20, 1960, again in New York. This time Patterson prevailed, regaining his title with a fifth round knockout of the Swede. With the public demanding a rubber-match, the two men met for the third time, this time in Miami Beach on March 13, 1961. The third fight was the most exciting of the series. Patterson and Johansson exchanged knockdowns in the first round, and Johansson floored Patterson two more times before being knocked out himself in the sixth.

The year after defeating Johansson, Patterson lost his title to the fearsome Sonny Liston, who was improbably conquered by the man who is generally regarded as the greatest fighter of all time, Muhammad Ali. Ali's career is too recent and too well-known to be recounted here, but there can be little doubt that Ali was a unique combination of size, speed, quickness, agility, endurance, durability, strength, and power—a combination seemingly possessed only by the descendants of the rain forests of West Africa.

Although, in the interest of space, I have chosen to concentrate on just the heavyweights, black fighters have historically also dominated a majority of the lighter weight divisions. Indeed, when Ali's claim as the greatest fighter of all time is disputed by some experts, the men who are most frequently substituted are all black. Leading most lists is usually the man who is almost always described as the greatest fighter, pound for pound, who has ever lived, the six-time welterweight and middleweight champion of the world: Sugar Ray Robinson.

Born Walker Smith in 1920, the elegant, dazzlingly fast Sugar Ray was the most acclaimed fighter in the world for almost fifteen years. A master boxer and deadly puncher, the handsome, charismatic champion ruled the welterweight division from 1946 to 1951. Although he was not quite as dominant in the heavier division, it was as a middleweight that Robinson waged his most memorable battles: winning the middleweight crown an extraordinary five times between 1951 and 1960.

The record is clear and indisputable. Athletes of West African descent, despite being a tiny percentage of the world's population, are the greatest athletes in the world, and they have dominated every sporting activity they have entered in significant numbers. Africans from other parts of the continent are the greatest distance runners in the world, and their dominance has increased as they have gained access to training and nutrition. Why this is so is the subject of Part Three.

Part
Three

The Biological Evidence

10

Disease, Biological Superiority, and Athletic Ability

When Christopher Columbus landed in Jamaica on May 5, 1494, the island was populated by 100,000 healthy and happy Arawak Indians. The Arawaks, who had migrated from their ancestral home on the South American mainland, had been in Jamaica for more than 800 years when the Spanish arrived. But by 1611, only 117 years later, a mere seventy-four of them remained.

Like the other Amerindian peoples, the Arawaks became victims, on a mass scale, of the common childhood diseases of Europe and Africa. Nor were they able to cope with the physical rigors of plantation slavery. To replace them, the Spaniards imported Africans, a race they described as "robust for labor." Despite extraordinarily brutal treatment, inadequate diet, and protracted exposure to the same diseases that had decimated the Amerindian populations, the Africans not only survived slavery but multiplied.

The story of why men and women from the isolated and disease-infested rain forests of West Africa became the "strength and sinews" of the Western world and the world's greatest athletes is a fascinating and little-understood one. In some ways, the West African story is part of a larger one about the extraordinary but little-known role disease has played in man's historical development. In other ways, the West African story is unique because it transformed critical physiological processes in at least some West African populations and created one of the preconditions for slavery in the New World, and, therefore, for the Industrial Revolution.

The historian William H. McNeill has convincingly argued that European diseases were far more lethal to the Amerindians than the horses and gunpowder of the Spaniards. As McNeill points out in *Plagues and Peoples*, Hernando Cortez, the leader of the Spanish forces, starting with fewer than six hundred men, conquered the Aztec empire, then a great civilization of some six million people spread over 80,000 square miles. In searching for an adequate explanation for the extraordinary triumph of the Spaniards, McNeill discarded as inadequate the conventional wisdom that Spanish gunpowder and horseflesh simply overwhelmed a primitive people who thought they were being assaulted by gods. "If Montezuma and his friends first thought the Spaniards were gods, experience soon showed otherwise," McNeill wrote. "If horses and gunpowder were amazing and terrible on first encounter, armed clashes soon revealed the limitations of horseflesh and the very primitive guns the Spaniards had at their disposal." Instead, the acclaimed historian looked to an incident that had been overlooked by conventional history for a more satisfactory explanation.

On the very night the Aztecs drove the Spaniards out of Mexico City, killing many of them, McNeill noted that a smallpox epidemic was raging in the city, and that the man who had organized the assault on the Spaniards was among those who died on that *noche trista*, as the Spaniards later called it. McNeill would come to believe that it was the paralyzing effect of the lethal epidemic that was primarily responsible for the failure of the Aztecs to pursue the badly beaten Spaniards. That failure would give them time and opportunity not only to rest and regroup, but also gather Indian allies, set siege to the city, and eventually achieve victory.

As McNeill pondered the psychological implications of a disease that killed only Indians and left Spaniards unharmed, he became convinced that the lopsided impact of infectious diseases upon Amerindian populations offered a key to understanding the ease with which the Spanish conquered America, both militarily and culturally. To the Indians, McNeill believes, such partiality could only be explained supernaturally, and there could be no doubt about which side of the struggle enjoyed divine favor: "The religions, priesthoods, and way of life built around the old Indian gods could not survive such a demonstration of the superior power of the God the Spaniards worshipped."

This bold hypothesis, McNeill quickly realized, raised other questions. Not only how and when did the Spaniards acquire the disease experience that served them so well in the New World, but also, why did the Amerindians not have diseases of their own with which to repel the invading Spaniards? His attempt to answer those questions, he wrote, soon began "to uncover a dimension of the past that historians have not hitherto recognized: the history of humanity's encounters with infectious diseases, and the far-reaching consequences that ensued whenever contacts across disease boundaries allowed a new infection to invade a population that lacked any acquired immunity to its ravages."

Perhaps no other population group better illustrated this observation than the Amerindians. At the time of Columbus' landing in Hispaniola in 1492, the total Amerindian population was about 100 million. Driven by a remarkable system of agriculture, which featured intensive cultivation of all available land by elaborate irrigation systems and reclamation of swampland, the Aztec society was still expanding when the Spaniards invaded. By 1568, less than fifty years after Cortez unwittingly but fatefully initiated epidemiological exchanges between Europeans and Amerindians, the population of central Mexico had shrunk to about three million, approximately a tenth of what it had been before Cortez. The stricken population of central Mexico continued shrinking relentlessly for another fifty years, declining to a pitiful 1.6 million in 1620. Recovery did not begin for another thirty years, and even then remained extremely slow until the eighteenth century.

The disease experience of the Spaniards was the result of the development by what the historian described as the "major civilized regions of the Old World," before 500 B.C., of their own peculiar mix of infectious diseases. The development of these diseases was the inevitable result of the growth of cities that became increasingly crowded and the adjoining areas of dense agricultural settlement. It is now obvious that these diseased and disease-resistant populations had become biologically dangerous to neighboring groups of people who were unaccustomed to such a formidable array of infections. This biological advantage would enormously facilitate the territorial expansion of European populations.

That is not to say, however, that these Old World populations were themselves immune to the devastation of lethal diseases. Biblical texts are replete with examples of deadly epidemics, and many modern scholars believe, for example, that there might well have been a historical basis for the plagues of Egypt described in the Book of Exodus. The same may also be true for the pestilence that punished David's reputed sin of numbering the people, reportedly killing 70,000 out of 1,300,000 able-bodied men in Israel and Judah; and the deadly visitation that "slew in the camp of the Assyrians one hundred and eighty-five thousand" overnight and forced the Assyrian King, Sennacherib, to withdraw from Judah without capturing Jerusalem.

Although such passages made it clear that the writers of the Old Testament were familiar with sudden outbreaks of death-dealing diseases, they were usually not severe enough to disrupt armies on a regular basis or suppress populations sufficiently to impede empire-building. The Assyrian and Persian empires could not have flourished as they did between the ninth and fifth centuries B.C. if that had been true. Although modern translators frequently use the term plague to describe those events, there is no reason to believe that they were outbreaks of bubonic plague. In fact, it is likely that any of the familiar civilized infections—such as measles, smallpox, influenza, typhoid, and dysentery—could have been responsible for the kind of dramatic outbreak of mortality recorded in the Bible.

But if the oldest population centers in the Middle East had developed significant levels of immunity to a wide range of infections five hundred years before the time of Christ, the fringe regions of the Old World had not. The Yellow River flood plain, the monsoon lands of the Ganges Valley, and the Mediterranean coastlands had become capable of supporting large populations at a far later date than had the Middle East. In China, as pioneers moved southward into more fertile farming areas, they encountered what McNeill described as "a rather steep disease gradient." Most insect carriers of disease were unable to survive in the cold and dry conditions of the north, but a far greater variety of parasites were able to flourish in the warmer, moister south. Consequently, it took almost a thousand years, from the time the taming of the Yellow River flood plain began, for the Chinese people to develop sufficient immunity to complete the southward trip across their vast country and begin similar development in the valley of the Yangtze River.

In India, powerful and extensive Kingdoms developed in the Ganges Valley from around 600 B.C; but in comparison to China, they remained unstable and were never truly unified. It is thought by some that a primary factor that heavily influenced Indian history was the enormous variety of microparasitic diseases that are typical of a climate as warm and wet as that of the Ganges Valley and the rest of India's best agricultural lands. Such a load of infestation and infection would have, inevitably, significantly reduced individual vigor and capacity for physical labor and may even have been a major reason why Indian empires were so fragile and short-lived.

Unlike China, and particularly India, the Mediterranean coastlands were relatively free of disease, and new patterns of cultivation did not create new forms of microparasatism. Although malaria may have limited agricultural expansion in some areas, the generally cool, dry conditions kept the Mediterranean a relatively healthy place for human beings, even as large cities became centers for intense disease circulation. Consequently, the population of the classical world grew rapidly, allowing Athens to overcome large war losses and to seize lands from weaker and less numerous peoples overseas. In later centuries, a similar increase in the Macedonian and Italian peasant populations would fuel the imperial expansion of Macedon and then of Rome.

By the beginning of the Christian era, the civilizations of China, India, and the Mediterranean, despite having very different environmental conditions, had all managed to develop populations of a mass and size comparable to the more anciently civilized Middle East: populations—large and dense enough to sustain modern types of infectious childhood diseases. But the Mediterranean population—with its far less intense disease experience—would prove to be far more vulnerable to unfamiliar infections, as the people of Athens would discover, to their sorrow, in 430-429 B.C. It is not possible to definitively identify the disease that wiped out about a quarter of the Athenian land army, but it apparently came by sea and disappeared as mysteriously as it had arrived. And although it lasted for a single season, some contend Athenian society was dealt a blow from which it never fully recovered.

At this time, at least four population centers had disease pools that were potentially lethal to the populations of each of the other centers. Since spillover from one pool to another could have been caused by some accident of communication, it is possible, even probable, that the mysterious attack on Athens could have been just such an episode. However, when travel across the length and breadth of the Old World—from China and India to the

Mediterranean—became routine, the homogenization of these infections became possible. Although the details of the earliest contacts are still not known, they probably began as early as the first century A.D. Initially, contact between the centers was limited to the daring journeys of explorers and soldiers, but all that changed with the development of the caravan trade and seafaring.

Regular movement across such distances involved the exchange of both goods and infections. Not surprisingly, the available evidence suggests that exposure to new infections had little effect in either India or the Middle East—the areas with the most intense disease experience. As an example, in Mesopotamia, a survey of ancient canal systems concluded that the population crested between A.D. 200 and 600, at about the same time that epidemics were sharply reducing the Roman and Chinese populations. In India, the vitality and cultural power of the Gupta age suggests that the merging of previously separate disease pools in the first Christian centuries caused no major demographic disaster in that country.

The opening of the oceans after A.D. 1500 allowed diseases to circulate more freely. By the sixteenth century, Western Europe would also be minimally affected by this phenomenon, while Amerindians and other vulnerable people suffered catastrophic losses. But in the early centuries of the Christian era, Europe and China (the Old World civilizations with the least disease experience) were in an epidemiological position similar to that of Amerindians after 1200: vulnerable to devastating attacks by unfamiliar diseases.

Starting about A.D. 165, a series of devastating pestilences—probably measles, smallpox, and the bubonic plague—significantly reduced urban populations in the most active centers of Mediterranean commerce and triggered a long process of economic decay, depopulation, loss of skills (including literacy), barbarian invasion, and the breakup of imperial administration. Some historians believe, as McNeill points out, that Justinian's failure to restore imperial unity to the Mediterranean was due largely to the reduction of imperial resources by the plague.

Equally, the inability of Roman and Persian forces to offer more than token resistance to the Muslim armies that swooped out of Arabia in 634 is easier to understand when viewed against the background of the demographic disasters that afflicted the Mediterranean coastlands during this period. It is also likely that the decline of the Mediterranean as the principal center of European civilization, and the resulting increase in the importance of areas to the north, was driven by a long series of plagues which were contained almost entirely in regions surrounding Mediterranean ports.

Epidemics were not absent from northern Europe during this period; however, the colder climate, coupled with the rural nature and lower population densities characteristic of the less-developed north, gave the region a microparasitic advantage despite its relative disease inexperience. As a result, the Germanic and Slavic populations grew rapidly during the fifth and eighth centuries A. D., as evidenced by the colonization of the Balkan Peninsula by Slavs, and of Britain and the Rhine and Danube frontier lands by Germanic settlers. Some experts believe that an enormous population increase in remote Scandinavian fjords and coastlands was largely responsible for the Vikings raids between A.D. 800 and 1000.

Significant increases in food production in northwestern Europe between the fifth and eleventh centuries drove and sustained "a new style of civilization-organized states, hierarchical churches, and expanded movement of goods by sea and land." As an inevitable by-product, it promoted more frequent and intensive contact with the Mediterranean lands to the south. The result, within limits imposed by climatic gradients and population densities, was for European populations to become sharers in a single disease pool.

During the centuries in which this process unfolded, diseases that had been highly lethal when they first appeared in Europe gradually became endemic, at least in those areas where population densities were sufficient to sustain a chain of infection indefinitely. Although costly epidemics continued to occur in less developed areas until the nineteenth century, death rates slowly decreased as repeated exposure gradually increased the percentage of people in the community with effective immunities.

This process of gradual epidemiological adjustment ended the crippling demographic consequences of sudden exposure to unfamiliar diseases, and made it possible for Western Europe to benefit from the technical and institutional innovations already instituted throughout Latin Christendom. While unfortunately there is not enough information to write a comparable history of gradual accommodation to new diseases for any other part of the world, it appears fairly certain that by the tenth century, the biological adjustments created by the reshuffle of infectious patterns was complete in both Europe and China. Consequently, populations in those areas began to increase both totally and in relationship to the Middle East and India, a fact with profound consequences for the subsequent course of history.

While people all across Asia, and in some parts of sub-Saharan Africa, were at least marginally affected by the disease circulation centered in the older, more developed lands, the New World was completely excluded. As a result, the relatively large populations of Mexico and Peru were highly vulnerable to Old World infections; civilized Amerindians, after 1200, were like the peoples of the Mediterranean and Far East earlier: disease-inexperienced populations, dense enough for epidemic decimation.

It seems fairly clear, with the possible exception of syphilis, that the Amerindians were not carriers of any serious new infection that was transferable to the European or African populations. This was apparently the case because the New World, as compared to the mass and ecological complexity of the Old, was little more than an enormous island. Life forms, generally, were more highly evolved in Eurasia and Africa, and consequently often displaced less-hardy native American species. As an example, Kentucky bluegrass, dandelions, and daisies, which today are integral parts of the American landscape, were all introduced from the Old World. Although some indications of disease and epidemic death have been found in Aztec codices, the New World—like the Mediterranean coastland—seemed enormously hospitable to human settlement. In fact, after the Spanish conquest, old men even denied that disease had existed in their youth.

But Africa remained a mystery, even for experts like McNeill. For there, on that puzzling continent, the usual rules did not always seem to apply. After noting that "diseases peculiar to that continent presented barriers to alien intrusion more formidable than anything present in other parts of the earth," McNeill concluded that "civilized encroachment" must have been restricted, and "African exposure to civilized diseases" may have been less thoroughgoing than was true in other fringe areas such as the Asian steppes. Nevertheless, as he noted (and here was the mystery), "when African slaves began to come to the New World after 1500, they suffered no spectacular die-off from contact with European diseases." That was sufficient demonstration, he concluded, without citing any evidence, "that in their African habitat some exposure to the standard childhood diseases of civilization must have occurred, if not before, then soon after 1200."

Although he at least implicitly excluded sub-Saharan Africa from the civilized world, a central tenet of McNeill's theory was that standard childhood diseases could only exist in civilized communities. "Only in communities of several thousand persons," he wrote, "where encounters with others attain sufficient frequency to allow infection to spread unceasingly from one individual to another, can such diseases persist. Those communities are what we call civilized: large, complexly organized, densely populated, and without exception directed and dominated by cities. Infectious bacterial and virus diseases that pass directly from human to human with no intermediate host are therefore the diseases of civilization par excellence: the peculiar hallmark and epidemiological burden of cities. They are familiar to almost all contemporary humankind as the ordinary diseases of childhood: measles, mumps, whooping cough, smallpox and the rest."

Not that McNeill is a racist—he correctly attributed Africa's relative lack of development to the enormous difficulty of increasing food production on that continent. Commenting on the failure of European colonial administrators to expand agricultural production in central and eastern Africa by altering traditional patterns of herding and cultivation, McNeill wrote: "These efforts, in fact, precipitated veritable epidemics of sleeping sickness in parts of Uganda, the Belgian Congo, Tanganyika, Rhodesia, and the end result, as colonial regimes came to an end, was a land more thickly infested with death-dealing tsetse flies than before government policy set out to utilize what looked like good agricultural land more effectively. Obviously, human attempts to shorten the food chain within the toughest and most variegated of all natural ecosystems of the earth, the tropical rain forests and adjacent savanna regions of Africa are still imperfectly successful. That, more than anything else, is why Africa remained backward in the development of civilization when compared to temperate lands."

In truth, McNeill's incoherence on Africa is understandable. Africa, at least West Africa, simply does not fit easily into the biological rules that apply everywhere else. How do you adequately explain how peoples from allegedly primitive (or at least rural), relatively underdeveloped, and historically isolated societies with relatively low population densities developed immunities to diseases which, theoretically, occur only in complex, densely populated, civilized societies? To a significant degree, populations developed immunities, the theory went, not primarily through a general increase in immunological ability (although that was clearly also a factor) but specifically through repeated exposure to diseases that were the "peculiar hallmark" of cities. This process gradually eliminated the individuals who were most vulnerable to these diseases, permitting only those with adequate immunities to survive and to reproduce increasingly less vulnerable populations.

In every other population for which we have records—even disease-experienced ones—exposure to unfamiliar infections had produced lethal consequences. In Europe, the demographically crippling consequences of exposure to unfamiliar diseases took centuries to repair. That is why the bubonic plague continued to be a significant demographic factor until early modern times throughout Europe. Outside the Mediterranean, European exposure to plague was less frequent and public administration in late medieval and early modern times was less expert. The result was to make visitations of plague rarer and, at least sometimes, also more catastrophic. It also explains why European populations were so vulnerable, as we shall see, to the unfamiliar infections of West Africa.

Although McNeill claims that the plague did exist in India and East Africa between 1200 and 1700, he makes no similar claim for West Africa, which until the circumnavigation of the continent by European seamen in 1499 was almost totally isolated from the rest of the Old World. For centuries, the states of the Forest Belt of West Africa had looked north to Ghana, Mali, Songhay, Kanem, and the Hausa city-states for trade. They, in turn, had looked further north, across the Great Dessert, to the Arab and Berber states of North Africa. But the arrival of the Europeans off the Atlantic coast transformed the West African seaboard from what the eminent British historian Basil Davidson described as "the edge of nowhere" into the focus of the trading aspirations of the West African peoples.

Not only did the previously isolated West Africans not succumb to the "civilized" diseases of Europe, as the Amerindians earlier had, but African pathogens proved to be formidable barriers to European expansion. Joao de Barros, a Portuguese explorer on the Guinea coast, more eloquently than most expressed the frustration of Europeans who coveted the riches and splendors of Africa: "But it seems that for our sins, or some inscrutable judgment of God, in all the entrances of this great Ethiopia that we navigate along, he has placed a striking angel with a flaming sword of deadly fevers, who prevents us from penetrating into the interior to the springs of this garden, whence proceed these rivers of gold that flow to the sea in so many parts of our conquest."

In fact, West African infections were almost as lethal to Europeans as the Europeans' infections had been to the Amerindians. Between 1793 and 1796, the British army in the Caribbean theater lost about 80,000 men, a greater amount than the Duke of Wellington lost in the entire Peninsula War; more than half succumbed to the yellow fever that the African slaves had brought to the New World. Even during a time of peace, from 1817 to 1836, the annual death rate of British troops in the West Indies ranged from 85 to 130 per thousand, compared to about 15 per thousand in Great Britain.

But those numbers pale into insignificance when compared to European death rates in West Africa itself. In West Africa, during the same period, the annual death rate of British troops exceeded an astounding 500 per thousand, or fifty percent. European death rates in West Africa were so high that during the 1820s, the popular press in Britain began to describe West Africa as "the white man's grave," a term borrowed from the Portuguese. A British parliamentary report published in 1826-27 found that as many as fifty-six percent of all British citizens who went to tropical Africa died within a few years of arrival. While the report was being discussed, three successive Governors of the Sierra Leone Crown Colony died of fever in 1827, 1828, and 1829.

This extraordinarily high European death rate forced the British government in 1830 to withdraw almost all of its white citizens from West Africa and replace them with blacks from Africa or the West Indies. The changes were enormously successful on the Gold Coast, where 200 blacks adequately replaced 600 whites, the majority of whom had been ill and incapacitated most of the time. Consequently, during the 1830s, there were usually less than 200 white British citizens living in all of West Africa. When the American Revolution made it impossible for Britain to send its convicts to Georgia, some were sent to the Gold Coast. But so many died that Edmund Burke described exile to Africa as the equivalent of a death sentence after a "mock display of mercy."

While unfamiliar West African infections were lethal to both Europeans and Amerindians, and unfamiliar European infections were lethal to Amerindians, unfamiliar European infections had virtually no impact on West Africans. This unique immunological trait, and the fabled strength and endurance of West Africans, were quite likely manifestations of the biological adaptations West African populations made to their uniquely lethal environment. It is noteworthy that this immunological trait was not shared by other Africans. As an example, a 1713 smallpox epidemic was the single most important factor in the destruction of South Africa's native San people by European settlers, a fact mentioned by Jared Diamond, a professor of physiology at the UCLA School of Medicine, in his Pulitzer Prize-winning book *Guns, Germs and Steel*. And like the San and unlike West Africans, East African population groups have also been seriously affected by outbreaks of European diseases during the last two centuries. It is probably no accident that West African countries have reported significantly lower percentages of AIDS infections than the rest of Africa.

In some areas of sub-Saharan Africa, the conversion from hunting and gathering to sedentary agriculture had been accompanied by an enormous increase in the varieties and numbers of parasites. The parasites generally came from domestic animals, which accompanied traders from the north, and then multiplied rapidly in favorable environments. The hot, wet, humid rain forests of West Africa—unlike the cool and relatively dry regions of East and South Africa—were particularly receptive to a vast array of disease-bearing insects, among them some sixty of the world's species of Anopheles mosquitoes.

While comparing the disease environments of West Africa and Britain, British physician Dennis G. Carlson pointed out in *African Fever* that the amount of rainfall along the coastal strip of West Africa, extending inland in some places for several hundred miles, is two to three times that of England. Consequently, the collections of water in forest pools, lagoons, and deltas are far more extensive than in the British Isles. Those factors, plus the humidity (which ranges from 70 to 100 percent throughout the year) and the mean annual temperatures (which range from 69°F to 95°F) make large areas of West Africa an ideal breeding ground for the Anopheles, which needs both high moisture and temperature to complete its life cycle.

The spread of slash-and-burn agriculture in West Africa placed enormous strains on an older ecological balance and created breeding places for many of these mosquitoes, including *Anopheles gambiae*, the most efficient carrier of falciparum malaria. It prefers to feed on human blood, and with the development of agriculture it replaced other mosquito species that were accustomed to feeding on creatures other than man. Consequently, the malarial cycle between man and mosquito became so intense that it affected practically every human being that dared to venture into the forest clearings.

By then, *Plasmodium vivax*, perhaps the oldest of the malaria types and once apparently ubiquitous throughout sub-Saharan Africa had disappeared entirely in Africa, presumably because of a lack of hosts. The evidence for this assumption is the complete absence of Duffy antigen from the blood of more than ninety-five percent of black Africans, and those of African descent around the world, which makes them absolutely immune to that type of malarial parasite. The genetic characteristics known as the Duffy Antigenic System determine whether the *P. vivax* malaria parasite is able to penetrate the wall of the red blood cell. If either Duffy "a" or "b" type is present, penetration and infection can occur, but the "Duffy null" pattern prohibits invasion.

However, immunity to *P. vivax* provided little protection against the new and far more deadly falciparum malaria. All types of malaria destroy red blood cells and cause vascular inflammation and splenic enlargements at some stage of the illness. But, as Dr. Carlson explained, "falciparum malaria involves the vasculature of the central nervous system to a much greater extent than do the other types. This probably accounts for its common name, malignant tertian, and for the pronounced symptoms of headaches, frequent comatose states, and higher mortality rates. In patients who died of falciparum malaria, autopsy shows that the brain is slate gray in gross appearance, and punctate hemorrhages are present throughout the brain substance."

A new genetic defense, sickle-cell trait, had to be created. This new defense and the biological adaptations it triggered, which apparently developed after the dispersion of the founders of the Bantu populations from their original West African homeland (between Cameroon and eastern Nigeria), would not be possessed by the rest of Africa. The development of sickle-cell trait, although the result of a single amino acid substitution in the hemoglobin molecule, would have considerable medical and physiological consequences.

This substitution or "language error" in nucleotide sequencing created the abnormal hemoglobin gene, which produces sickle-shaped red corpuscles. Because these sickle-shaped cells are less hospitable to the malarial plasmodium than normal red blood cells, the debilitating effects of malarial infection are reduced in individuals who inherit this kind of red corpuscle from just one parent. But the cost of this biological protection, particularly before the advent of modern medicine, was very high. Individuals who inherit the sickling gene from two asymptomatic parents who are both carriers of the recessive sickle-cell trait have a one-in-four probability of being afflicted with sickle cell disease. Almost invariably, even today, these individuals die young.

The inevitably heavy child mortality is further increased by the fact that those born entirely without the sickling gene are extremely vulnerable to lethal malarial infection. Just how lethal can be measured by the fact that in the most intensive malarial regions of West Africa, even among populations bearing the sickle-cell trait, half the infants born are biologically vulnerable.

While it is now indisputable that heterozygous individuals—those with one copy of the sickling gene—possess a selective advantage in areas of high malarial infection, the connection between sickle-cell trait and athletic ability is far less clear. In fact, since the sickle-cell gene reduces oxygen transportation in the circulatory system, the evidence apparently points in the opposite direction. Despite this biological handicap, people of West African descent, by developing "compensating mechanisms," were able to supply the enormous stores of human energy that powered the industrial revolution, and have now enabled them to become the greatest athletes in the world.

There is overwhelming evidence that the source of the natural athletic superiority of people of West African origin is their physiological uniqueness, which began, but did not end, with the mutation of the hemoglobin molecule. Apparently, a series of mutations created biologically minor but athletically meaningful genetic differences between these West Africans and all other groups, including all other black Africans. Such mutations might or might not have occurred in other population groups, but were preserved in some West Africans because of the biological advantages they conferred in that uniquely lethal malarial environment. These differences include testosterone and human growth hormone levels, skeletal muscle fiber type proportion and density, and respiratory rates.

The thesis that the athletic superiority of people of West African origins is linked to their development of biological defenses against falciparum malaria is not as new or as radical as it might seem. A British physician, A. C. Allison, first advanced the concept of sickling as an instance of natural selection in humans in 1954. Allison had spent several years in Africa drawing the blood of native people as part of an extensive colonial project to establish racial and tribal affinities. His familiarity with the findings of the malaria association allowed him to marshal the evidence required to support the hypothesis that carriers of the sickle-cell trait were immune to malaria.

The recognition that sickling could be an indication of biological superiority shattered a widely held view that the mere presence of sickle-shaped cells in the blood was a sign of constitutional degeneracy and racial inferiority.

Four years later, biological anthropologist Frank B. Livingstone would become the first person to link the agricultural revolution in West Africa to the sickle cell. "The agricultural revolution," he argued, "has always been considered an important event in man's cultural evolution, but it also seems to have been an important event in man's biological evolution." Livingstone attributed this change in the role of disease in human evolution to two byproducts of West Africa's agricultural revolution: the great changes in the environment, and the huge increase in the human population. Both of these events, he argued, seemed to have been involved in what he described as "holoendemic malaria."

By "blundering on the scene," man apparently caused the extinction of the previous host of the *Anopheles gambiae* mosquito and caused his own substitution as the most available blood meal. Under these conditions, Livingstone explained, "holoendemic malaria" became an important factor in human evolution. The sickle-cell gene, he concluded, "thus seems to be an evolutionary response to this changed disease environment. Hence, this gene is the first known genetic response to a very important event in man's evolution when disease became a factor determining that evolution."

But it is also important to recognize that not all the athletic advantages enjoyed by West Africans over Europeans and Asians are the result of mutations that took place in West Africa. Some, such as body proportions and low subcutaneous fat percentages, are shared with other Africans. The relatively shorter arms and legs and higher subcutaneous body fat of Europeans, Asians, and all other non-African groups, which were adaptations to colder climates, are the result of mutations that occurred outside of Africa. These non-African mutations were detrimental to the relative athletic abilities of those populations because they eroded the original anatomical equality between all human populations without adding any apparently athletically beneficent physiological ones.

11

Body Structure, Physiology, and Athletic Performance

S ome philosophers associated it with a flame; others believed it indistinguishable from air or breath. Aristotle thought it too insubstantial to be associated with any of the four physical elements. To neo-Platonists of the fourth and fifth centuries, it was a radiant emanation. And to the Florentine mystics of the fifteenth century, it was a very subtle body, almost soul, or again, not soul and almost body. It verified everything everywhere and was the immediate cause of all generation and motion.

The mysterious subject of these philosophical musings was the elusive medium thought responsible for translating mental activity into physical action. Not surprisingly, man has long been curious about the functioning of his body, but so little was known for so long that despite the extraordinary literary and artistic advances of the Renaissance, philosophers of the period were convinced that an ingredient they deemed "Animal Spirits" was responsible for translating the impulses of the soul into movements of the muscles.

It was not until the seventeenth and eighteenth centuries that physiologists began developing a rudimentary outline of the physical processes involved in muscle contraction, and a more complete explanation was not made until after World War II. But long before those physiological functions were properly understood, man was aware of a connection between body shape and athletic ability. Inspired by Egypt, where they became acquainted with monumental sculpture in hard stone, Greek artists developed a form, which, within three hundred years, achieved remarkable realism in anatomy, action, and expression. Abandoning an earlier focus on an abstract, decorative format, the classical Greeks established an idiom of representational art based primarily on the nude human figure. Demonstrating their understanding of the link between body shape and physical prowess, Greek artists depicted their gods and athletes as beings both graceful and powerful.

It was fitting, therefore, that in the twentieth century, the earliest attempts to study the connection between body type and athletic performance were focused on Olympic athletes. Rudimentary studies based on competitors in the 1928 and 1948 Olympic Games were published in 1929 and 1951. But a truly detailed study of the physique of the Olympic athlete was not done until after the Olympic Games in Rome in 1960. This study, which was reported in *The Physique of the Olympic Athlete* by anthropologist J.M.Tanner, included 137 track and field athletes from twenty-three countries. Only athletes who had achieved the 1960 Olympic standard were included. The great majority of subjects were of European origin, but the test group included a number of blacks from North America, the Caribbean, and Africa, plus a few Asians from Japan and Korea.

The primary purpose of the study was to scientifically determine whether body structure limited certain types of physical performance. The assumption was that if any relationship between physique and success in one event rather than another existed, it would show up most clearly in groups like Olympic athletes, where the intensity of the competition had equalized other influences, such as motivation and training.

The methods used to compare the athletes were impressively detailed. They included fourteen different anthropometric measurements—specially posed photographs using an aerial mapping technique—so that measurements could be taken from the photographic prints and x-rays to delineate the bone, muscle, and fat in the upper arm, calf, and thigh. The photographs and x-rays were then analyzed and classified to determine if there were any reliable physical differences between athletes from different events—for example, between sprinters and hurdlers, or 400-meter and marathon runners.

Somatotyping, the method used to compare the x-rays and photographs of the athletes, was then, and perhaps still is, the best method of classifying physiques by reliance on external appearances alone. Samotyping allows physiologists and other experts in this area to compare both single measurements—such as height, or weight, or calf muscle width—to determine differences in size, and multiple measurements—such as the proportion or relationship, between leg length and trunk length—to determine differences in body proportions. The results confirmed in the most unambiguous way the relationship between success in certain athletic activities and body size and proportion.

An expected but interesting finding was that only half of the somatotypes present in the general population were represented on the Olympic teams— the clear implication being that it is virtually impossible for those with certain body types to become Olympic athletes. All of the Olympians, for instance, had the naturally muscular-mesomorphic body type and none had the naturally heavy-endomorphic body type. The results also clearly established that there are very striking differences in body size, shape, and structure between competitors in different events.

Although some of the greatest sprinters of all time, such as the incomparable Carl Lewis, have been relatively tall, as a group sprinters are generally relatively short and very muscular compared with middle- and long-distance runners, and all their limb muscles are larger in relation to their bones than those of other runners. The study also found that there is a clear gradient of build, running from competitors in the 400 meters to those in the marathon, with the men in the 1,500 and 5,000 meters occupying an intermediate position. Men competing in the 400 meters are large, long-legged, and broad-shouldered in relation to their hips and are relatively heavily muscled. On the other hand, long-distance runners tend to be small, short-legged, narrow-shouldered, and relatively lacking in muscle. The 110-meter hurdlers are large, long-legged sprinters, as muscular as the sprinters, with legs as long as the 400-meter runners. As expected, weightlifters are extremely mesomorphic and generally short-limbed.

To close observers of athletes, Tanner's findings were hardly surprising. While there are examples of outstanding athletes who have apparently defied the limitations of their physiques, the truth is that even these remarkable people are operating at the outer limits of their physical capabilities, but within the apparent iron rule that in athletics genetics is destiny. Although it is generally recognized that environmental factors can influence the shape and composition of the body, it is increasingly apparent, even if the precise mechanisms are still unknown, that genetics prescribe the limits of such variations. As an example, studies on hundreds of pairs of twins have demonstrated that sports performance—while influenced by factors such as training, social environments, and economic levels—is also significantly determined by hereditary factors. Dedication and fierce determination will maximize individual potential, but success at the highest levels of athletic competition is possible only if genetically endowed physical gifts are equal or at least similar.

More importantly for the purposes of this book, the study also found strong evidence, despite the limited size of the sample, of significant differences in body proportions between blacks and whites of comparable size competing in the same events. Among competitors in both track and field events there were "large, significant racial differences in leg length, arm length, and hip width." White sprinters had a greater average sitting height than their black counterparts, 93.5 cm to 92.5 cm, but the leg length of blacks averaged 86.2 cm, to only 83.0 cm for whites. The arm length of black sprinters averaged 81.9 cm compared to a mere 76.7 cm for whites, and the hip width of the blacks averaged 26.8 cm while whites averaged 28.5 cm.

These differences were not limited to sprinters. The ratio of leg length to sitting height for sprinters, 400-meter runners, and high jumpers averaged 0.88, 0.92, and 0.93 respectively in whites, and 0.93, 0.97, and 1.01 respectively in blacks. The same differences were also found between black and white weightlifters. But the differences were not limited to these anthropometric measurements. Black athletes in the study were also found to have had significantly less subcutaneous fat, slightly larger and more muscular arms and legs, and calves with wider bones and narrower muscles.

The findings of Tanner's study were similar to an earlier one conducted in 1939 by Eleanor Metheny, a physical educator from Iowa State University. Prompted by an explosion of black athletic talent throughout the decade, the study compared the body measurements of 102 students who were evenly divided by race. The white students were from a variety of ethnic backgrounds, but almost all of the blacks were of West African origin. Her study, probably the most extensive of its kind until Tanner's effort, revealed that relative to body stature, African Americans surpassed European Americans in the following characteristics: weight, shoulder breadth, chest depth and width, neck and limb girth, and length of arm, forearm, hand, leg and lower leg. European Americans, on the other hand, exceeded African Americans in sitting height, total fat, and hip width.

Not content to merely publish her findings, Metheny went on to consider the athletic consequences of these racial differences in body measurements. She concluded that several physical features of African Americans offered obvious advantages in a variety of sports. She pointed out that greater body weight, which was the result of heavier bones and greater musculature, coupled with lower body fat, conferred an advantage in contact sports such as football. Longer forearms and hands were advantageous in throwing and provided greater momentum in jumping. Longer legs and narrower hips, she argued, combined with greater musculature, gave African American athletes advantages in running. Metheny also claimed that African Americans were disadvantaged in endurance events because of lower breathing capacity.

The findings and conclusions reported by Metheny and Tanner were confirmed and amplified by a far larger and more elaborate study of Olympic athletes from the 1968 Games in Mexico City. More than 1,000 athletes—this time of both sexes, of every racial group, and from all parts of the world—participated in the project, which was named the Program of Genetics and Human Biology. Unlike the previous studies, which were limited to the morphological basis of performance, the Mexico City study attempted to examine the possible genetic bases for body structure and sports performance. As a result, in addition to samotyping (using Tanner's methodology), the Mexico City study collected and analyzed a number of genetic and anthropological characteristics of the athletes.

Among the factors included were investigations of the sports histories of the families of the athletes; genetic traits of the athletes, especially those that might be correlated with sports ability; and those aspects of the athletes' physiques that represented the interaction of their genetic endowments with the environmental factors involved in training. The 1,265 athletes, representing 129 separate Olympic events, were grouped into four major racial categories: Caucasoid, Mongoloid, Mestizo (Indian plus Caucasoid), and Negroid. The classifications were based on identification and somatotype photographs, as well as physical characteristics including skin color; general body shape; proportions of segments of the limbs; facial structure; form of eyes, lips, and nose; and color and texture of hair.

Like the Tanner study of the athletes from the 1960 Olympic Games, the Mexico City survey confirmed the relationship between body type and athletic performance as well as the differences in body proportions between the Negroids and the other groups. Not only were the Negroids significantly narrower in hip breadth than the Caucasoids (slightly less so with the two other groups), but the Negroids were found to have longer arms and legs, and a shorter trunk, than the other groups. Despite these differences, the study concluded, "it would appear that the same somatypes excel at the specified events regardless of race, and that the functional requirements of the events demand similar somatypes."

The most interesting and important finding of the study was not produced by anthropometric measurements, but by tests to determine a possible association between athletic ability and single gene systems. Investigated were the ABO, MN, and Rh red cell types; haptoglobin, glucose-6-phosphate dehydrogenase, and acid phosphatase. Although the study failed to link athletic ability to a single gene system, the authors expressed "surprise" that "a sizable number of Negroid Olympic athletes manifested the sickle-cell trait."

The authors noted, "In view of the importance of hemoglobin in the transport of oxygen to tissues, one might expect very slight differences in function or amount of hemoglobin to be reflected in athletic potential. Especially in the case of hemoglobin S (the sickle gene), one might suppose that the great oxygen demand, which accompanies certain athletic activities, might cause a certain amount of *in vivo* sickling of red cells even though this is not observed in heterozygotes under other conditions. Such persons might, therefore, be at a disadvantage, and even a small disadvantage would be expected to prevent such persons attaining Olympic status. It was surprising to discover that this was not the case."

The surprising finding, that a shortage of hemoglobin—which enables red blood cells to transport oxygen—had not adversely affected the athletic capabilities of black athletes, was magnified by the fact that the 1968 Olympics were staged at the high altitude of Mexico City. "One could imagine," the authors wrote, "that a greater oxygen deficit would be associated with this altitude and that persons heterozygous for hemoglobin S would be more likely to form sickle cells in vivo than at lower altitudes."

Despite their failure to link athletic ability to a single gene system in the Mexico City study, the authors were undaunted. "That athletic ability is indeed associated with specific genetic markers is an assumption which needs little proof," they wrote. "Within the normal population, many persons lack the biological potential to become an outstanding athlete ... whatever biological limitations may exist, they are almost certainly largely genetic in origin. These limitations must be attributed ultimately therefore, to the action of a series of single genes. One may reasonably expect to find associations between athletic ability and single genes if the search is continued long enough."

After pointing out that the genetic systems selected had been dictated primarily by the large number of athletes in the study, they noted that when the study was planned, "the number of polymorphic protein and enzymes known was limited." However, they wrote, "This situation is changing rapidly, with new polymorphic enzyme systems being reported frequently." The systems, which with considerable foresight they found to be "of particular interest," were those "related to energy metabolism, where one might expect small differences in normal function to become important under the severe stress of athletic competition."

Almost thirty years after Tanner's, another study, this time of the general population, would confirm the racial differences in body proportions. The authors compared data on the relative proportions of the legs and trunks of black Americans, non-Hispanic whites, and Mexican Americans ages 2 to 17. They found that, on average, there were only small differences in the proportion of leg length to height in the Mexican American and non-Hispanic white groups, while blacks had proportionately longer legs. Speculating on the reasons for racial differences in body proportions, the authors concluded that they were both environmental and genetic.

As an example of the former, they pointed to the recent height increase of the Japanese that is due almost entirely to an increase in leg length: an increase they attributed to the significantly greater protein consumption of the postwar Japanese population. On the other hand, according to the authors, the difference in body proportions between children of African and European ancestry appear to be genetic since they are evident even at birth and have not been significantly affected by protein consumption patterns. Other more recent studies have also supported the Metheny-Tanner-Mexico City anthropometric findings, and there is now widespread agreement that there are real and meaningful differences in body measurements between Americans of African and European descents. But there is probably far less agreement regarding the athletic significance of these differences; some researchers, such as anthropologists Carleton Coon and Edward Hunt, while agreeing that there are racial differences in body proportions, also argued that African American dominance in some sports is based on socioeconomic factors.

All of this was before the chemistry of muscle contraction was properly understood. Tanner himself speculated that since the "Negro had slightly more muscle in the arms and thighs than the corresponding white but considerably less muscle in the calves... it is hard to suppose that he produces more muscular force. In theory his muscles might be capable of a more explosive action; that is, they might produce a more rapid development of force by contracting faster, but there is no evidence for this and it does not seem very likely from a physiological point of view." Ironically, as the Mexico City researchers suspected and as we now know, this is exactly what happens.

Six years after the Tanner study and two years before the one in Mexico City, Harvard anthropologist Albert Damon probably became the first American to venture an explanation of black athletic success that has stood the test of time. Although it is unlikely that his conclusions were based on a deep knowledge of cell biology, Damon predicted that "physiological factors" were more likely than anthropometric ones to explain "the much greater success of Negroes in track events requiring short bursts of power."

A decade after Professor Damon's prediction and eight years after the Mexico City report, an article in the *Journal of the National Medical Association*, the official organ of the African American medical group, provided the first concrete clue to the puzzle of African American athletic superiority. The Mexico City study had expressed surprise that Negroid athletes with sickle-cell trait had been able to compete effectively at the very highest levels, despite deficiencies in their oxygen transportation systems. This article would reveal, astonishingly, that it was not only individuals with sickle-cell trait who had lower than average hemoglobin levels, but that African Americans generally had significantly lower hemoglobin levels than their white counterparts. It would also raise, for the first time, the critical issue of how African Americans coped so well with this apparent biological handicap.

Although the article attracted very little attention at the time, the question posed was central to any attempt to understand the mystery of African

American athletic dominance. For not only do average black Americans have significantly lower hemoglobin levels than their white counterparts, but as the authors pointed out, "studies of athletes who tend to higher hemoglobins and hematocrits still show evidence of differences between blacks and whites."

Conducted in ten states and in New York City, the study involved nearly 30,000 individuals, divided into twenty-four age groups, from the first year through the ninth decade. To eliminate the possibility that the racial differences in hemoglobin levels were caused by socioeconomic factors, the study included matched comparisons of blacks and whites with reported high levels of iron intake and higher incomes, and athletes of both races. Nonetheless, the results clearly indicated that, without exception, there were significant racial differences in hemoglobin levels, at every age group, and for both sexes. This "systematic difference," the authors wrote, "is fully evident even during the period of rapid adolescent gain in hemoglobin levels in the male, and during the period of declining hemoglobin levels in the 7th and 8th decades."

Speculating on whether the observed difference in hemoglobin levels between the races was of environmental or genetic origin, the authors explained that if it were the latter, then this "would also raise the possibility of mechanisms for oxygen transport beyond those provided by the respiratory pigments." Or, more plainly, if the lower hemoglobin levels of healthy African Americans were caused by genetic factors, then it was clear that African Americans had developed an extra-normal system for transporting oxygen, since the "normal" system provided by the red blood cells was clearly inadequate. In fact, as we now know, what African Americans did develop was not an extra-normal system for transporting oxygen but a "compensating" mechanism—-that we shall examine in far greater detail in Chapter 13—for coping with this apparent handicap.

Since hemoglobin, the main constituent of red cells in the blood, not only makes blood red but also gives it the ability to collect oxygen from the lungs and deliver it to the tissues, significantly lower levels should have had, as the Mexico City researchers had explained, a significant negative effect on the muscular strength and stamina of African Americans. The fact that the muscular system of black Americans and other West African-descended groups has not been impaired, indeed has even been enhanced, by an apparent biological handicap, is the clearest and most obvious indication that significant adjustments in energy metabolism have occurred in that population group.

Two years later, another team of researchers, also writing in the *Journal of the National Medical Association*, came closer to the truth. Surely, they wrote, "some compensatory mechanism must exist to counteract this relative deficiency of hemoglobin, since a significant difference has even been demonstrated in healthy athletes." It is difficult to overemphasize the importance of this finding, and yet, mystifyingly, it has attracted very little attention and commentary in the heated debate over the basis of black athletic dominance.

Perhaps because the implications of lower hemoglobin levels in healthy black athletes were not fully understood, the second major clue to the puzzle of black athletic dominance was not uncovered for another decade. It was not until almost two decades after the authors of the Mexico City study had pointed to genetic systems related to energy metabolism as areas where explanations for differences in athletic ability might be found, that a study to determine whether there are racial differences in fiber type proportion and how the skeletal muscles receive energy was proposed. By that time, in 1986, research over the previous decade or so had established that not only was skeletal muscle composed of two types of fibers—fast-twitch and slow-twitch—that deploy different metabolic pathways, but that the proportion of those fibers influenced athletic performance.

Conducted at Laval University in Quebec, Canada, the study consisted of forty-six men: twenty-three black African students from Cameroon, Senegal, Zaire, Ivory Coast, and Burundi, and an equal number of Caucasians. Since training influences enzyme activity in both fast-twitch and slow-twitch fibers, all the men selected had either never trained or had been inactive for several months. The groups were also matched by age, height, body weight, and body mass index.

The study, conducted by geneticist and exercise physiologist Claude Bouchard and exercise biochemist Jean-Aime Simoneau, revealed that the groups differed in both fiber type proportion and muscle enzyme activity levels. Muscle biopsies clearly showed not only that the mixed group of Africans had a higher percentage of fast-twitch fibers and a lower level of slow-twitch fibers than their Caucasian counterparts, but also that the Africans had significantly higher activity, about 30 to 40 percent, in their phosphagenic, glycolytic, and lactate dehydrogenase metabolic pathways. The authors concluded that "the racial differences observed between Africans and Caucasians in fiber type proportion and enzyme activities ... may well result from inherited variation. These data suggest that sedentary male black individuals are, in terms of muscle characteristics, well endowed for sports events of short duration."

For Professor Damon of Harvard and the authors of the Mexico City study, the findings of the Laval University study were sweet vindication. Damon had boldly predicted that physiological factors were more likely than anthropometric ones to explain black athletic success in athletic events requiring short bursts of power. The authors of the Mexico City report had not only (like Damon) targeted energy metabolism, but had correctly identified the metabolic systems involved. But despite its obvious importance, by treating West Africans from Cameroon, Senegal, and the Ivory Coast; Central Africans from Zaire; and East Central Africans from Burrundi as a single group, the study probably, inadvertently, understated the differences in fiber proportion and enzyme activity between athletes of West African origin and others.

It may also be true that the study, by excluding African Americans, Afro-Caribbeans, and other West African-descended groups in the Diaspora, significantly underestimated the differences between Europeans and those West Africans whose ancestors had been transported across the Atlantic. Such differences may exist not only because of the eugenic effects of the slave trade, but also because there is reason to believe that not all West Africans are equally endowed with fast-twitch muscle fiber, and that the ancestors of many of the most outstanding athletes of West African descent in the Diaspora may have come, disproportionately from a relatively small area of West Africa.

During the hundreds of years of the slave trade and slavery itself, millions of Africans perished from disease, overwork, undernourishment, and other kinds of brutality. The British historian and author Basil Davidson believes that at least one and a half million slaves died during the passage to the New World—about thirteen percent of all the slaves taken on board. Millions of others perished after arriving at their destinations in the Americas and the Caribbean before they had an opportunity to reproduce at all, or before they contributed their expected share of genetic material to future generations. If it was not quite true that in New World slavery only the strong survived and reproduced, it was certainly true that the strongest survived the longest and contributed the most genetic material to future generations. It also seems clear, as shall soon be explained, that the ability to survive the rigors of the Middle Passage and then of slavery itself was not unrelated to area of origin and fiber type proportion.

In addition to these natural selection processes, there is some evidence that the eugenic effect of slavery may have been aided by selective breeding on some slave plantations. Although, as noted earlier, the sports commentator Jimmy "The Greek" Snyder was fired from his television job in 1988 for suggesting that the success of African American athletes originated with selective breeding by slave owners, a doctoral dissertation completed some years earlier by Gerald S. Norte had concluded that slave breeding was indeed a common practice. After examining advertisements that offered thousands of female slaves for sale each day, Norte noted that many of them emphasized the reproductive abilities of the women. As an example, an advertisement in the *Charleston Mercury* explicitly boasted: "She is very prolific in her generating qualities and affords a rare opportunity for any person who wishes to raise a family of strong and healthy servants."

But it was natural selection and not selective breeding that was the primary eugenic agent during slavery. It seems clear that the vast majority of the slaves who perished during the Middle Passage died of disease, as a result of the "absolutely pestilential" conditions in the holds of the ships. Perhaps the most explicit, vivid, and harrowing account of the Middle Passage came from an Ibo slave, Oludah Equiano, who published an account of his own trip across the Atlantic. "The closeness of the place," he wrote, "and the heat of the climate added to the number in the ship, which was so crowded that each had scarcely room to turn himself, almost suffocated us. This produced copious perspiration, a variety of loathsome smells, and brought on a sickness amongst the slaves, of which many died."

We also know that one of the most significant aspects of the Middle Passage was the unequal impact its rigors had on captives from different parts of West Africa. According to observers of the period, slaves from the Gold and Slave Coasts, whom he claimed were fed on Indian corn, "had in general little or no mortality." Those from the Windward Coast, whose diets supposedly consisted primarily of rice, were "next to degree most healthy," while those from Nigeria, whom he said were fed mainly on yams, were "subject to the greatest mortality."

Today, with our far greater understanding of disease, it is fairly safe to conclude that the differences in death rates between various West African groups probably had little or nothing to do with differences in diet. Although it is clear from the height data that the diet of West Africans was poor relative to slaves in the Caribbean or in the United States, the Africans selected for slavery were usually young, healthy, and relatively well fed: But it probably had a great deal to do with differences in disease experience and relative immunological ability.

There is ample testimony to the existence of these differences. A British physician, Dr. Thomas Winterbottom, provided perhaps the best-documented and most reliable account of the unequal impact of malaria on various groups of West African people. Winterbottom, who spent seven years in Sierra Leone studying and documenting the disease experience of several local groups, published his findings in two well-received volumes in 1803. Winterbottom noted that the clinical signs of malaria, which he described as "intermittents," were very uncommon among the Bulloms and Timmanees, two coastal people who would have had the most constant infection of malaria. It was so uncommon, he explained, that many of them had never even seen the disease, except perhaps among Europeans, and therefore had no "specific name for an ague, but generally term it the shaking sickness." That was in sharp contrast to the inland Foola, Soosoo, and Mandingo peoples, who were probably only exposed during the rainy seasons and consequently had a lower tolerance for the deadly disease. Particularly vulnerable were the people of Foola country, where "intermittents" were "more usual" than in either Soosoo or Mandingo.

It is highly probable that the West Africans, who survived the Middle Passage and then slavery itself, were most likely to have come from areas of the most intense malarial and yellow fever infection. This would have made them the most likely to have acquired genetic defenses to those pitiless killers, and as a consequence, they would have also been the most likely to have developed the genetic mutations—including an increased percentage of the fast-twitch fiber—which are biological byproducts of the genetic defense against falciparum malaria, as explained earlier. This means, of course, that West African-descended populations in the New World are likely to have a higher percentage of fast-twitch muscle fiber and therefore greater average athletic ability than West Africans whose ancestors did not leave the mother continent.

Some support for this hypothesis, apart from the dominance of African American athletes, can probably be seen in the performance of Afro-Caribbean athletes in a number of sports, including track and field, boxing, cricket, and baseball. The tiny countries of Jamaica, Barbados and the Dominican Republic have produced world-class athletes disproportionate to their share of the world's population. Despite a population of just over two million—a significant percentage of whom are too poor to participate in organized athletics—Jamaica has historically produced some of the greatest male and female track athletes in the world, plus a quite remarkable number of outstanding boxers, including the former world heavyweight champion, Lennox Lewis. The Dominican Republic, with a population of just over eight million, millions of them also too poor to participate in organized athletics, has consistently produced some of the finest baseball players in the world. And the tiny island of Barbados, from an area of just over 150 square miles, has over many decades managed in almost miraculous fashion to produce many of the greatest cricket players in the world, including the greatest of them all, Sir Garfield Sobers.

But, however flawed, the Laval University study provided the first evidence that there is, in fact, a compensatory mechanism to counteract the relative deficiency of hemoglobin in even healthy African American athletes. The Laval study also made it clear that the mystery of African American athletic dominance could be solved by a careful examination of the biological processes involved in the conferment of this compensation.

The importance to athletic performance of fiber type distribution and muscle energy production was confirmed by another study. Conducted at the University of Jyvesta in Finland, the subjects were nine national-caliber male high jumpers and fourteen males who trained regularly with weights. The result of muscle biopsies indicated that reaction time and vertical jumping ability were both affected by fiber type proportion. The authors concluded that subjects who "had a high percentage of fast-twitch fibers were able to reach certain force levels in a shorter time and jump higher than subjects who had a lower percentage of fast-twitch fibers."

The result indicated no relationship between strength and vertical jumping ability. For example, the high jumpers produced their force faster and jumped higher than the weight-training group. The study concluded that "reaction time and vertical jumping height were interrelated and that both of these factors are significantly related to muscle structure."

The following year, 1987, brought the third clue and an example of the compensatory mechanism at work. For years, studies examining racial differences in lung function had found that the lung volume of whites was greater than those of blacks of similar size, age, and fitness level. As with decreased hemoglobin levels, a smaller lung capacity should have been a handicap to hard physical labor and high-level athletic performance. Since it clearly had not done so, a study was conducted at the State University of New York at Buffalo to "determine whether the lower FVC (forced vital capacity) observed in healthy blacks results in a ventilatory adjustment to exercise which differs from that observed in healthy Caucasians."

Eighteen white and fourteen black subjects were studied, ages eight to 30, and were matched for sex, age, height, and weight. The results confirmed that lung volumes were ten percent to fifteen percent greater in white subjects than in blacks of the same sex, age, and size; that there were clear differences in the breathing patterns of the two racial groups during exercise; and, most surprisingly, that blacks, despite their smaller lung capacity, consumed more oxygen in every phase of exercise than their white counterparts. This was possible, the researchers determined, because minute ventilation—the provision of oxygen to the total area of the lungs—was higher in blacks at all work loads and became more significant as the workload increased.

Blacks, the study found, compensated for their smaller lung capacity by increasing the frequency of their breathing, which was achieved by a proportionate reduction of both the inspiratory and expiratory cycles. In effect, they breathed more rapidly and more shallowly than whites.

Speculating on the differences in lung volume and the ventilatory response to exercise in his black and white subjects, the author pointed to a possible link with hemoglobin levels. Other researchers, he explained, had reported altered lung pressure-volume relationships in healthy black subjects with hemoglobin sickle-cell trait, the mild form of the disease, which conveyed genetic superiority in the deadly malarial environment of West Africa. While noting that there was no direct evidence of differences in lung compliance between the races, the author pointed out that "on indirect evidence in the literature, however, this possibility cannot be ruled out at this time." The likelihood that the high exercise breathing frequency in black subjects is influenced by genetic factors was also strengthened by findings, from other researchers, that breathing patterns during exercise are, to a large extent, genetically determined.

While the Buffalo University study fully explained the mechanism that allows individuals of West African descent to get adequate supplies of oxygen to their lungs despite volume restrictions, it left unanswered the larger question of just how that oxygen is transported to the tissues. Of course, it is in the answer to that question that the solution to the puzzle of African American athletic superiority is to be found.

For more than a decade, there has been more than sufficient scientific evidence to make it clear that there are intriguing and athletically meaningful physiological differences between black and white Americans. Why so little has been written about these differences is best understood by examining the controversy surrounding the fourth clue.

African American men have one of the highest rates of prostate cancer in the world; almost double that of white American men. Research undertaken to explain this phenomenon, found that black men have higher levels of both testosterone and human growth hormone than their white counterparts. After adjustment for the time of sampling, age, weight, alcohol use, smoking, and use of prescription drugs, the research found a fifteen percent difference in total testosterone levels between the races. Since testosterone and growth hormone promote the growth of lean muscle mass, significant racial differences in these hormones could be athletically meaningful. But some saw in these differences in hormone levels something far more sinister and fundamental than differences in athletic ability.

Ellis and Nyborg, the hormone theorists, seized on the difference in testosterone levels to revive old theories of black intellectual and moral inferiority. After noting that "recent evidence has shown that black men exhibit biochemical responses to stress that are, on average, distinct from white men, i.e., black men produce higher beta-endorphin levels in response to stress," they concluded, ominously, that they were aware that average racial/ethnic differences in testosterone levels may not only help to explain group variations in disease, but could also be relevant to group differences in "behavior patterns" since "testosterone and its metabolites are neurologically very active."

Nyborg's 1994 tract, *Hormones, Sex and Society*, helped to clarify what group behavior patterns meant. After piously warning against the misuse of this kind of research, Nyborg advanced the theory that low testosterone males "are predicted to show a higher level of brain-based, so-called intellectual activity" than high testosterone males, who are "physically more active." His theory resurrected what has been described as the old economy principle, and which was first articulated by Goethe and supported, with reservations, by Darwin in *The Descent of Man.* "Nature," Goethe claimed, "in order to spend on one side is forced to economize on the other side."

Although Darwin wrote that "it can hardly be maintained that the law is of universal application," and that only when a "structure, before useful, becomes less useful, its diminution will be favored," Nyborg used it as the basis for challenging the intellectual capacity of black Americans. "The economy principle," he wrote, "implies that this [body-brain relationship] requires intrasystemic energy resources that detract from complete brain development." To make sure his meaning was clear, Nyborg added, "A much less sophisticated formula is the old saying, too much muscles, too little brain."

Even more direct than Nyborg was the Canadian psychologist J. Philippe Rushton, a professor at the University of Western Ontario. An unrepentant racist, Rushton revealingly described the theory this way: "Even if you take something like athletic ability or sexuality—not to reinforce stereotypes or some such thing—but, you know, it's a trade-off: more brain or more penis. You can't have everything."

For those determined to portray blacks as intellectually inferior, evidence of genetically determined athletic ability is just one more arrow for their quivers of hatred. White racial theorists have not always, of course, regarded physical prowess as evidence of intellectual inferiority. The more intelligent ones surely know that most movements involved in athletic activity are controlled and coordinated through the higher brain centers, specifically the motor cortex, the basal ganglia, and the cerebellum. It is no accident that the athletes competing in the "Special" Olympics have as much difficulty with muscular coordination as with clear and logical thought. Perhaps that is one reason why speed, power, and strength have been instinctively celebrated, in poetry and verse, in cultures around the world, long before man understood the functioning of the brain and the nervous system.

From Hercules to Rambo, physical prowess has been the primary requisite quality of the hero. The legendary explorer Richard Francis Burton boasted of his strength, and after climbing one of the highest peaks in the Cameroon

Mountains was lionized by white commentators for his "tremendous animalism." He later wrote of his physical exploits: "To be first in such matters is everything, to be second nothing." Another nineteenth century European explorer, Eduard Foa, warned other white men who were thinking of coming to Africa that they would lose their authority and perhaps their lives if they lacked the strength and stamina to maintain the respect of the Africans.

While some white intellectuals may be sanguine about the physical superiority of blacks, their indifference to physical prowess is hardly shared by the vast majority of their race—male or female. Witness the enduring popularity of white heroes—fictional and real—and white America's extraordinary psychological embrace of white baseball players such as Babe Ruth, Joe DiMaggio, Mickey Mantle, and Mark McGwire. For decades the greatest white action heroes were mere celluloid fantasies. Tarzan, John Wayne (in whatever role he played), Rocky, Rambo, and Schwarzenegger action movies kept the myth of the omnipotent white male alive.

Then came the real thing in Mark McGwire: muscles bulging, bat flashing, a real, genuine, authentic white stud-hero. Never mind the talk of possible steroid use, America was in no mood to tarnish the reputation of its first real white action hero in a long, long time. McGwire was the first white man, since blacks were allowed in substantial numbers to compete against whites, to prove that he was, perhaps, more than a match for any black man. White America cheered Sammy Sosa of course, for being a splendid and gallant loser, and out of a sense of fairness and decency. For McGwire, the response was deep and intensely emotional.

The ability to run, jump, and catch is, inherently, in this technological age, of little real-life consequence. But Americans with their vast amount of leisure time and discretionary income have bestowed on ballplayers fame, riches, and worship wildly disproportionate to the intrinsic value of their functions.

For reasons that lie outside the scope of this book, man, in every culture and age, has created and worshipped gods and heroes. In Greek legend the hero was a demigod, the offspring of the mating of men and gods. Today, in America, heroes are primarily athletes, superstars, created by fan need and mass media greed. But, in one of natures little ironies, the most despised Americans—African Americans—once allowed to compete, were found to possess in great abundance the physical gifts of which great athletes and modern heroes are made.

Naturally, in a country such as the United States that is highly conscious of race and addicted to sports, numerous theories, most hardly worthy of the term, have been developed to explain African American physical supremacy. We now know that African Americans are athletically dominant because they are biologically unique. The more important and interesting questions are, why are people of West African descent physiologically different from all other racial and ethnic groups on the face of the earth, including other black Africans, and, of course, what are the implications of this West African biological uniqueness? The former is the focus of the next chapter, and the latter is the subject of Part Four.

12

Natural Selection and the
West African Biological Miracle

Before the publication of Darwin's *The Origin of Species* in 1859, white European males by dint of species, race, gender, culture, and might of arms stood unchallenged as the natural, preordained masters of the universe. Wherever their glances fell, at home or abroad, submissive women and subjugated races affirmed their special status. A major tenet of Western thought was that man was created by God to have control and dominion over the earth and every living thing on it. Man, in that biblical injunction, was widely interpreted as meaning white males of European origin, and their dominance, however recent and temporary, was seen as the fulfillment of God's design.

The publication of *The Origin of Species,* and the acceptance by the thinking world of the theory of evolution, initially rocked the pedestal white males had erected for themselves. Man was robbed of the privilege of having been specially created and was now relegated to "descent from the animal world." In time, however, Europeans would seize upon Darwin's theories of natural selection and evolutionary descent to explain their leadership in technology and political organization. "Technologically primitive people," Professor Jared Diamond explained in *Guns, Germs and Steel* "were considered evolutionary vestiges of human descent from apelike ancestors.

The displacement of such peoples by colonists from industrialized societies exemplified the survival of the fittest."

It was not only against "primitive" peoples from other societies that Darwinism would be directed. In the United States, the doctrine of the survival of the fittest would also be used by the captains of industry to justify the exploitation of their workers. Beginning in the late nineteenth century, the rise of science and industrialization would be accompanied by a growing tendency among wealthy and successful Americans and Europeans to see, in the tenets of Darwinism, justification for competitive individualism and untrammeled capitalism.

However, in the context of its time, Darwin's theory was so revolutionary that he delayed its publication for an amazing twenty-one years. He finally published his work only because a competitor, A. R. Wallace, had arrived at a similar conclusion and was about to publish his own theory. It was not the concept of evolution itself that was so disturbing to the status quo; indeed evolution was a common enough heresy during the first half of the nineteenth century. But while other evolutionists expressed themselves in terms that permitted a Christian god to work through evolution instead of creation, Darwin, uncompromisingly, spoke only of "random variation and natural selection." Nowhere was there any acknowledgment of man's special status.

When *The Origin of Species* was first published, the great majority of naturalists believed that species were immutable productions and had been separately created. An exception was the great French evolutionist, Jean-Baptiste Lamarck, who had attracted a great deal of attention as early as 1801 with his claim that species, including man, descended from other species. Darwin acknowledged that Lamarck "first did the eminent service of arousing attention to the probability of all change in the organic, as well as in the inorganic world, being the result of law, and not of miraculous interposition." But by insisting that animals responded creatively to their needs and then passed on these acquired traits (a longer neck for giraffes, or bulging biceps in a bodybuilder, for example) to their offspring, Lamarck demonstrated that he did not fully understand what Darwin would describe as "the means of modification." Variation, Darwin insightfully concluded (before the laws of inheritance were properly understood) is random, and natural selection is the means of modification.

Darwin arrived, he claimed, at this central insight while reading Malthus' *On Population*, amazingly, for pleasure. As he later explained in his autobiography, "Being well prepared to appreciate the struggle for existence which everywhere goes on from long continued observation of the habits of animals and plants, it at once struck me that under these circumstances favorable variations would tend to be preserved and unfavorable ones to be destroyed." The result of this would be the formation of new species.

The great naturalist views on natural selection were explained at greater length in *The Origin of Species*. "Can it, then, be thought improbable," Darwin wrote, "seeing that variations useful to man have undoubtedly occurred, that other variations useful in some way in the great and complex battle of life, should occur in the course of many successive generations. If such do occur, can we doubt (remembering that many more individuals are born than can possibly survive) that individuals having any advantage, however slight, over others, would have the best chance of surviving and of procreating their kind. On the other hand, we may feel sure than any variation in the least injurious would be rigidly destroyed. This preservation of favorable individual differences and variations, and the destruction of those which are injurious, I have called Natural Selection, or the Survival of the Fittest."

Darwin's theory of natural selection did not achieve widespread popularity during his lifetime, did not prevail until the 1940s, and even today, as Stephen Jay Gould reminds us, "is widely misunderstood, misquoted and misapplied." One reason, perhaps the most important, why Darwin's theory failed to gain general acceptance until the middle of the twentieth century, was widespread ignorance of the nature of life.

Two great permanent revolutions occurred in the twentieth century, and as we now know, neither was in Moscow or Peking. Both were scientific, and one, the revolution in biology, made Darwin understandable and made this book possible. Both revolutions, the other and first was in physics, created transformations so broad and so deep that they changed forever our understanding of the world and of ourselves.

The revolution in physics began at the very start of that century, with Max Planck and the quantum theory and Albert Einstein and the theory of relativity, and included the interior of the atom and the structure of space and time. The revolution in biology began later, in the mid-thirties, coincidentally at about the same time that Jesse Owens and Joe Louis were changing the world's perception of the black athlete. Its first phase, the early stages of molecular biology, lasted until about 1970, and during that period a preliminary outline of the nature of life was constructed.

The centerpiece of this revolution was the discovery and elucidation of the structure of the genetic material deoxyribonucleic acid, or DNA. The discovery of DNA allowed biologists to glimpse the extraordinary complexity of the process of life in higher organisms, and to begin the still uncompleted pursuit of complete and explicit understanding of the precise molecular sequences that encode the hereditary message, instruction by instruction.

Because of its versatility and its conspicuous role in the function of the cell and the organism, as late as 1951 most biologists still thought that the hereditary message, the gene, was almost certainly made of protein. But once the structure of DNA was fully understood, its function as a blueprint became clear and incontrovertible. As the biologist Max Penitz explained, "The structure of DNA gave to the concept of the gene a physical and chemical meaning by which all its properties can be interpreted." Horace Judson, author of *The* eighth *day of creation: makers of the revolution in biology*, described the discovery of the unity of structure and function of DNA as the "master concept" of the next twenty years of biological investigation.

Since biology's primary concern—the origin and history of life—is also man's most fundamental interest, the progress of knowledge in this science has often been intensely controversial. For thousands of years it was religion, not science that guided man's belief in the origin and processes of life. Aristotle regarded the soul as inseparable from its body and believed that the soul was characterized by "self-nutrition, sensation, thinking and motivity." Perhaps because of Aristotle's enormous reputation and influence, the concept that living processes are regulated by a non-material vital force, outside the law of physics and chemistry, was not one that was easily extinguished among even the highly educated.

The scientific era in biology can be said to have begun in 1665 when Robert Hooke became the first person to describe cells, which he had discovered after examining a sliver of cork under his microscope and observed "microscopic pores." But the significance of his discovery was not appreciated by his contemporaries, and it was not until almost two centuries later that a conversation between two German scientists, Mathias Schleiden and Theodor Schwann, led to the creation of a general cell theory. Schwann realized that plant cells described by Schleiden were very similar to those he had observed in the nervous tissue of animals. Eventually, he would prove that all tissue—blood, skin, bone, nerve and muscle—is composed of cells.

Creation of the cell theory was an intellectual breakthrough of seminal importance. The discovery that all living things, plant and animal alike, are composed of living cells which are, without exception, organized in basically the same way, provided biology with what is probably its most important and fundamental tenet. That discovery led, logically, to the construction of evolutionary theories; it also led inevitably, to the then-revolutionary and, to some, blasphemous theory that life had a single origin. Aided and abetted by the steadily greater resolving power of the microscope, and the invention of test tubes and high-speed centrifuges, the cell theory also led to an understanding of embryological development and the laws of inheritance.

DNA functions as an information storage mechanism for the next generation; and the molecule must be replicated faithfully; sometimes an error occurs, and the result is an important change of code in the new cell. This sudden, random change or mistake in the duplication of the DNA sequence, which may cause it and all cells derived from it to differ in appearance or behavior from the normal type, is known as a mutation. There are two kinds of mutations. The less significant is the somatic type that occurs in the non-reproductive cells and is therefore not passed on to the next generation.

Germline mutations, on the other hand, occur in the reproductive cells, or the precursors, and may be transmitted to the organism's descendants. Most mutations are harmful, but a very small proportion may increase an organism's fitness; these, typically, spread through the population over successive generations by natural selection. Mutations, because of their importance in introducing new genetic forms into a population, are the ultimate source of variability of a species and, as such, are the foundation for the wide diversity we see in the biological world, including racial and ethnic variation in man. But, as we shall see in Part Four, anatomically modern man is a very young species; consequently, despite wide differences in physical appearance, ethnic and racial variation in man is genetically minor and biologically inconsequential.

To fully understand the miracle of West Africa, it is important to first understand how great the odds were against West Africans becoming valuable and famous for their size and strength. Malaria in West Africa was not just more malignant, more severe, and more widespread than in the rest of the world, but epidemics in tropical climates are essentially different from those in temperate ones. Bacteria or viruses cause almost all epidemics in temperate regions, and however severe or lethal, survivors usually recover fully, without disability, and often with lasting immunity.

In sharp contrast, many equally severe and lethal tropical diseases are caused by organisms that persist in the body, creating continuous disabilities and recurrent bouts of the disease. Malaria and schistosomiasis, a disease caused by worm infestation, although by no means the only examples, probably best exemplify the debilitating nature of tropical diseases. But tsetse flies, jiggers, locusts, water-snails, and fever-bearing clouds of flying creatures all took their toll.

In comparison to the conditions in Africa in general and in West Africa in particular, mankind faced simpler and far less challenging environmental conditions in temperate climates. Generally, lower temperatures are less hospitable to various life forms, and humans inhabiting these areas were able to escape many of the parasites and disease organisms of the tropics. The spread of human communities across the globe in diverse climatic zones created what McNeill described as a "parasitic gradient." As climates became colder, the variety and lethality of life forms capable of tormenting humans decreased, health and vigor improved accordingly, and human populations increased to levels unparalleled in warmer climates.

The extraordinary variety of human parasites that distinguish Africa from the rest of the world was not the only handicap inhabitants of the continent faced. The production of adequate food supplies required far more energy and ingenuity in Africa than in temperate climates. I have already explained that, in West Africa, the unexpected result of the initial efforts to establish agriculture in the rain forest was to give malaria a new epidemic intensity. Sleeping sickness did not seem to seriously affect the wild animals, but it took such a serious toll on domestic animals that most West African peoples were unable to keep horses and cattle.

Perhaps the clearest and most convincing explanation of the difficulties Africa faced with food production has been provided by Professor Jared Diamond at of the UCLA School of Medicine. In *Guns, Germs and Steel*, Diamond contended that the development of food production in sub-Saharan Africa was delayed (compared with Eurasia) "by Africa's paucity of domesticable native animal and plant species, its much smaller area suitable for indigenous food production, and its north-south axis, which retarded the spread of food production and inventions."

The invention of agriculture was a critical precondition for the development of any complex civilization. Nowhere was the advantage of the European continent over Africa greater than in the amount of energy and ingenuity required to create the food surpluses that allowed non-food-producing specialists to concentrate on other activities. Since historic times, the African continent has been handicapped by a shallow lateritic soil of low fertility and the most challenging ecosystem in the world. Geography, it has been said, is the mother of history, and nothing illustrates this more clearly than the contrasts between Africa, south of the Sahara, and Europe. While much of the vast African landmass was, and to a considerable degree still is, naturally hostile to man, the European continent has long provided (and still provides) a relatively pleasant human habitat. In fact, the differences between the two continents are so great that it is tempting to conclude they were designed by the Creator to play very different roles in human development. Sub-Saharan Africa, with its deadly environment and rapid cycles of birth and death, is the perfect laboratory for the creation of modern man. Europe, because of its location and physical geography, is the ideal vehicle for gathering the accumulated wisdom of the ancient world and creating modern civilizations.

In West Africa, the initial efforts to establish agriculture in the rain forest gave falciparum malaria, as we have seen, "a new epidemic intensity." For those inclined to somehow blame this development on black African ineptitude, it should be instructive to remember the ill-conceived and ultimately disastrous attempts of European colonial administrators, in the nineteenth and twentieth centuries, to alter traditional patterns of herding and cultivation in central and eastern Africa. Those efforts to utilize what appeared to be good agricultural land more effectively instead precipitated sleeping sickness epidemics across wide swaths of the continent. As a result, by the time colonialism came to an end, parts of Uganda, the Belgian Congo, Tanganyika, Rhodesia, and Nigeria were more thickly infested with the deadly tsetse fly than before the arrival of the Europeans. That failure underlined the difficulty of shortening the food chain within what McNeill described as "the toughest and most variegated of all natural ecosystems of the earth, the tropical rain forests and adjacent savanna regions of Africa."

It is no coincidence that the most important early agricultural societies, like the one in Egypt, were located in areas where the ecosystems were all intrinsically less resistant to human intervention and alteration than those of tropical Africa. In temperate zones, parasites were fewer and less formidable and human populations were able to increase more rapidly. Not surprisingly, the temperate Mediterranean area, the cradle of European civilization, was extremely receptive to human existence. Not only did the Mediterranean coastlands offer a relatively disease-free environment, but also the new patterns of cultivation did not create new forms of micro-parasitism. Olive trees, as an example, were probably a part of the wild flora of Greece: Since they generally prospered on rocky hillsides that were hostile to almost all other forms of plant life, they could be cultivated with only modest disruptions of the pre-existing landscapes. Wheat and barley were native plants of the Middle East and, some experts believe, may have been two of the grasses of Mediterranean regions before they were domesticated by man.

The creation of food surpluses not only required far less ingenuity and effort in Europe, but unlike Africa, most of the continent, in modern times, has been suitable for human settlement. Europeans, generally, were relatively free of the disease organisms that sapped the energy and shortened the lifespan of their tropical counterparts. In Europe, it took the buildup of significant population densities and the creation of cities to introduce anything like the level of infestation that was endemic to much of tropical Africa. Europe's advantage even extended to the species of mosquito that was the effective transmitter of malaria in each area. Unlike the West African *Anopheles gambiae,* which as we have seen prefers human blood and transmits the deadliest form of malaria known to man, the European type transmits a far less lethal form of malaria and is partial to cattle. Consequently, if sufficient alternate sources of blood are available, European vectors will ignore humans, thereby interrupting the deadly chain of infection since cattle are not susceptible to malaria.

Religion and technology were not the only artifacts of civilization that were more easily and rapidly diffused in Eurasia than in Africa. So too were domesticated animals and plants, the very basis of food production. Not only were far fewer of Africa's native wild plants and animals domesticable, but because of wide differences in climates and day lengths across the continent, plants or animals domesticated in one part of the continent were frequently unable to survive or prosper in other parts of the continent. Of the approximately 200,000 wild plant species in the world, only a few hundred have ever been domesticated, and a mere dozen represent more than eighty percent of the modern world's annual food production. Astonishingly, almost all of these major crops were domesticated in Eurasia, and only one in Africa, south of the equator. Of the 148 species of large wild terrestrial mammals, only fourteen were domesticated before the twentieth century, and only five—the cow, sheep, goat, pig, and horse—became important and widespread around the world. Even more astonishingly, given Africa's abundance of big wild animal species, not a single large wild mammal domesticated before the twentieth century originated in Africa.

The relative failure of tropical Africans to domesticate their wild plants or large wild animals had nothing to do with their intelligence or industriousness. The record is clear that Africans made the most of what they had. The vast majority of wild plant and animal species are either not edible or worth hunting or gathering. Most species are useless to humans as food because they are indigestible, poisonous, low in nutritional value, difficult or time consuming to prepare, difficult to gather, and/or dangerous to hunt. In fact, the vast majority of the living biological matter on land is in the form of wood and leaves, most of which cannot be digested by humans. Tropical Africans were as successful as any other group in identifying and domesticating those few species of animals and plants native to the continent that were suitable for human use and consumption.

The cereal sorghum, which is currently one of the dozen major crops in the world and is grown in areas with hot, dry climates on every continent, was domesticated in Africa by Africans. So was pearl millet, which along with sorghum, is one of the staple cereals of much of modern sub-Saharan Africa. The coffee plant was domesticated by ancient Ethiopian farmers, and it remained confined in that country until it became popular in Arabia and then around the world. The oil palm and the kola nut, the latter a vital component of the beverage industry around the world, were domesticated from wild ancestors that flourished in the wet and humid climate of West Africa. Other products of the West African rain forests proved less attractive to the rest of the world while playing an important role in food production on the continent. West African yams are popular throughout tropical Africa, and West African rice is a staple throughout the West African region.

It is difficult to overstate the importance of domestic animals to human societies. Not only do they provide meat and milk, the primary source of animal protein, but big domestic animals also increase crop production by pulling ploughs and providing fertilizer. Domestic animals such as cows, sheep, goats, llamas, alpacas, and silkworms provided material for clothing. Until the development of the railroad in the nineteenth century, the only method of transporting goods and people overland, other than on the backs of humans, was by using domestic animals. Horses revolutionized warfare thousands of years before the birth of Christ, and their primary role on the battlefield was not supplanted until the introduction of trucks and tanks in the twentieth century.

Domestic animals are animals that have been selectively bred in captivity and modified from their wild ancestors in ways to make them more useful to humans, who control their breeding and food supply. Domestication altered the size of many species: cows, pigs, and sheep became smaller; guinea pigs grew larger; and dogs became both larger and smaller than their wild ancestor, the wolf. Size is not the only difference between domestic animals and their wild forebears. Cows produce more milk, sheep and alpacas retain more wool, and several species have smaller brains and less developed sense organs because they no longer need them to escape from predators.

No indigenous large mammal has ever been domesticated in sub-Saharan Africa. Elephants have been captured and tamed, but they have never been domesticated. And, unlike in Eurasia, where the native cows, sheep, goats, horses, and pigs were among the few large wild animals in the world that were sufficiently domesticable (because they were docile, cheap to feed, fast-growing, and immune to disease), the African equivalents—such as the buffalo, zebra, bush pig, rhino and hippopotamus—have never been domesticated, even by modern geneticists. In sharp contrast, not only were some Eurasian domesticated animals independently domesticated in several parts of the world, but also cows, sheep, goats, horses, and pigs were quickly adopted by African societies wherever conditions were suitable.

Africa was not only handicapped by a shortage of domesticable plants and animals. Unlike Eurasia, where crops and animals moved easily between societies thousands of miles apart, crops and animals acquired or domesticated in one part of Africa frequently could not be transferred to other parts of the continent. This, too, had nothing to do with the relative intelligence or industriousness of the African and Eurasian peoples, but with the orientation of their continents' axes: east-west for Eurasia, and north-south for Africa. Regions located to the east or west of each other on the same latitude, even when thousands of miles apart, are exactly alike in day length throughout the year and share similar diseases, temperatures, rainfall, and types of vegetation.

In contrast, regions on the same longitude, less than a thousand miles apart, vary in day length, rainfall, vegetation, and disease. An example is that Portugal, northern Iran, and Japan, which are all located on about the same latitude but 4,000 miles to the east or west of each other, are more alike in climate than locations 1,000 miles to their south. Plant populations are genetically programmed through natural selection to respond to seasonal changes in day length, temperature, and rainfall. Since changes in climate tell plants when to germinate, grow, and mature, mismatches between genetic programs and climate are, invariably, disastrous. Although little understood and rarely mentioned by traditional historians, plant geography has had a profound impact on the course of African history.

For example, it is unlikely that southern Africa would have been colonized by Europeans if the Mediterranean crops that had been domesticated in Egypt could have been grown successfully south of the Sudan, or if the wet-climate crops that had been domesticated south of the Sahara could have been grown successfully in the Mediterranean climate at the Cape of Good Hope. Because neither of these factors was true, the Khoisans—the indigenous people of southern Africa—never developed agriculture at all, and the expansion of Bantu agriculture was halted outside the Cape itself.

Starting in about 3000 B.C., the Bantu, armed with the wet-climate crops they inherited from their West African homeland, swept across the continent in one of the most rapid colonizing advances in recent prehistory. Bantu farmers first engulfed the Pygmy hunter-gatherers in the equatorial forests of the Congo Basin and then moved into the more open country of East Africa's Rift Valley and Great Lakes, where they encountered a polyglot of Nilo-Saharan and Afroasiatic farmers and herders, as well as Khoisan hunter-gatherers. Utilizing their wet-climate crops, the Bantu were able to farm areas that were unsuitable for millet and sorghum, the principal crops of the Afroasiatic and Nilo-Saharan farmers.

After acquiring iron, millet, and sorghum and reacquiring cattle, Bantu pioneers left the increasingly crowded East African area and turned south, advancing into 2,000 miles of thinly occupied country. Standing in their way were scattered groups of Khoisan hunter-gatherers who had acquired neither crops nor iron. The outcome was never in doubt; within just a few centuries the Bantu almost completely replaced the Khoisan population. Overnight, in historical time, only Bantus lived in areas where Khoisans had lived for tens of thousands of years. If history is a reliable guide, the Bantu invaders probably decimated their Khoisan neighbors by murdering and enslaving the men, abducting the women, and infecting both genders with diseases against which they had little or no immunity. The evidence of intermingling can be seen today in the Khoisan-like appearance of southern African Bantu people, such as Nelson Mandela, and can be heard in the clicking sounds in Xhosa and a few other Niger-Congo languages of southern Africa.

The failure of the Khoisan peoples of southern Africa to develop agriculture also had nothing to do with their intelligence or industriousness. They had acquired sheep and cattle centuries before the onslaught of the Bantu, but it was the historical misfortune of the Cape Khoisan that their homeland contained few wild plants suitable for domestication. While the failure to develop a society with an agricultural base was not the result of any genetic deficiency, the genetic consequences were enormous. Not only were they replaced by the Bantu in most of southern Africa, but they were killed or driven out of those areas the Bantu had not occupied because they were unsuitable for tropical summer-rain agriculture, by the Europeans.

After rapidly advancing all the way to Natal, on the east coast of present-day South Africa, the Xhosa, the southern-most Bantu people, had stopped at the Fish River on the south coast, 500 miles east of Capetown. The Cape of Good Hope is today the breadbasket of modern South Africa, but its Mediterranean climate of winter rains made it inhospitable to the summer-rain crops of the Bantu. Consequently, when the Dutch settlers first arrived at the Cape in 1652, they were opposed by only a relatively small number of Khoisan herders instead of huge numbers of steel-equipped Bantu farmers. The consequences were enormous. A half-century later, when the Europeans began expanding east and encountered the Xhosa at the Fish River, an enormous struggle began that would last almost two hundred years. As Professor Diamond has pointed out, "Even though Europeans by then could supply troops from their secure base at the Cape, it took nine wars and 175 years for their armies, advancing at an average rate of less than one mile per year, to subdue the Xhosa. How could whites have succeeded in establishing themselves at the Cape at all, if those first few arriving Dutch ships had faced such fierce resistance?"

Ironically, the winter-rain crops that the Dutch brought with them were not inherited, as Diamond claimed, from "their ancestors of nearly 10,000 years ago," but from the ancestors of the very Africans who were now being displaced. The wheat and barley the Europeans brought with them had been domesticated in Egypt, and it is only in a broad cultural sense that Northern Europeans can claim ancient Egyptians as ancestors. Northern Europeans colonized Africa not because of any inherent racial superiority, but in large part because the east-west axis of Eurasia, and the absence of any significant physical barriers between the Mediterranean world and North Europe, allowed people, ideas, inventions, animals, plants, and germs to move easily from one side of the region to the other.

By the time of Christ, cereals domesticated in ancient Egypt were being cultivated over a vast area that ranged from the Atlantic coast of Ireland to the Pacific coast of Japan. That 8,000-mile west-east expanse of Eurasia is the largest land distance in the world. The contrast with Africa was striking. Not only did Africa have far fewer wild animals and plants suitable for domestication, but it had less land area and less fertile soil, more numerous and more deadly pathogens, and more numerous and far greater physical and ecological barriers. The wheat and barley of Egypt penetrated into the cool highlands of Ethiopia, but the 2,000 miles of tropical territory separating Ethiopia from South Africa was an insuperable barrier. If Africa's axis were east-west instead of north-south, not just the history of Africa, but history itself, would have been different.

The spread southward of animals domesticated in Eurasia was also slowed or halted by climate and disease in tropical Africa. The tsetse fly prevented the horse from penetrating beyond the West African savannah kingdoms north of the equator, and for 2,000 years halted the advance of cattle, sheep, and goats at the northern edge of the Serengeti Plains. Daunting physical barriers not only isolated tropical Africa from the rest of the world, but also impeded development inside the subcontinent as well. The dense equatorial forests erected formidable barriers to free movement inside the subcontinent. This is reflected, even today, in the linguistic map of areas like West Africa. Not only are some languages spoken by millions and others by mere thousands, but there is also a marked correlation between the boundaries of the major language families and the old boundaries of the forest. That kind of fragmentation made it extremely difficult for African rulers to create the concentration of population groups that led to the large nation states of Europe and Asia.

Other natural barriers, such as the falls and rapids that reduced the navigability of rivers, and the absence of prominent inlets and peninsulas or even good natural harbors, significantly reduced the ability of medieval Africans to move freely inside the continent, or to develop a shipping industry and travel to other parts of the world. To Professor Diamond, Europe's triumph and colonization of Africa had nothing to do with the African and European peoples themselves. "Rather, it was due," he wrote, "to accidents of geography and biogeography—in particular, to the continents' different areas, axes, and suites of wild plant and animal species. That is, the different historical trajectories of Africa and Europe stem ultimately from differences in real estate."

Although burdened by disease and handicapped by the difficulty of providing adequate food supplies, West Africans became the world's greatest athletes because of a series of mutations that altered how their bodies process, store, and utilize energy for skeletal muscle contraction. These adjustments, as indicated earlier, were triggered by the mutation of the hemoglobin molecule and were biological responses to falciparum malaria. Although the precise mechanism that allows individuals with a single copy of the sickle gene to successfully resist malarial infection has not been proven, it is presumed that the basic cause is the reduced vigor of the parasite in the AS (one normal and one sickle gene) environment. It is believed that the parasite derives much of its nutrition from the hemoglobin in the red blood cells, and it seems likely that the plasmodium is unable to digest the sickle-cell hemoglobin when it becomes grossly distorted and forms crystalline groupings in the veins, where the oxygen level is lower than in the arteries. Additionally, it appears that the presence of the parasite in the red blood cells may cause the cells to stick to the walls of the capillaries long enough for a significant reduction in oxygen to take place. The oxygen reduction leads to sickling, and the sickle cells are more likely to be devoured by phagocytes, blood cells that ingest and destroy foreign particles, bacteria and other cells.

Whatever the process, the fact is that in West Africa, the individuals most likely to survive should have been physically handicapped by the diminished oxygen-transporting capacity of their bloodstreams. It is not surprising, therefore, that the mutations most likely to be biologically beneficial and therefore spread throughout a considerable segment of the West African population, would be ones that compensated for this apparent inadequacy in energy-generating capacity.

It is worth repeating here that the enabling mutation was the result of the substitution of a single amino acid-valine for glutamic acid-encoding the sixth amino acid from the end of the beta chain of hemoglobin. To put the biological consequence of this mutation into perspective, it first has to be understood that hemoglobin is composed of two pairs of proteins, alpha and beta, and that alpha is 141 amino acids long and beta 146 amino acids long. It should also be noted that sickle-cell disease is not the only genetic disease resulting from a mutation of the hemoglobin molecule. Thalassemia, which is widespread in Southeast Asia, also developed as a genetic adaptation to malaria. Unlike in the sickle-cell adaptation, where the body produces a structurally abnormal protein, in thalassemia the hemoglobin molecule remains structurally intact but is reduced in quantity. In beta-thalassemia, the gene is transcribed inefficiently, while in alpha-thalassemia, an entire gene is deleted.

Clearly, therefore, it was not inevitable that the genetic reaction to malaria in West Africa would initiate a series of physiological adjustments with favorable athletic consequences. That it did can be seen as lucky or providential, but it was certainly improbable. Not only are mutations rare, but beneficial mutations are even more so. Evidence suggests that as few as one of every thousand mutations is beneficial and, therefore, spread through the population over successive generations by natural selection. Even more improbable is the likelihood that multiple mutations, involving a variety of organs and tissue types, would occur in a manner beneficial to the entire organism.

The human body, even in the resting stage, is the site of countless events occurring simultaneously and in perfect coordination. Therefore, a positive mutational change in one system, or in certain tissues, could easily be harmful to other systems or other tissues in the same system. Take, for example, a mutational change that results in the synthesis of a previously unknown digestive enzyme. To be useful, the enzyme has to be produced in specialized cells in the digestive tract. If its actions are not limited to those cells, the results could be disastrous, because other cells could be destroyed—digested away.

Since it is virtually certain that, even in West Africa, there must have been hundreds of harmful mutations for every beneficial one, the process of differentiation must have taken thousands of years and required very special environmental conditions. Africa, for reasons not entirely clear but certainly related to the intensity of the selection process, has been what author Michael H. Brown described as "simply the fountain of creation. But also the fountain of renewal, regeneration and permanent change." In *The Search for Eve*, Brown wrote, "something dynamic seemed to occur down there, something spawning advantageous mutants." Geneticist Rebecca Cann, who helped to discover the mitochondrial Eve, called Africa the "cradle of human polymorphism."

Africa's size and diversity, as Lee R. Berger pointed out in his book *In the Footsteps of Eve*, certainly created conditions conducive to evolutionary change. For millions of years, Africa was far more habitable than the continents of the Northern Hemisphere, which were locked in the frozen grip of an ice age. The great Miocene rain forests, which covered the entire African continent for some fifteen million years, provided more than adequate food and shelter for a wide range of primate species. There is mounting evidence that a series of climate changes ignited a chain of events that would push some populations of archaic *Homo sapiens* over what Berger described as a "morphological behavioral boundary" into their present forms.

As explained by Berger, about 300,000 years ago, an expansion of desert conditions in areas of the South African interior known today as the Kalahari and the Karoo forced the dispersal of the archaic human populations then occupying the area. Some of these ancient humans—those who moved southward and westward—were soon trapped by the Atlantic and Indian Oceans, the Namib Desert to the north, and the Kalahari and Karoo deserts from which they had fled. For tens of thousands of years, the groups on the western and southern Cape coastal plains would have been forced by the low nutritional value of the plant life in the area to turn increasingly to marine resources for survival. Thousands of years of this intensive protein-rich marine diet, the theory posits, spurred the growth in brain size, which transformed these archaics into anatomically modern men.

Ample evidence supports this proposition. The earliest indication of a human marine diet, dating back more than 100,000 years, has been found along the coastlines these groups inhabited. The archaeological record makes it clear that a conceptual leap, evidenced by the appearance of sophisticated tools like bone harpoons and the use of ocher as a cosmetic, took place along the Cape coast during this period. Berger believes that this conceptual leap "coincided with another shift in climatic conditions in the southern African subcontinent, which allowed these isolated populations to migrate northward into Africa once again. The seeds of contemporary human culture that may have sprouted during this phase of coastal isolation are suddenly found farther a field."

Even if the reasons for African prodigality are not entirely clear, it is clear that if the miracle of West Africa was possible anywhere in the world, the conditions were most propitious in West Africa itself. In West Africa there was time and the circumstances were right. Agriculture began in West Africa before 2000 B.C., which was about the time serious desiccation of the Sahara set in. As we have already learned, it was the spread of agriculture in the rain forests of West Africa that disrupted existing ecological balances and gave malaria a new, epidemic intensity. It was the unexampled virulence of falciparum malaria, once unique to West Africa, which forged out of long, bitter cycles of early death and ruthless selection a people immunologically and physically strong enough to survive and multiply despite the holocaust of slavery. And those people are now the greatest athletes in the world.

13

The Biology of Speed

Perhaps the easiest way to understand the biomechanical and biochemical processes that have conferred a small but absolute advantage on people of West African descent in athletic events requiring speed and power is to visualize two sprinters at the starting line of a 100-meter contest. The athletes, one black and one white, are the very best of their races. They are similar in height, weight, age, experience, technical ability, motivation, and determination. Any differences between them have been genetically determined.

As they walk slowly to the starting line, to the practiced eye, some physical differences are immediately evident. The black runner seems leaner and more muscular: the muscles in his legs, arms, back, and shoulders are more visible, seem larger and more defined, and appear somehow closer to the surface of the skin. In fact, because of less subcutaneous fat, they are. The white runner, you realize, although the same height has shorter arms and legs and a longer torso; but his calves are larger and more muscular. They kneel and wait for the sound of the gun, which frustratingly has jammed. As they rise and turn away impatiently to wait the resetting of the starter's pistol, you also notice that the black athlete has, improbably, both narrower hips and larger, more muscular buttocks.

To the initiated, these visual clues are by themselves extremely compelling. The mechanical advantage of a longer and more efficient stride—caused by longer legs, narrower hips and lighter calves—and greater power-to-weight ratio—caused by more muscle and less fat—would probably, by itself, be sufficient to guarantee victory for the black athlete. But the biggest difference between these athletes, and the primary reason for African American athletic dominance, is not externally visible.

Before the race even begins, as they listen to the starter's instructions and get set in the blocks, the white athlete, in addition to his biomechanical shortcomings, will also be at a clear biochemical disadvantage. This biochemical disadvantage is based, primarily, on one simple difference between them: how their bodies convert the carbohydrate glucose into energy. The black athlete, as we shall see, primarily because of a higher ratio of fast-twitch muscle fiber, will convert glucose into energy more rapidly than his white counterpart. Glucose is the major source of energy for all cellular functions in the body, including muscle contraction. Energy is required even during rest since muscles are involved in contraction to help maintain posture, breathing and other bodily functions.

Energy for muscle contraction, including all physical and athletic activities, is created by the breakdown of glucose to produce a compound called adenosine triphosphate (ATP). The conversion of glucose to ATP occurs in two stages and by two different metabolic processes. The first stage takes place outside the cell nucleus in the semifluid portion of the cell called the cytoplasm (sarcoplasm in muscle cells) and does not require oxygen. The second stage is in the mitochondria, subcellular bodies within the cells and does require oxygen.

The first stage, which is known as glycolysis, converts glucose into ATP at a rate more than twice than that of the second phase but is also far less efficient, producing far less energy per glucose molecule.

Both athletes will convert glucose to ATP by both glycolysis—anaerobic metabolism (oxygen not required)—and by mitochondrion metabolism (oxygen required), but in different ratios. This difference in the relative efficiency or effectiveness of these metabolic pathways in the athletes will play a decisive role in the outcome of this race and is largely responsible for the greater athletic success of African Americans and others of West African descent.

Skeletal muscle, as we learned earlier, is composed of two types of fibers—slow-twitch and fast-twitch—classified by their speed of contraction, oxidative capacity, and resistance to fatigue. Slow-twitch or red fibers, with their high myoglobin content and resulting greater oxidative capacity, generate ATP primarily by the slow but efficient process of aerobic metabolism. In this process, oxygen, bound to hemoglobin in red blood cells, is carried to the muscles by the capillaries. Myoglobin, an iron-protein compound, is essential for the transfer of oxygen from the cell membrane to the mitochondria, where the oxygen is consumed.

In sharp contrast, fast-twitch or white fibers, with their lower myoglobin content and considerably lower oxidative capacity, are less able to utilize aerobic metabolism for the production of ATP and are therefore more dependent on glycolysis or anaerobic metabolism. Glycolysis is not only fast and relatively inefficient—only two of the 36 or 38 molecules of ATP produced by the breakdown of each glucose molecule are generated at this stage—but the supply of glycogen, which is how glucose is stored in the muscle and liver, is exhaustible. This is why the ability to regenerate ATP during activities requiring short bursts of power is so physiologically meaningful.

As the race begins, the white runner's muscles and probably his liver will hold smaller reserves of glucose than those of his black opponent. This will be true, as will be explained in greater detail later, because of less activity in his creatine phosphate pathway during his training, however anaerobic and rigorous. This means, of course, that he will have comparatively less readily available fuel for something as anaerobically demanding as world-class sprinting. This disadvantage could, theoretically, be overcome if his muscular system produced or regenerated more ATP more quickly, during the race, than his black counterpart. But, because his skeletal muscles contain a lower percentage of fast-twitch muscle fibers than his black opponent's, this is not what happens.

Muscle biopsies have concluded, as we learnt in Chapter 11, that people of African descent have significantly higher levels of activity in their phosphagenic, glycolytic, and lactate dehydrogenase metabolic pathways than their Caucasian counterparts. The production and regeneration of ATP takes place in the glycolytic and phosphagenic pathways; higher levels of activity result, therefore, not just in faster production of ATP but also in its more efficient regeneration. When ATP is depleted, it is very rapidly replaced through a reaction that consumes creatine phosphate. Creatine phosphate acts like a battery, storing ATP energy and recharging itself from the new ATP that is generated by cellular oxidations when the muscle is resting. Skeletal muscle converts chemical energy into mechanical work with relative efficiency; only thirty to fifty percent is wasted as heat. In contrast, an automobile engine typically wastes eighty to ninety percent of the energy available from gasoline. As a result, even small differences in chemical energy generation are physiologically meaningful.

As the athletes explode out of their starting blocks, the biochemical advantage of the African American athlete should be evident, as he will, in all probability, take the lead immediately. There is some evidence that the reaction time of black athletes is generally less (or faster) than that of whites, probably because of the greater contractile speed of fast-twitch muscle fibers. The white biochemical disadvantage only grows as the race continues. It is true that, because of a greater percentage of slow-twitch fibers, his metabolic system is more efficient. He produces more energy from less glucose, but he does it less rapidly because he has a lower percentage of fast-twitch muscle fibers. So, not only did he start the race with less available fuel for an anaerobic activity like sprinting, but also during the race he produces less than his black counterpart. This is because the activity level of the glycolytic pathway—where ATP is produced anaerobically—is directly related to the percentage of fast-twitch muscle fibers in the muscle groups—such as the buttocks, quadriceps and hamstrings—involved in running and jumping.

At the halfway mark, given his advantages in stride length and efficiency, power-to-weight ratio, glucose storage, and speed of glucose conversion to ATP, the black athlete should be well ahead. But, at about this point, muscle fatigue caused by a buildup of lactic acid and a rapid depletion of ATP levels could begin to become a factor. Glycolysis, as we have already seen, is fast but inefficient. Additionally, the rapid breakdown of glycogen during glycolysis leads to a buildup of pyruvic acid and its conversion to lactic acid, which causes muscle fatigue. All of this means that the advantage in glucose conversion rate—which, literally and figuratively, fueled his blazing start—should at this stage become a serious liability for the black athlete.

Therefore, despite his advantages in glucose storage and energy conversion rate, he should be running out of fuel (because of the inefficiency of anaerobic metabolism) and he should be getting fatigued (because faster lactic acid formation is an inevitable byproduct of faster anaerobic metabolism). However, as we know, this does not usually happen. Although the black athlete's advantage is greatest at the very beginning, it is still formidable at 400 meters. This is partially because of the biomechanical factors noted earlier and partially because ATP is rapidly regenerated by the activity of creatine phosphate produced in the phosphagenic pathway. This explains the athletic importance of the significantly greater levels of activity of this pathway in athletes of West African origin.

Faster production and increased regeneration of ATP, however, does not fully explain African American biochemical superiority in athletic events requiring speed and power. There is also, as also noted earlier, considerably greater activity in the lactate dehydrogenase pathway of people of West African descent. A primary function of this pathway is to reduce muscle fatigue by converting lactic acid back to glucose and refeeding the muscles. This cyclic set of reactions, from muscles to liver and back to muscles, is known as the Cori cycle.

The postponement of muscle fatigue during prolonged anaerobic activity is dependent on a number of factors, the most important of which is the rate at which lactic acid is removed and reconverted to glucose. The removal of lactic acid from the muscles by the circulatory system reduces muscle fatigue, and its reconversion to glucose by the liver provides the muscles with additional supplies of energy. The rate of lactic acid removal is partially regulated by the activity of the lactate dehydrogenase metabolic pathway, which explains why increased activity in this pathway is so athletically meaningful.

The recycling of waste products, such as lactic acid, by the liver is vital to the proper functioning of the muscular and nervous systems, among others. If the glycogen reserves stored in the muscles were depleted during intense physical activity, blood glucose would become the major source of energy. This sequence could lower blood glucose levels sufficiently to seriously compromise the nervous system. Additionally, during prolonged intense activity, if glucose is not available, muscle resorts to the use of fat for fuel, which is less efficient for combustion than carbohydrates. Consequently, an athlete engaged in fairly prolonged anaerobic activity—sprinting, for example—would be far less effective without a mechanism to increase the supply of glucose. This is what is accomplished during the Cori cycle, the cyclic set of reactions initiated by increased activity in the lactate dehydrogenase pathway.

Armed with such formidable biomechanical and biochemical advantages, the absolute dominance of athletic events involving speed and power by people of West African origin is hardly surprising.

There is now widespread agreement that fiber type proportion is genetically determined, remains constant throughout life, and is unaffected by training. During the past several years, researchers have examined the fiber type ratio of athletes in a wide range of activities. Muscle biopsies have demonstrated that athletes who compete successfully in activities requiring speed have a high percentage of fast-twitch fibers, while those who are successful in activities requiring endurance have a high percentage of slow-twitch fibers.

Researchers from the Copenhagen Muscle Research Center have recently confirmed not only that individuals vary widely in the percentage of fiber type in major muscle groups like the quadriceps, but also that fiber type percentage determines the nature of athletic success. The researchers did not identify the racial identity of their subjects, but they reported encounters with people with a slow-twitch fiber percentage of as little as nineteen percent and as high as ninety-five percent in the quadriceps muscle. While there is only one type of slow-twitch fiber, there are actually two types of fast-twitch fibers. One type, the faster fast type, contracts ten times faster than slow-twitch fibers, while the slower fast type contracts at a rate somewhere between the faster fast type and the slow-twitch type. As the Copenhagen team pointed out in published charts, the percentage of these fibers in the quadriceps muscles of world-class runners accurately predicted the distance at which they would be successful.

The researchers found that a typical world-class sprinter would have a fairly small percentage of slow-twitch fibers and a slightly larger percentage of the slower fast fibers than the faster fast fibers. A top middle distance runner would have a larger percentage of slow-twitch fibers than fast fibers, about sixty percent to forty percent, and almost all of his or her fast fibers would be of the slower type. A world class marathoner would have a large percentage of slow-twitch fibers and a small percentage of fast fibers, and just about all of the fast fibers would be of the slower type.

Surprisingly, however, despite the difference in basic oxidative capacity, experiments have also demonstrated that endurance training can dramatically increase the oxidative metabolic capacity and fatigue resistance of both fast-twitch and slow-twitch muscle fibers. This is due to increases of up to 120 percent in the size and membrane surface area of skeletal muscle mitochondria and the double and triple increase in some mitochondrial oxidative enzymes. This ability of fast-twitch fibers to increase their oxidative capacity is probably another reason why athletes of West African origin are able to sprint effectively up to 400 and 800 meters.

On the other hand, the biochemical changes caused by resistance training are both relatively minor and inconsistent. While there are some increases of ATP and glycogen within hypertrophied muscles, there is virtually no change in glycolytic enzyme activity, and it appears that a high percentage of fast-twitch fibers are a prerequisite for maximal gains from strength training. What this means, of course, is that while fast-twitch muscle fibers can be trained to increase their resistance to fatigue, slow-twitch fibers cannot similarly be trained to increase their speed of contraction.

Theoretically, therefore, athletes with high percentages of fast-twitch fibers can be trained to be effective at distances beyond a sprint, but athletes with low percentages of fast-twitch fibers cannot become sprinters, however hard they train. In the words of the old aphorism: You cannot teach speed.

Nor can one teach fiber density. One of the more obvious differences between African American athletes and their white counterparts is in apparent muscularity. Typically, when comparing black and white athletes of similar size, weight, fitness level, and ability, the black athletes will appear to be fitter, leaner, and more muscular. As previously mentioned, this is in part due to lower levels of subcutaneous fat in African Americans, which, like darker skin, curlier hair, longer limbs and narrower hips, is a legacy of evolution in a warm climate. Or more accurately—since all humans once shared these physical qualities—the lighter skin, straighter hair, shorter limbs, wider hips, and greater levels of subcutaneous fat of Europeans and other non-African groups were adaptations to less sunlight and colder temperatures. There is also, unquestionably, a difference in muscle fiber density, which apparently is related to the observed racial differences in metabolic pathway activity.

Responding to a question from a reader of *Muscle and Fitness* magazine who wanted to know if the composition of the muscle tissue of African American bodybuilders was different from that of their white counterparts, professors from the Universities of Michigan and Massachusetts cited a 1984 study which had found, they wrote, that the difference in the lean body mass of blacks and whites was at least twenty percent, and may be as high as thirty-six percent. In a practical sense, they explained, this meant that there is more compactness or a closer network of muscle fibers in blacks than in whites.

Not only is fiber density physically attractive, it is also biochemically useful. Anaerobic metabolism, as we've noted again and again, is fast but inefficient. Consequently, each fast-twitch fiber generates far less energy for anaerobic activity than each slow-twitch fiber generates for aerobic activity. Therefore, if a given number of fast-twitch fibers are required for an effective anaerobic performance, far fewer slow-twitch fibers are needed for a similar aerobic performance.

Some commentators, who should know better, have found the very prospect of racial differences in metabolic pathway activity alarming. In registering his disapproval of the concept that that African American athletic superiority was genetically based, Professor Hoberman, in his book *Darwin's athletes* expressed his concern about the implications of "an exotic physiological pathway reserved for black athletes alone." Mindful of the continuing power of racial folklore, Hoberman wondered, "whether data that offered a physiological rationale for black athletic superiority was more attractive than environmental factors precisely because they confirmed a pre-existing conception of the hardy black organism possessing special adaptive powers."

An "exotic physiological pathway reserved for black athletes alone" conjures up vivid images of otherworldly black athletes who belong, almost, to another human species. The truth, of course, is far more prosaic. Metabolic pathways (the type of physiological pathway to which Hoberman was referring) are simply the organized sequence of enzymatic chemical reactions that supply humans and other living organisms with the energy and raw materials needed for growth and maintenance. It is therefore arguable that any change in the exact sequence of any of the countless reactions involved in metabolism—however minor—could create a new metabolic pathway. But that seems to be stretching the meaning of a new pathway, and to label them exotic is a form of racial profiling.

The final question that confronts us now is the one that has been most responsible for society's failure to more openly discuss the topic of this book. What are the implications of black biological difference? It is beyond the imagination of some to conceive of a response that might not be negative. Deviation from the European norm, by this reckoning, can never be positive. As Part Four will demonstrate, the fear that inherent black intellectual inferiority is the flipside of inherent black athletic superiority is utterly and completely unfounded; it is nothing more than a chimera of the propaganda to justify slavery, segregation, and discrimination.

Part Four

The Implications

14

Standard Tests and the Definition of Intelligence

When John Thompson, then the basketball coach of Georgetown University, led his team off the floor during a nationally televised game in 1989 to protest the National Collegiate Athletic Association's adoption of Proposition 42, he dramatically highlighted the apparently unending power that scientific racism continues to exercise on Americans and demonstrated the widespread confusion about the goals and capabilities of standard tests and between functional and inherent intelligence. Proposition 42, which prevented students with either a sub-2.000 grade point average or a sub-700 SAT score from receiving financial aid, was as harshly denounced in sections of the black community as it was warmly welcomed by some white commentators, no doubt for the same reason: that it would disproportionately affect young black athletes.

Although the Scholastic Aptitude Test (SAT) is a test of preparation and what can be called functional intelligence, the relatively poor performance of blacks in the SAT was not seen by those white commentators as an almost inevitable consequence of centuries of slavery, oppression, and segregation, but as further proof of inherent black intellectual inferiority. Although the concept that the SAT is capable of measuring a biologically based, genetically inherited quality that is tied to race or ethnicity was rejected as

199

long ago as 1928 by its inventor, that premise was precisely the viewpoint of the best-selling racist tract *The Bell Curve*. The authors, two professors from Harvard and MIT, adamantly rejected the very idea that differences in black and white scores are attributable to differences in opportunities, educational levels, incomes, exposure, and expectations. They did not even acknowledge, let alone attempt to measure, the bitter legacy of segregated, inferior schools, or the long exclusion of black Americans from a range of occupations, which were reserved exclusively for white men.

The book's dust cover, in a clarion call to the faithful, proclaimed, "despite decades of fashionable denial, the overriding and insistent truth about intellectual ability is that it is endowed unequally, for reasons that government policies can do little to change." Another truth, the authors insisted, was the "taboo fact: that intelligence levels differ among ethnic groups" and that "for a wide range of intractable social problems, the decisive correlation is between a high incidence of the problem and the low intelligence of those who suffer from it: this holds for school dropouts, unemployment, work-related injury, out of wedlock births, crime, and many other social problems. Though we stubbornly deny it, those social problems correlate to a significant degree with intelligence." The new information age, they argued, "has created a new kind of class structure led by a cognitive elite," and simultaneously perpetuated a class of people deficient in these endowments and abilities, and increasingly doomed, if they found work at all, to find it outside the information economy.

The popularity of *The Bell Curve* and the apparent agreement with its basic thesis by even some critics who worried that no good would come from talking about "this kind of truth" underlines how deeply embedded these ideas remain in the nation's psyche. However, it is difficult to condemn the people who embrace these "truths" when the objective evidence seems to support a biological explanation. After all, as Diamond points out in *Guns, Germs, and Steel*: "It is perfectly obvious to everyone, whether an overt racist or not, that different peoples have fared differently in history. It seems logical to suppose that history's pattern reflects innate differences among people themselves. Of course, we're taught that it's not polite to say so in public… We read of technical studies claiming to demonstrate inborn differences, and we also read rebuttals claiming that these studies suffer from technical flaws. We see in our daily lives that some of the conquered peoples continue to form an underclass centuries after the conquests or slave imports took place. We're told that this too is to be attributed not to any biological shortcomings but to social disadvantages and limited opportunities. Nevertheless, we have to wonder. We keep seeing all those glaring, persistent differences in peoples' status… Until we have some convincing, detailed, agreed-upon explanation for the broad pattern of history, most people will continue to suspect that the racist biological explanation is correct after all."

Like many of the other pioneers of IQ testing, Carl Bingham, the man who invented the SAT, had been an ardent eugenicist and a good friend of the most prominent race theorists of the early twentieth century: men like Madison Grant, who authored *Decline of the Great Race*, and Charles W. Gould, who wrote *America: A Family Matter*. Both men believed that the country had been pushed to the brink of disaster because the "native stocks" had been dangerously diluted by immigration, and Bingham enthusiastically shared their view. Bingham's own book, *A Study of American Intelligence,* advanced the prevailing eugenicist theory of the period, which held "that there were three distinct white races in Europe—in descending order of intelligence, Nordic, Alpine and Mediterranean—and that the United States had been initially and successfully populated by the highest but was now being filled up with the lowest. Mediterraneans were not only immigrating but also reproducing in alarming numbers. On the Army IQ tests, Nordics scored higher than Alpines, who scored higher than Mediterraneans. The test results as a whole were like a photograph of American culture, so faithfully did they reproduce the social order."

Nevertheless, by 1928, only two years after the unveiling of the SAT, Bingham publicly recanted his earlier views at a meeting of eugenicists. He had by that time, as Nicholas Lemann explained in *Test: The Secret history of the American Meritocracy,* "come to the point of specifically renouncing his best-known book." Two years later, Bingham published a formal retraction, declaring his book and its conclusions "pretentious" and "without foundation." He also began trying to make a clear distinction between the SAT and IQ testing. Initially, the SAT had been a single number, like the intelligence quotient, and Bingham had even published a crude scale for converting it to an IQ score. Eventually, as Lemann reveals, Bingham was "persuaded by his assistant… to divide the SAT score into two parts, one for verbal and one for mathematical ability, and to drop the conversion scale."

The enthusiasm of the leaders of the IQ testing movement, Bingham concluded, had led them to make what he felt was an unwarranted and dangerous leap: That because the test could reliably predict the college grades of some high school seniors, what it measured must be a biological trait of the brain, although there was no physical evidence for the truth of this belief. In 1929 he wrote to Charles Davenport, head of the Eugenics Record Office, an old friend who had sent him a manuscript on differences in test scores by race, to explain his new position. "The more I work in this field, the more I am convinced that the psychologists have sinned greatly in sliding easily from the name of the test to the function or trait measured," Bingham wrote. "I feel we should all stop naming tests and saying what they measure... if we are to proceed beyond the stage of a psycho-phrenology."

Five years later, Bingham was even more blunt. In a manuscript that was not published, he wrote the following: "The test movement came to this country some twenty-five or thirty years ago accompanied by one of the most glorious fallacies in the history of science, namely, that the tests measured native intelligence purely and simply without regard to training or schooling. I hope nobody believes that now. The test scores very definitely are a composite including schooling, family background, familiarity with English, and everything else, relevant and irrelevant. The native intelligence hypothesis is dead."

The development of the SAT had been driven by two powerful ideas: one ancient and the other peculiarly American. James Bryant Conant, president of Harvard University, like Thomas Jefferson and Plato himself, passionately believed that a nation's rulers should be drawn from an elite whose members were selected early in life without reference to their station at birth. Once identified, this natural aristocracy, which Plato described in *The Republic* as a class of "guardians," would be elaborately trained by educators for positions in government that they would hold for their entire adult lives but which could not be automatically passed down to their children.

The other had originated with Frederick Jackson Turner, the dominant American historian at Harvard during Conant's undergraduate years. Turner, who invented the terms "social mobility" and "equal opportunity," argued persuasively that America's open Western frontier had made those terms, which he regarded as embodying the most distinct qualities of American life, possible. The frontier's disappearance in the final decade of the nineteenth century, he warned, imperiled the future stability of the country. To replace the opportunities the frontier had formerly supplied, Turner and later Conant and others proposed the adoption of public education. To its advocates, this distinctive American institution, like the frontier in an earlier age, would provide the opportunity for every citizen to rise in the world.

In the American context, therefore, the idea of an elite class of guardians transmogrified into what Conant envisioned as a means of testing and selecting that would be used, in Lemann's words, simply to "direct each person to the most appropriate place for service to the nation" and to make full use of individual talents. In an uncompleted and unpublished book titled *What We Are Fighting to Defend*, Conant argued that the United States, historically a classless society, had in recent times developed a hereditary aristocracy whose existence placed the country's future at risk. To correct this ominous development, he proposed public education as "a new type of social instrument whose proper use may be the means of salvation of the classlessness of the nation...a means of recapturing social flexibility, a means of approximating more nearly the American ideal." In public schools, he wrote, "Abilities must be assessed, talents must be developed, ambitions guided."

Interestingly, Conant, who was one of a small group of scientists who advised President Franklin Roosevelt during World War II, for all of his concerns about social mobility for white men, was seemingly unconcerned about "the most obvious departures from the American democratic ideal during the 1940s." Legal segregation in the South, informal segregation elsewhere, as Lemann points out, "and the relegation of women to a secondary position in society—went unmentioned by Conant in his writings during the war." This was not his only blind spot. Without realizing it, Lemann charges, Conant "had set the stage for a fundamental clash. He had helped to enshrine the idea that an absolute, formal guarantee of opportunity for all—not just for people with high IQ scores—was the central premise of American society. But he had also created a system for serially ranking people by a supposed innate worth expressed in the scores made on standardized intelligence tests, on the basis of which their place in society— their prosperity and their prestige—would be apportioned. This was the fundamental clash: between the promise of more opportunity and the reality that, from a point early in the lives of most people, opportunity would be limited."

Not surprisingly, therefore, given the nation's pre-existing contempt for the inherent intelligence of its African American citizens, the lack of a clear distinction between inherent and developed or functional intelligence, and the related confusion about the precise nature of the mental quality measured by the SAT, a vast majority of white Americans were convinced that the relatively low SAT scores of African American youngsters reflected not centuries of oppression but inborn incapacity. Today, some three-quarters of a century after its founder publicly declared that the SAT did not and could not measure native or inherent intelligence, the debate rages on. The triumph of those who wanted to apportion merit through mental testing is complete. Not only is the individual future of every American youngster, of every race and ethnicity, largely dependent on his or her personal performance on the SAT, but the group reputation and individual destiny of African Americans is still being colored by their collective performance. As with athletic ability, the question is: Which is more important in shaping the human brain, nature or nurture?

That African Americans have not had the same access to education and its benefits as their white counterparts is undeniable. During the more than 250 years of slavery in America, even the most rudimentary education was routinely denied to black slaves. But the final three decades of slavery, between 1830 and 1860, were particularly oppressive, as the Southern states, where the vast majority of blacks then lived, made the education of black children a crime. Not surprisingly, at the time of emancipation, virtually all slaves were illiterate. Not much improved after the end of the antebellum period. After a brief honeymoon during Reconstruction, white America moved decisively to extinguish, one by one, all the gains made by the freed slaves during the period. In 1883, the Supreme Court decided, in *Plessy v. Ferguson,* that segregation was not a violation of the 14th Amendment; in 1899, the Court decided in *Cummings v. Board of Education* that segregated education was constitutional. Segregated education meant, of course, inferior education.

Once the "Redeemers" took control of the Reconstruction governments, there was a conscious effort to limit the amount of education blacks received. Senator James K. Vardaman, of Mississippi, made the intentions of the South's leaders very clear. "Too much education," he said, would render blacks "unfit for the work which the white man has prescribed, and which he will be forced to perform." So determined were Southern whites to deny blacks a decent education that they were prepared to harm the educational opportunities of poor white children in the process. Redeemer governments not only sharply reduced funds for all schools, but, tragically for the South, they also rejected the Blair Bill of 1885, which would have channeled large amounts of surplus federal money into the region for educational purposes. The South rejected the bill, which would have provided some $11 million to the region, because of "race prejudice," as one Southern educator who fought for the bill explained, and a "fear that the education of the Negroes would make them less easily manipulated."

The centuries of slavery, the decades of scientific racism, and the Supreme Court's Dred Scott decision that blacks "had no rights which the white man was bound to respect" left the vast majority of white Americans, until after the middle of the twentieth century, hostile, or at best indifferent, to even rudimentary black aspirations. Remarkably, as Thomas Sowell pointed out in *Ethnic America*, "Although blacks suffered in body and mind under slavery, they did not emerge as a spiritually crushed people." Great numbers of black men fought bravely during the Civil War, and several of them were awarded the Medal of Honor, the nation's highest military award, for outstanding bravery. But the centuries of brutality had taken their toll on the psyche, expectations and habits of black Americans. Not only did they emerge from slavery illiterate and destitute, but, as Sowell so eloquently explained, like "other very poor agricultural peoples," the former slaves had very little experience in "budgeting or in managing their own daily lives."

They had developed, he pointed out, "habits of carelessness, little foresight and dependence on whites." Slaves, he wrote, "had long been careless and wasteful with food, firewood, clothing, and other necessities issued to them by slave owners and had cherished such small luxuries as they have acquired, often as castoff items from slave owners' family members. The economic weighing of necessities against luxuries, which was common and taken for granted among other peoples of the world, was something that slaves in the United States had not experienced for centuries."

The war on black self-confidence and self-respect was not to end with slavery. In some ways, what was to follow after emancipation was more destructive than slavery itself. To be trapped temporarily in a monstrous and clearly evil system was, for many, far less spiritually crushing than to be repeatedly told that second-class citizenship was what your entire race deserved. Instead of a tool of rehabilitation, education (or, more accurately, the denial of it) became a weapon for a new form of oppression. The first black public high school in the United States was established in Washington,

D.C., in 1870, but not until 1916 in New Orleans and 1924 in Atlanta did the same thing take place.

Things were even worse in rural areas. As late as 1911, so many rural areas were without schools for black children that the Jewish philanthropist Julius Rosenwald established a fund that helped to build black schools in the South. During the next twenty years, more than 50,000 such public schools were built with contributions of more than $4 million from the fund. Even after Southern states began constructing public schools for blacks, however, the amounts allocated were a mere fraction of those spent on white children. Consequently, it was not until 1930 that the average black American had as many as six years of schooling, compared to ten for whites. But the educational discrepancy was even greater than those numbers indicated, as in many parts of the South black children were only allowed to spend about two-thirds as many days in school per year as white children. For the South generally, the amount spent on each black pupil in 1912 was less than one-third the expenditures per white pupil; in the Deep South, not surprisingly, the disparity was even greater. Black teachers also had less training and taught larger classes in significantly inferior facilities.

That was not all. As late as 1910, the states of Alabama, Georgia, and Louisiana, home to millions of blacks, between them did not have a single public high school for black students; approximately a half of the elementary schools in these states were operating in makeshift quarters (such as homes and churches) rather than in school buildings. As a consequence, in the 1930s, seven decades after the end of slavery, a mere fourteen percent of black children in the South even entered high school. Not surprisingly, as late as 1963, the income of black families was only fifty-three percent of that of white families.

But since the biological explanation for racial differences in income and status is widely accepted and communicated both explicitly and implicitly, it is hardly surprising that millions of young black Americans have come to equate academic achievement with whiteness and racial treachery. So convinced are they that books and ideas and college and homework are foreign concepts to their race that they frequently threaten, reject, and even physically attack academically ambitious black students for "acting white." So completely have these young black Americans accepted and internalized the propaganda of black intellectual inferiority that they have become, unwittingly, its fiercest and most assiduous proponents and enforcers.

This disdain of education, which is rampant in some sectors of the African American community, is even beginning to attract the alarmed attention of some of the black community's most unrepentant liberals. The Rev. Al Sharpton, one of the country's preeminent black leaders, recounted in an interview with the *New York Times* the story of a black student who was the first person in her family to attend college. When her brothers and sisters learned that she was making straight A's, they said to her, Sharpton recalled, "'Oh you acting white now?' Like there is something black about flunking," Sharpton commented, explaining that he was not just speaking as a civil rights leader but as a father with two daughters whose marriage prospects deeply concerned him. He was, he said, saddened by the younger generation of black Americans, who were captivated by hip-hop, inured to violence, and indifferent to public life and politics. "Here's the real problem: The drive, the ambition, the desire to reach higher goals seem to have been lost in this new generation, particularly of black men," Sharpton said. "This whole glorification of decadence, of acting like this is black culture. Black culture is striving, it's achieving."

Ironically, the primary vehicle for the dissemination of this new anti-intellectualism is music, which was at the forefront of the black cultural renaissance of the early twentieth century. Unlike earlier forms of black musical expression, which were widely acclaimed for their aesthetic beauty and transformative power, hip-hop too frequently unabashedly embraces and celebrates the most violent and decadent aspects of black street life. Misogynic and crudely and mindlessly hedonistic and materialistic, "gangsta rap" is the very antithesis of its predecessors. In his 1903 book *The Souls of Black Folk*, DuBois described black musical culture as a gift to American society and as a vehicle for African American liberation. The Negro folk song, he wrote, "stands today not simply as the sole American music, but as the most beautiful expression of human experience born this side of the seas... It still remains as the singular spiritual heritage of the nation and the greatest gift of the Negro people."

At a time when many white critics saw African American popular music as the product of mere instinct, and were attempting to distinguish between what they regarded as the "authentic" vernacular of "jazz" from its commercial cousin "swing," Duke Ellington insisted that both were part of a deliberate attempt to create an "authentic Negro music" that was "a genuine contribution from our race." As Eric Porter explained in *What Is This Thing Called Jazz?* "Ellington's musical project was consistent with some of the fundamental goals of the diasporic, black cultural renaissance of the early twentieth century. Like other artists and intellectuals of the period, he believed that the production and reception of black music would have an effect on the social standing of African Americans. In other words, Ellington tried to define a socially relevant black aesthetic under conditions that limited black creativity."

Despite the mindless nihilism of much of hip-hop, the monumental achievements of the often poorly educated and even illiterate black musical geniuses who largely created American popular music, as it is known today, are positive indicators of inherent black intellectual capacity. Neuroimaging and neurological studies of music performance, perception, and comprehension confirm the obvious: that music as a whole, which is a complex stimulus and activity, is represented in mechanisms widely distributed throughout the brain. For example, the data indicate that specific subareas of major areas, such as the cerebellum and the frontal and temporal cortex, perform different functions for particular subtasks of musical comprehension; that areas in the right auditory association cortex are involved in the reception and expression of melody; and that activations in the temporal, frontal, and midbrain may be involved in processing the temporal grouping structure of rhythms. Clearly, musical ability is related to intellectual ability and appears to be as much a measure of inherent intelligence as the mastery of English on which much of the SAT is based.

We now know that the human brain, which holds about 100 billion nerve cells, or neurons, is a physical system; that its development is influenced by external factors, such as nutrition and environmental stimulation; and that the established connection between poverty and SAT scores is not accidental. "The human brain," as Dr. Richard M. Restak explained in his book, *The Brain*, "approaches its adult size, weight, and number of cells by age two. It does so in a series of steps starting before birth. In the second trimester of pregnancy until about the age of six months, there is a brain growth spurt marked by rapid cell multiplication. The first extends throughout the second trimester and is largely restricted to nerve cell multiplication. In fact, most researchers believe that the majority of our neurons are established during this period."

That means, in effect, that by the age of six months, the intellectual potential of human beings has been largely determined. How much of that potential is reached is then determined by events that occur before the end of the second year of life. "In this stage," Restak explained, "are formed the supporting cells of the human nervous system (the glia) along with the neuronal branches (dendrites) that extend from one neuron to another and establish the functional connections—the synapses—between neurons." Dendrites are numerous tiny extensions of the nerve cell and "can be thought of as nerve-cell antennae which pick up impulses sent from other neurons."

This process of dendritic extension establishes nerve cell connections and forms the basic foundation of intellectual activity. "In many ways," Restak wrote, "the number of dendritic connections is considered even more important than the total number of neurons in the brain, since the density and complexity of dendritic connections probably has greater psychobiological consequences for brain development and human intelligence." Similarly, Dr. Irving Lazar, a professor of special education and resident scholar at the Center for Research in Human Development at Vanderbilt University in Nashville, believes that the complexity of the synaptic web laid down early may very well be the physical basis of what we call general intelligence.

Underlining the impact of external factors on the development of the brain, Dr. Patricia Kuhl, a neuroscientist at the University of Washington, points out that scientists "now know that neural connections are formed very early in life and that the infant's brain is literally waiting for experiences to determine how connections are made." We did not realize until very recently, she explained, "how early this process begins. For example, infants have learned the sounds of their native language by the age of six months." And, according to Dr. Esther Thelen, a neurobiologist at Indiana University, experience in the first year of life forms the basis for networks of neurons that enable us to be smart, creative, and adaptable in all the years that follow.

Dr. Betty Hart, a professor emeritus of human development at the University of Kansas in Lawrence and her colleague, Dr. Todd Ridley of the University of Alaska, are authors of *Meaningful Differences in the Everyday Experience of Young American Children.* They are among a growing number of researchers in this area who have concluded that constant exposure to adult speech is perhaps the single most important factor in early brain development. To test this thesis, the authors studied a mixed group of forty-two children from professional, working-class, and welfare backgrounds.

During the first two and a half years of the children's lives, they spent an hour every month recording every spoken word and every parent-child interaction in every home, compiling data that included 1,300 hours of everyday interactions.

The children were then tested at age three using standard tests. The children of professional parents scored highest and the key variable, according to Hart, was spoken language. On average, a child with a professional parent heard 2,100 words an hour, children of working-class parents heard 1,200 an hour, and those with parents on welfare heard only 600 words an hour, less than a third of what children from professional families heard. Additionally, the researchers pointed out, children with professional parents received positive feedback thirty times an hour, a rate twice as often as children of working-class parents and five times that of children whose parents were on welfare. By age two, all the parents began speaking more frequently to their children, but by that age, Hart explained, the differences among the children were already so great that those left behind could never close the gap. Unfortunately but unsurprisingly, the differences in academic achievement between the groups remained throughout primary school.

To test whether environmental factors can influence the physical structure of the brain, Dr. Mark Rosenstein and his associates carried out a series of experiments on rat brains. Rats were placed in environments with varying degrees of stimulation, from minimal to enriched. Their heads were then removed and their brains extracted. In every instance, Dr. Restak reported, "the rats from the enriched environment showed an increase in the number of nerve cells and a greater weight of cerebral cortex, along with a thicker cortical covering. In addition, important brain enzymes showed significant elevations, which are thought to correlate with a greater number of connections between nerve cells and heightened cerebral arousal. But the most consistent effect of experience on the brain turned out to be a boost in the ratio of the weight of the cortex compared to the rest of the brain. Enrichment doesn't just act like an all-purpose tonic, but has specific and localized effects on the development of the cerebral cortex."

It is hard to believe that the authors of *The Bell Curve* were not aware of the undeniable link between prenatal nutrition and early environmental stimulation on one hand, and cognitive ability on the other. Yet, while admitting that the size of the black-white IQ gap "shrinks when socioeconomic status is statistically extracted," Herrnstein and Murray argued that controlling for socioeconomic status was not valid. That was so, they argued, because controlling for socioeconomic status "is guaranteed to reduce IQ differences in the same way that choosing black and white samples from a school for the intellectually gifted is guaranteed to reduce IQ differences."

On its face this is an astonishing argument, which even they admit is a "hard point to grasp." The difficulty has nothing to do, however, with either subtlety or complexity, but rather with its clear and obvious prejudice. They offered no evidence that the intellectually gifted, of both races, are not also the socioeconomically favored. Indeed what their argument appears to amount to is that comparing socioeconomically favored whites against less favored blacks is a more accurate measure of racial intellectual aptitude than comparing black and white students from similar socioeconomic backgrounds.

The suspicion of preconceived prejudices can only be strengthened by their attempts to support their contention. "Suppose," they wrote, "we were asking whether blacks and whites differed in sprinting speed, and controlled for varsity status by examining only athletes on the track teams in Division 1 colleges. Blacks would probably still sprint faster than whites on the average, but it would be a smaller difference than in the population at large. Is there any sense in which this smaller difference would be a more accurate measure of the racial difference in sprinting ability than the larger difference in the general population?" Of course, no evidence of any kind is offered to support this contention, and one is left to conclude that like so much else in this book, the authors are merely venting personal and unfailingly biased opinions.

Despite the refusal of *The Bell Curve* authors and other conservatives to acknowledge the devastating impact of slavery, segregation, and discrimination on the socioeconomic status and cognitive ability of its black citizens, there are several ways of measuring the negative impact of these policies on black America. One way is to compare the present condition of blacks presently living in America, who, for a variety of reasons, were either not subject to, or were able to avoid the full effects of those policies, to those who *were* subject to the full effects of those policies.

In spite of significant barriers, including the enactment of Black Codes designed to control both enslaved and free Negroes, literacy was the rule rather than the exception among urban free Negroes, even in states where they were not allowed to attend either public or private schools. Clandestine private schools for free Negro children flourished throughout the South. The head start gained by the antebellum free persons of color over the rest of the black population had enduring consequences.

Beginning generations ahead of other African Americans in education, urbanization, acculturation, and economic conditions, by 1850 three-fifths of all free persons of color were literate, a level of literacy not reached, as late as 1900, by the black population as a whole. In fact, by the mid-nineteenth century, free persons of color were not only more urbanized than the white population, but also more urbanized than the black population, as a whole, would be until 1940. As a consequence, the majority of black students attending college were descendants of free persons of color, until after World War II, when the G. I. Bill allowed the children of the black masses to attend college. Although a small percentage of the black population—only eleven percent in the 1940s—descendants of free persons of color played a disproportionate leadership role in black American life for most of the twentieth century. The black founders of the NAACP were descendants of antebellum free persons of color—so were most holders of doctoral degrees in the mid-twentieth century and the majority of blacks who worked as professionals in the nation's capital.

Perhaps an even more accurate measurement of the negative consequences of slavery, segregation, and discrimination is the relative prosperity of West Indians, the largest black immigrant group in the United States. West Indians, who began immigrating to the United States in the nineteenth century, are an absolute majority of black immigrants to this country. Despite a common genetic heritage and a shared history of slavery in the New World, West Indians and black Americans, are, or for many decades were, culturally very different. The West Indians, because of greater opportunity, were more urban, more skilled, more likely to save, and more entrepreneurial. Not surprisingly, their children outperformed native American black children in the public schools.

As was the case with the free persons of color, the cultural advantages the West Indians brought to the United States had enduring consequences. By 1969, black West Indians were earning ninety-four percent of the average income of all Americans, as compared to sixth-two percent for native blacks.

Even more impressively, second-generation West Indians out-earned Americans of all races by fifteen percent. That was not all. In New York State, more than half of all black-owned businesses were owned by West Indians, despite huge disparities in population numbers. And astonishingly, in the 1970s, all of the highest-ranking blacks in New York City departments were West Indians, as were all black federal judges in the city and the vast majority of directors of black-studies programs in American universities. Underlining this extraordinary West Indian performance is the fact that both parents of General Colin Powell, the first black person to become Chairman of the Joint Chiefs of Staff of the United States Armed Forces and later Secretary of State, were among the Jamaicans who immigrated to New York in the early part of the twentieth century.

Since there were no meaningful genetic differences between the African slaves in the West Indies and those in the United States, the differences in educational achievement and economic status can only be explained by the differences in formative environments. Perhaps the most important difference was demographic, and the most important demographic factor was the enormous numerical advantage slaves held in the West Indies. That advantage, despite a range of laws, which theoretically restricted movement outside the plantation, gave West Indian slaves the kind of freedom from direct white supervision that was almost unimaginable in the United States.

Demographic reality also meant that West Indian blacks not only grew their own food but also supplied the larger society. While white males dominated the economy, there were simply not enough of them to restrict blacks to menial jobs, as was generally the case in the United States. West Indian blacks were carpenters, masons, plumbers, farmers, and small businessmen of all kinds. It was this ability to participate meaningfully in the economy, to exercise initiative, to develop practical skills, and to value education that gave West Indian blacks an enormous cultural and psychic advantage over many of their American counterparts.

The achievements of these West Indians and the ancestors of antebellum free persons of color is, of course, far more representative of the inherent intellectual ability of their African forebears, as the next chapter will explain, than the intellectual underachievement of too many African Americans. That underachievement is the continuing legacy of slavery and the propaganda that attempted to justify it.

15

A Clearer View of African History

For many, many years, millions of young men and women of African descent around the world were introduced to Africa by comic books written by white males, about white males, for white males. Africa was, of course, merely a backdrop and its peoples stereotyped foils for the heroics of white men. Nobody, least of all the colonial officials in British colonies like Jamaica, ever objected to the selling of these comics to young, impressionable black children. To the young so indoctrinated, the concept of an illiterate scion of an English aristocratic family as the king of the African jungle seemed natural and normal. They knew, although it was never explicitly stated in the comics, that Tarzan's class, race, and gender were more important than his inability to read, write, or even speak a human language. Nobody questioned the right or ability of a white man, more ape than human, to be the master of Africa and the Africans.

Africa was, after all, a dark and savage continent peopled by barbaric subhumans with the nauseating habit of broiling and consuming their enemies. Fortunately, there was more to Africa than its primitive and unattractive natives. As any fan of Tarzan knew, the jungles of Africa were filled with magnificent animals, many of them apparently more intelligent and certainly more admirable than their human counterparts. It was, remember, a female ape that Tarzan's creator, Edgar Rice Burroughs, selected as his surrogate mother. Although the ancestors of apes and humans separated more than thirty million years ago, Burroughs, who accurately reflected the racial sentiments of his time, selected an ape rather than an African woman to raise and nurture his hero.

Burroughs, an American, had little or no personal knowledge of Africa, but his fantasies were based on popular prejudices. He was, however, neither the only nor the first popular writer to enlist in the propaganda war against Africans. In 1865, Dean Farrar, the English clergyman and author of the famous nineteenth century school story *Eric*, wrote that the features of Africans were "invariable and expressionless," and that their minds were "characterized by a dead and blank uniformity." Although the good parson had not traveled to Africa himself and there was little photography at the time, Farrar was certain he understood what kind of creatures these Africans were. They had not, he asserted, "originated a single discovery...not promulgated a single thought...not established a single institution...not hit upon a single invention."

Despite the conspicuous paucity of written native sources, and the inaccuracy of much of what has been written about Africa by Europeans, the truth about the history of Africa and its people has not been completely lost. In the words of the great African scholars Paul Sinclair, Thurstan Shaw, and Bassey Andah in *The Archaeology of Africa*, the story of Africa "has been written not by contemporary historians, but in the earth; accordingly this story is revealed by the methods of archaeology and of paleoenvironmental study, assisted where appropriate by oral history and ethnography, including the history of languages, as far as this can be elucidated." In delicate understatement the authors noted that not only was "The history of the archaeological interpretation of Africa....riddled with assumptions," but because of colonialism, "any innovations within the continent of Africa were only considered to be derived from people migrating to Africa from elsewhere."

The most prominent of these assumptions was, of course, the determined attempts of European Egyptologists to deny black Africans a meaningful role in the creation of the Ancient Egyptian civilization. For more than one hundred and fifty years Ancient Egypt's identity has been concealed and its progenitorial role in Western civilization marginalized as European historians decreed Greece the fountainhead of modern civilization. But a new day is dawning. Slowly and grudgingly, but relentlessly and irrevocably

European contempt for Africa and Africans is being slowly melted by the fierce assault of science.

The British historian Basil Davidson has written that Ancient Egypt was essentially an African civilization, and that when Classical Greek civilization began to take shape not long before the middle of the last millennium B.C., it owed much to the influence of Pharonic Egypt, then more than 2,000 years old and of immense prestige. And late in 1998, German archeologists announced that they had unearthed evidence which suggests that Egyptians, not Sumerians, were the first people to write. Egyptian inscriptions discovered in an ancient royal cemetery dating back between 3,200 B.C. and 3,400 B.C. were judged more advanced and readable than those of the same time period in Mesopotamia. A logical explanation for the superiority of the Egyptian inscriptions, the Germans believe, is that the Sumerians, who are known to have traded extensively with Egypt, copied the Egyptian inscriptions, imperfectly.

Despite this slight thawing of traditional European hostility to black achievement, white historians and archeologists, with notable exceptions, are still a long way from acknowledging what their Greek counterparts attested to thousands of years ago: that Egyptian science and philosophy prepared the way for Classical Greek philosophers and scientists, many of whom made a special point of studying in Egypt, often for periods of many years. The renowned Greek historian, Herodotus, who famously described Egyptians as black-skinned and wooly-haired in his *Histories*, made his admiration for the intellectual achievements of the Egyptians clear. It was the Egyptians, he wrote, who by their study of astronomy discovered the solar year and were the first to assign altars and temples to the gods, and to carve figures in stone.

The enormous contributions of black Africa to the religious ideas and practices of the entire word were well understood and acknowledged in Greece. Diodorus Siculus, who completed his history of the world approximately four centuries after Herodotus had written his, was expressing conventional Greek wisdom when he described the black people of Africa as the first to be taught to honor the gods and to hold sacrifices and processions and festivals and other rites by which men honor the deity. As a consequence, he explained, their piety had been published abroad among all men and that it was generally held that the sacrifices practiced among the Ethiopians (the black peoples) were the most pleasing to heaven.

To support his claim, Diodorus called on no less an authority than Homer, who he described as a poet, who is perhaps the oldest and certainly the most venerated among the Greeks. He pointed out that in the *Iliad*, Homer's magnificent epic poem, the poet in tribute to the piety of black Africans, represented Zeus and all the other gods of Greece as being absent because they had traveled to Ethiopia to feast with Ethiopia's faultless men.

The attempt of Egyptologists to separate Ancient Egypt from black Africa was predictable, given its origins. Egyptology, the study of Pharonic Egypt, which spanned the period from 4,500 B.C. to A.D. 461, began when the scholars accompanying Napoleon Bonaparte's invasion of Egypt (1789-1801) published the *Description de Egypte* (1809-28), which made large quantities of source material about Ancient Egypt available to European scholars. Since the release of the materials came at a time when European historians, archeologists and scientists were feverishly devising new ways of justifying slavery, it is not surprising that European Egyptologists did their best to conceal the fact that this magnificent civilization had been created by the ancestors of men and women they were presenting to the world as nothing more than savage brutes.

It now seems clear that in spite of the great antiquity of the ancient Egyptian civilization and its now copiously documented native African origins and character, the earliest pages of African history were not written there. Any attempt to understand the truth about African history, the origins of the West African peoples, and indeed the history of civilization itself must begin with an understanding of the history of the Sahara. It is now clear, from both archaeological and linguistic evidence, that the Sahara, which for thousands of years was the site of innovative and dynamic black societies, was also the birthplace of modern civilization.

The Indian historian K. Madhu Pannikar wrote in his book *The Serpent and the Crescent* that "It is only on the basis that thousands of years ago the Sahara was an extremely fertile area where a civilization of considerable antiquity existed that ancient West African history, which archaeologists have started unearthing, can be understood." Rock paintings document the evolution of this society, from the early Stone Age to about 1500 B.C. Although most of the Sahara is now too dry to support even the most rudimentary forms of plant and animal life, it was once a fertile area dotted by lakes and filled with game. Remnants of tropical and Mediterranean fauna and rock paintings support this contention. When it rains, frogs still appear in the Ahaggar, ostriches and antelopes can still be found in many areas, crocodiles in a degenerate form are still found at Ennedi, cypress still flourishes in the Tassali des Ajjer, and rock paintings of elephants, hippopotamuses, and giraffes all vividly demonstrate that the unknown artists were personally familiar with these animals.

The Saharan rock paintings, which are among the most important archaeological discoveries of our time, have, in tandem with recent developments in linguistic geography, completely revolutionized the traditional view of Saharan, and consequently, African history. The quality of the paintings, which document the long history of a civilization that evolved through at least sixteen stages, from hunting to cattle raising, have been compared favorably with the finest artistic efforts of any period. The rendition of the movement of camels in silhouette, and horses pulling chariots and galloping in full extension with both front and back legs raised symmetrically, for example, have been widely praised.

Almost all of the paintings were found near the two great trade routes in what must have been the heavily populated regions of Tessali-Fezzan and Atlantic-South Morocco. Horses, chariots, and the wild rush of desert warfare are vividly and convincingly illustrated. The people depicted, some armed with javelins, are clearly Negroid in type, and a painting of a mask similar to ones still being made in the Ivory Coast was found near Aurohet in the Tassali range. Although dating the paintings in chronological sequence has proven to be extremely complex and difficult, two broad historical periods have been recognized. During the first period, when the Sahara was still fertile, the animals shown (such as the hippopotamus and the giraffe) are primarily tropical. In the later period, when the Sahara began to dry up, it became cattle country, and the engravings of oxen become more frequent and prominent.

The desiccation of the Sahara and the isolation this imposed on sub-Saharan Africa made the area, as Panikkar so aptly phrased it, "one of the very few areas in the world which was almost wholly thrown on its own resources." Unlike the forest dwellers of Central and North Europe, those of the African rain forests were unable to borrow the ideas and inventions of other civilizations. Unlike the Europeans, who were able to avail themselves of the accumulated wisdom of the Mediterranean world, including the black civilizations of North Africa, the people of tropical Africa were left to fend for themselves, and the societies they created were almost totally the result of their own native genius.

If the rock paintings initiated the rethinking of Saharan history, developments in linguistics have greatly expanded our understanding of its peoples and societies. Starting about 10,000 years ago in areas that included what is now southwestern Egypt, some of the Saharan peoples began a three-stage development of food production, the cornerstone of what we call civilization. Although the Sahara was at the time densely occupied by speakers of all three major African language families—Nilo-Saharan, Niger-Congo and Afroasiatic—the three most important African cereals were all domesticated in areas occupied by Nilo-Saharan speakers.

Because of the remarkable convergence of the archaeological record and the linguistic history of Nilo-Saharan food production, there is widespread agreement that pastoralism in the Sahara began long before the earliest known date for the arrival of food production in ancient Egypt. Cattle tending, in the first stage, was followed by what the linguists Christopher Ehret describes as "prima facie evidence for a second development, of cultivation, by the second half of the eighth millennium, and at a still later point in time, possibly about 6000 B.C., by the first evidence of sheep and goat."

These first food producers probably spoke proto-Northern Sudanic, one of two daughter languages of proto-Nilo-Saharan, the original mother language of Nilo-Saharan, and the oldest of Africa's three major language families. These widely used genetic metaphors imply, as Ehret pointed out, "a linguistic relationship not unlike that found in many single-cell organisms." Languages are regarded as related when they descend from a common mother language called a proto-language. Typically, proto-languages evolve into two or more daughter languages, in much the same way the mother cell divides into daughter cells. The daughter languages can become proto-languages themselves, diverging into daughter languages of their own, repeating this process over and over during the long run of language history.

By itself, linguistic history is usually not the most reliable method of precise dating. However, it provides powerful tools for probing and examining the history of communities and societies as a whole. Languages contain many thousands of individual artifacts of the past, words that are hard evidence of a society's gamut of knowledge, range of experience, and cultural practices. As ideas, behaviors, and practices evolved and changed, so too did, inevitably, the vocabulary that described those aspects of the society's life. New meanings were applied to existing words, new words were invented or adopted from other societies, and older words were discarded or forgotten. The history of that society, the changes and developments across the whole gamut of its culture and economy, is therefore reflected in the individual histories of the thousands of words used by the members of that society to express every element of their lives.

Languages exist solely as vehicles for social and cultural communication, so when the speakers of a common language no longer share common experiences and practices, the mother or proto-language they shared will begin to diverge into daughter languages. The breakup of a mother language is always gradual: a slow, progressive accumulation of small changes in vocabulary, grammatical usages and pronunciation. At first, different dialects of the language will emerge in different parts of its speech territory, and then, over centuries, the dialects will become distinct languages, no longer intelligible to each other's speakers. It should be noted that the mother language does not give birth to its daughters and remain separate and distinct from them. Instead, "it evolves directly into each of its daughters as part of a continuing historical process."

The process of recovering history from language evidence is a complex one, which begins with the establishment of a linguistic stratigraphy or family tree of the languages being studied. Like all other family trees, the purpose of the language stratigraph is to reconstruct relationships and historical connections, and to establish linkages to a common founding ancestor, or in this case, a mother or proto-language. Instead of family names, the linguistic stratigraphy will be comprised of "root" words describing everyday activities.

To qualify as a root word (a word used in an earlier proto-language), a word in current usage must, generally, meet two criteria. Firstly, the word must appear in at least one language in each of two primary branches of the family. Secondly, there must be some correspondence in how these words are pronounced. Differences in pronunciation will develop during the normal course of history. But since sound shifts in all languages proceed largely under regularly formulatable rules, it is usually possible to determine whether two closely similar words are cognates (from the same family), borrowings, or just chance resemblances.

Words reveal more than historical connections; they can also tell us about the history and cultural practices of the people who use them. Some words used today in daughter languages have not changed in meaning since the mother language was spoken. This is, of course, eloquent testimony to long-term cultural continuity, perhaps to conservatism, but certainly to a significant degree of stability and cultural retention. As an example, the current widespread use of an inherited word for goat in Bantu languages of the Niger-Congo family has been traced back to the proto-Bantu period and even earlier in Niger-Congo history. This is indisputable proof that proto-Bantu speakers knew about and probably raised goats, and that this knowledge was maintained until the present by all of the groups using the word today.

In contrast, the changed meaning of some words can tell us a great deal about older, now discarded, practices and concepts. For example, at around 1000 B.C., near the great Western Rift Valleys of Africa, speakers of proto-Mashariki, a daughter language of proto-Bantu, began using a new word to describe the planting of crops. The word was not new, but its meaning was new. Because in Bantu history it had previously meant, "to split," the new meaning revealed a great deal about the agricultural practices of the proto-Mashariki people. It meant that they continued to utilize an older rain forest-based agricultural technique, which was developed to protect fragile soils, of cutting a narrow slit in the ground and planting a new cutting of yam or some other similar food plant in the slit. Over time, the Mashariki people would settle on lands with richer soil and would change their crops and their method of cultivation. Without the linguistic evidence, this insight into their earlier agricultural practices would have been lost.

It is also happens that the meaning of some words, which have been in use since the mother language was spoken, will change in one or more daughter languages. As an example, in the Horn of Africa, several words in the proto-Somali language of the Afroasiatic family originally described the life-stages of cattle. In Northern Somali, where the daughter language Maxay was spoken, these words instead came to refer to the equivalent life stages of camels. This meaning shift tells us that the early Maxay replaced their cattle with camels when they moved into very dry areas of the Horn, where cattle could not thrive, about 1,200 years ago.

Cross-cultural influences can also be revealed by borrowed words—words adopted from another language rather than inherited from the proto-language.

However, the borrowing of a single word tells a very different story than the borrowing of a very large number of words from a single language in a relatively short period of time. The borrowing of a single word usually indicates that the item or idea named by the word was adopted from another society. On the other hand, large numbers of new words usually mean that large numbers of people who spoke the new words were assimilated into the society of the people who adopted the words. Between these extremes, other patterns of word borrowing, all of which must be carefully interpreted, reveal the extraordinary variety and intensity of intersocietal contact that have taken place between peoples all over the world.

Linguistic testimony, however compelling, is not by itself sufficient evidence on which to base a fully credible history. Correlation with other datable evidence of the past, such as archaeology or written documents, is also needed. Correlation requires the application of two other forms of linguistic historical analysis. One method is to try to establish the areas where the proto-languages would have been found by using the most recent locations of the languages. The other way is to estimate the general timeframe within which the proto-languages would have been spoken by applying a tool called glottochronology.

Establishing the most likely location of mother languages is probably most accurately done by applying the "least moves" theory. This theory assumes that the most likely locations are the ones that require the least population displacement and the fewest population movements to account for the modern locations of the languages of the family. Therefore, the analysis begins with the most recent branching of the family and moves backward in time. As an example, the final of the three stages in which food production developed among the Nilo-Saharan peoples took place among the proto-Sahelians. With the single exception of Eastern Sahelian, today the Sahelian groups are all located in the Sahel geographical belt, along the southern edges of the Sahara Desert. Languages range from Songay, spoken in Mali in the interior delta of the Niger River, to the For language of the Marra Mountains in Sudan. But the most likely location of the proto-Sahelians, because it requires the "least moves" to explain, is somewhere along the southern edge of the Sahara region.

Glottochronology assumes that there is a recurring pattern of lexical change in the basic or core vocabulary of all languages, and that the time of divergence between related languages can be estimated by calculating the percentages of these core words that have retained their original meanings over specified time periods. Scholars have discovered, by using a standard list of one hundred to two hundred meanings that are shared by almost every language in the world—sometimes referred to as the 'Swadesh' list—that words are replaced by new words with the same meanings, at the same rate, in every language. Although criticized by some, Ehret argues that glottochronology "has been shown to fit well with known language histories in the Americas, Europe, Asia and Africa."

Generally, approximately 86 percent of the words on the 100-meanings lists will retain their meaning over a 500-year period. Therefore, two languages that have been diverging from their common mother language for 1,000 years should continue to share about 74 percent of the same words. After 2,000 years, the percentages should decline to a median of 53 percent; after 3,000 years to about 39 percent, and so on. Since the Kunama and Saharo-Sahelian sub-branches of the Northern Sudanic branch of Nilo-Saharan share only three percent to six percent of the same words, the divergence of proto-Northern Sudanic began more than 9,000 years ago.

Although the recovery of early African history from the continent's major language families is really just beginning, we already know that Nilo-Saharan societies played key roles in the creation and spread of agriculture on the African continent. The Nilo-Saharan language family is at least 12,000 years old, and it reflects the complex history of the Nilo-Saharan people. Although it is comprised of a relatively low number of languages—only 78—it is the most diverse and therefore the oldest of the three major African language families.

The oldest of the African language families, Khoisan, which was probably first spoken about 20,000 years ago, is today a minor group with considerable internal differentiation, despite the distinctiveness of its sound. Khoisan languages were spoken by hunter-gatherers who once occupied much of the eastern side of the continent, from northern East Africa to the Cape of Good Hope.

Although Nilo-Saharan is the oldest of the three major African language families and Nilo-Saharan speakers were the first food producers, the other two are far more widespread and influential. Afroasiatic, which as the linguist Roger Blench observed was once known as "Hamito-Semitic with its slightly bizarre racist undertone," is comprised of more than 250 languages including ancient Egyptian, the Berber languages of northern and Saharan

Africa, and the Semitic languages of southwest Asia including Arabic, Aramaic (the language of Christ and the Apostles), and Hebrew. Niger-Congo, which includes the majority of the languages spoken in West Africa and the more than 700 recognized sub-groupings of the Bantu language, today has the widest distribution on the African continent.

Perhaps nothing more vividly illustrates the centrality of the Sahara to African and world history than this startling fact: The original mother languages of all three major African language families were first spoken in that region, and the youngest of them, Afroasiatic, is the ancestral language of all the Semitic languages. Niger-Congo probably began on the southern margins of the Sahara; Nilo-Saharan, somewhere on the eastern half of the southern regions of the Sahara; and Afroasiatic, on what is today the Sudan-Ethiopia border.

Since the original mother languages of all three language families were first spoken in the same ecological zone, in areas roughly adjacent to each other, at approximately the same period of history, it would not be surprising if all three of these so-called mother languages were, instead, daughter languages of an even earlier proto-language. In fact, the possibility of a deep-level relationship between Nilo-Saharan and Niger-Congo—a Kongo-Saharan proto-language—has already been raised. But most researchers believe that this question cannot be definitively answered until more solid reconstructions are completed for both language families.

What is already clear from both the archaeological and a linguistic record is that the period between 11,000 and 7,500 years ago was one of enormous innovation and change in the Sahara. Only a few thousand years earlier, the last Ice Age had ended, and what geologists term the Recent Era had begun. It was a time when all of the peoples of the world were still hunter-gatherers, and when the archaeological records undisputedly indicate that the peopling of the Americas had already begun. At the time, the Sahara, a region of steppe, grassland, and dry savanna environments, was already fairly densely populated by a physically heterogeneous collection of Africoid types speaking a wide variety of languages and dialects.

For the first two stages of this history, when the original mother language, proto-Nilo-Saharan, and the first daughter language, proto-Sudanic, were spoken, the vocabulary did not contain any words describing any type of food production. It was not until the third stage, when proto-Sudanic had evolved into proto-Central and proto-Northern Sudanic, that words indicating the deliberate raising of domestic animals first appeared in the proto-Northern Sudanic language. However, the first words describing cultivation of some kind did not appear until the subsequent proto-Saharo-Sahelian era. Finally, during the time of its daughter languages (proto-Saharan and proto-Sahelian), the linguistic evidence indicates that sheep and goats were added to the economy.

The unpredictable, even random distribution of human genius (or alternately, the decisive impact of chance and opportunity on human history) has rarely been more unambiguously demonstrated than in the very different responses of two early groups of Nilo-Saharan people to the challenge of food production. For reasons now unknown and perhaps unknowable, the speakers of proto-Northern Sudanic, as we have seen, learned how to domesticate wild cattle and made them their primary source of meat. On the other hand, their cultural and genetic brothers and sisters, who had migrated to areas either more or less challenging, did not participate in the origination of cattle-raising. It was not until much later that those ideas were diffused to the Central Sudanic branch from other Nilo-Saharan societies.

Perhaps no other single development has more potential to alter the traditional view of African history than the confirmation that Afroasiatic, the ancestral language of the Semitic languages, was first spoken in Africa. Ehret explains: "Because of the association of the Semitic languages with several world religions, the Afroasiatic family has long been uncritically presumed by non-Africanist scholars to be of south-west Asian origin." The great American linguist Joseph Greenberg was the first to determine that Semitic languages formed just one of six or more branches of Afroasiatic, and that all of the other branches and more than 200 other surviving languages are confined to Africa. The Semitic subfamily is itself mainly African, with twelve of its surviving nineteen languages spoken only in Ethiopia.

The importance of this development has probably been best explained by Professor Diamond, who described it as "a big shock for Eurocentric believers in the superiority of so-called Western civilization. We're taught that Western civilization originated in the Near East, was brought to brilliant heights in Europe by the Greeks and Romans, and produced three of the world's great religions: Christianity, Judaism, and Islam." We now that this view of history is simply wrong, that it was Africa, not the Near East, which gave birth to the languages spoken by the authors of the moral pillars of both

Western and Muslim civilizations, the Old and New Testaments, and the Koran.

The proto-Afroasiatic vocabulary included words for flour, for edible food taken from grasses, for grindstone, and for donkey. Apparently, for thousands of years, the first Afroasiatic speakers lived within the natural range of wild donkeys and subsisted on wild grasses, which they collected and ground into flour. Wild donkeys are known to have ranged the regions around the Red Sea hills and the far northern fringe of the Ethiopian Highlands, in just about the areas where linguistic geography places the early Afroasiatic speakers. We also know from the archaeological evidence that more than 15,000 years ago, in that general region, people with grindstones began collecting wild grasses for food.

The first divergence of the Afroasiatic family tree led to Omotic, consisting entirely of languages that would be spoken only in the Ethiopian Highlands and to the far more widely spread Erythraic branch. At the proto-Erythraic stage, the word for cow was added, but nothing in the vocabulary indicated that either herding or cultivation had begun. There is evidence that when wetter climates began spreading across the eastern Sahara sometime after the start of the Recent Era, wild cattle began moving from the Mediterranean area to as far south as the north edge of the Ethiopian region. But the first firm evidence of livestock raising and cultivation does not appear until far later, during the proto-Cushitic, proito-Chadic, proto-Berber, and proto-Semitic periods.

The archaeological evidence seems to confirm that food production among Afroasiatic speakers did not begin until about 6000 B.C.—thousands of years later than among the Nilo-Saharans—when the knowledge of livestock raising began spreading to the Caspian cultures of the northeastern Sahara. Afroasiatic speakers expanded in several directions: to the northern parts of the Ethiopian Highlands, to western parts of Africa, to North Africa, and, most notably, to far southwest Asia. Proto-Chadic, a member of the North Erythraic branch, was taken south from the Central Sahara into the eastern Lake Chad Basin sometime around 6000 B.C. From about 5000 B.C. to 3000 B.C., descendant languages spread over a great part of what is now Northern Nigeria and Central Chad. Today, more than 100 Chadic languages are spoken, including the best-known, Hausa.

Another subgroup of the North Erythraic branch, the Berber languages, expanded not once, but thrice. The first expansion took place around 3000

B.C., when speakers of proto-Berber spread across an area extending from the central Maghreb to the borders of Middle Kingdom Egypt. The second, during the last millennium B.C., covered large parts of North Africa and produced many of the Berber people mentioned in the Roman records. The third and final Berber expansion took place during the first millennium A.D., when the Tuareg, who had by that time tamed the camel, occupied the Central Sahara.

It is not yet clear just when the Semitic languages such as the ancient Egyptian, Chadic and Berber languages—a subgroup of the North Erythraic branch—spread to southwest Asia, but it is thought to have been before 5000 B.C. If so, it is probable, despite the relatively late start of food production among Afroasiatic speakers, that the black African ancestors of the Semtic peoples left Africa speaking an African language that had been spoken in Africa for thousands of years; these people were armed with the knowledge of cattle raising and grain cultivation, both of which had been developed in Africa after thousands of years of trial and error.

Although most experts believe Nilo-Saharan is the oldest of the three major African language families, some concede that distinction to Niger-Congo, which may have first been spoken some 15,000 years ago. While Nilo-Saharan never expanded much beyond its original territory, Niger-Congo speakers are now scattered over much of the continent. Today, more than 1,000 Niger-Congo languages are spoken by some 400 million people, about 200 million of whom are Bantu speakers. Nevertheless, the estimated 500 to 700 Bantu languages constitute a single subfamily of the Niger-Congo language family. The majority of the other 176 subfamilies are located in West Africa, a relatively small fraction of the entire Niger-Congo range.

Despite this West African concentration, the Niger-Congo language family did not begin in West Africa, as Diamond claims and as has been widely held. Ehret places the first expansion of the Niger-Congo peoples from an area as far east as the Nuba Mountains of Sudan, where proto-Kordofanian would have been spoken. Some of these people apparently ventured as far west as Mali, historically the territory of the Mande and Atlantic-Congo branches. Just when this expansion began and how long it lasted is not currently known.

It was during a second but still early phase of Niger-Congo history, the proto-Mande-Congo era that the first words for food production appeared. The evidence indicates that the peoples of the Atlantic and Ijo-Congo branches began cultivating the Guinea yam and perhaps other crops, such as the oil palm, sometime between 10,000 and 8,000 years ago. During that period, Niger-Congo speakers began spreading across the woodland savannas of West Africa, the natural environment of the Guinea yam.

Following the great aridity that began at the end of the Pleistocene, higher levels of rainfall over most of Africa, from about 9,500 to 8,500 years ago, greatly increased the habitable portions of the continent. As an example, the westward expansion of the Niger-Congo peoples was greatly facilitated by the extension of the woodland-savanna environment hundreds of kilometers further north into the Sudan belt than it is today.

Another shift in the weather pattern, this time to a somewhat drier climate, apparently triggered another expansion of Niger-Congo peoples. The proto-Benue-Kwa descendants of the proto-Volta-Congo people expanded south into the rainforest belt of West Africa between 7,000 to 6,000 years ago. The archaeological record of peoples with polished stone axes expanding into the rain forest about the sixth millennium not only correlates extremely well with the glottochronological dating, but is also a logical development. Yams and oil palms, as Ehret pointed out, "require sunlight to grow, and stone axes would have been essential tools of the incoming Benue-Kwa cultivators for converting forest into clearings."

After thousands of years of apparently rapid population growth and expansion into much of the West African region, one offshoot of the Benue-Kwa peoples left from the eastern Nigeria-Cameroon area and moved into the equatorial rain forest of the Congo, about 5,000 years ago. These were the Bantu speakers, and during the next 3,000 years, Bantu peoples would spread over much of subequatorial Africa, engulfing and replacing most of the original Pygmy and Khoisan populations. Today, with two exceptions, the distinctive Khoisan languages that once extended far further north are confined to southern Africa. The plight of the Pygmies is even more poignant; today they are the only African peoples without a distinctive language. Each band of Pygmies speaks the language of the area in which it lives, with only traces of its original language in some words and sounds.

The first great civilization founded by the emigrants from the Sahara was not the Egyptian one. The first stop was Nubia, which the *New York Times* has described as "a black African culture long overshadowed by Egypt but brilliant and innovative in its own right." Just how brilliant and innovative it was is only now becoming clear. The reconstruction of Nubia's reputation was occasioned by the recovery of tens of thousands of artifacts rescued from sites that were once part of ancient Nubia.

Some thirty years ago, during the construction of the New Aswan High Dam, many of the world's leading geologists, in a race against the rising Nile waters, joined forces to salvage the monuments, tombs, and other remnants of ancient Nubia. Among the rescued items were thousands of artifacts attesting to a distinct culture some six thousand years old. Scholars, the *New York Times* reported, were finding in the artifacts striking evidence of Nubia's influence on Egyptian culture and its development of kingly rule, a political innovation that some believe may have influenced the rise of pharaohs in Egypt.

Higher levels of rainfall, which began falling all over the African continent about 9,500 years ago and lasted for one thousand years, apparently triggered waves of emigration from heavily populated areas of the Sahara. In one wave, as we have seen, Niger-Congo speakers began moving west, where they would create the great West African civilizations. In another wave, Nilo-Saharan speakers moved north into what is now Egypt's Western Desert, which the increased rainfall had made suitable for human colonization for the first time in thousands of years. The origin of the colonists, whether from the Nile Valley or the Sahara, was once in dispute. But both linguistic and archaeological evidence indicates that they arrived with the kind of pre-existing knowledge of animal husbandry and grain utilization that they could only have gained from the more developed Saharan civilization.

Although there is considerable evidence of the presence of wild barley in the Nile Valley more than 18,000 years ago, food production did not begin there. While it appeared to offer a more suitable environment for the development of agriculture than the semi-arid Sahara, the Nilotic environment was probably less suitable for the kind of agriculture that developed in the Western Desert. Some experts believe that the relatively narrow Nile Valley of the period, with its limited floodplain comprised primarily of contracting silts, and handicapped by major seasonal variations in water levels, would have required technology more advanced than was used in the Western Desert.

Food production, with both domestic grain and animals, did not appear in the lower Nile Valley until near the end of the fifth or early in the fourth millennium B.C., when the technology to overcome the enormous problems of floodplain agriculture became available. Apparently, during the dry period of 6,000 to 5,500 B.C., the farmer-pastoralists of the Western Desert were driven into the Nile Valley because they were no longer able to continue their traditional methods of food production in their homeland. It was, very likely, these technologically sophisticated newcomers who developed the basin irrigation techniques that made possible the development of agriculture in the Nile Valley.

This does not mean that the early inhabitants of the Nile Valley did not participate in any aspect of the cultural revolution transforming the societies of their neighbors. A number of sites containing highly decorated pottery and bone and stone tools, some more than 8,000 years old, have been found in various areas of the Nile Valley. But, at even the largest of the sites, those along the Nile in Central Sudan, subsistence was based on intensive fishing and hunting, and there are no traces of domestic animals or the use of grains.

It would be another 2,000 years, during the fourth millennium B.C.— about when the Saharans arrived—before domestic animals and agriculture appeared at sites such as Shaheinab and Kadero. Further evidence that the direction of the Neolithic Revolution was from south to north is provided by the appearance in Nubia, at approximately the same time or slightly later, of three other apparently fully developed Neolithic groups.

The ancient Kingdom of Nubia covered an area, which today is southern Egypt and northern Sudan, stretching from Aswan in the north to Khartoum, about 1,100 miles to the south. Nubians were a sophisticated people who developed their own writing system and built cities, roads, and palaces rivaling those of Egypt. Nubian rulers also left monumental tombs, but instead of pyramids, they built huge gravel mounds or tumulus-covered internal chambers. Like the Egyptians, the Nubians apparently believed that their leaders should be well provided for in the afterlife. Magical figurines, known as shawabties, were placed in the tombs, apparently to work for the deceased in the heavenly grain fields.

One of the prized exhibits in the Nubian Gallery at the Royal Ontario Museum is a shawabty of King Taharquo, who ruled over both Nubia and Egypt in about 690 B.C. and revived art and architecture in both countries. The shawabty is inscribed with the king's name and carries a customary hoe and basket for moving dirt.

In the Old Testament, Kush (Nubia) is depicted as one of the world's great military powers, a distant and powerful people in the extreme south, and was contrasted with the Assyrians in the far north. Its inhabitants were described as tall and smooth-skinned and their blackness was proverbial. Kushite ambassadors traveled along the Nile in vessels of reed. Moses married a Kushite woman, and when Aaron and Miriam rebuked Moses for this—most likely because she was a foreigner and not because of her skin color— "the anger of the Lord was aroused against them and he left them; and there was Miriam, her skin diseased and as white as snow." A Kushite carried the report of Absolom's defeat and death from Joab to David. Ebed-melech, a Kushite eunuch in the palace of Sedekiah, upon hearing of Jeremiah's imprisonment and impending death from starvation, interceded with Sedekiah and helped ease Jeremiah's pain as the prophet was lifted from a pit.

More than 5,000 artifacts—including clothing, weapons, jewelry, sandals, a bronze statuette of a Nubian king, brightly painted pottery, and a sandstone sculpture of a human-headed bird representing the soul after death—were recovered during the salvage excavations of 1960 to 1968. The artifacts have allowed archaeologists to fill many of the pages in the history of ancient Nubia that earlier surveys had left blank. Probably the most important artifact discovered was an incense burner made of stone, which was excavated at the site of Qustual, capital of the Nubian Kingdom called Ta-Seti, the land of the Bow.

A seated ruler, a palace portal, and a crown and falcon—motifs that would become symbols of Egyptian pharaohs—were engraved on the side of the burner. Dr. Bruce B. Williams of the University of Chicago, author of a continuing series on the Nubian excavations, has written that the incense burner, dated about 3,100 or possibly two centuries earlier, is "the first self-evident Pharaonic monument from the Nile Valley."

The incense burner has made Williams and other scholars rethink their views on the origination of the Egyptian civilization. The concept of kingship, which traditionally was thought to have originated in Egypt about 3,100 B.C. and which was fundamental to ancient Egyptian civilization and power, could have been, they now acknowledge, a Nubian inspiration. Nubia, Williams concedes, was deeply involved in the formative stages of Pharaonic civilization. The incense burner, he wrote, "is making me something of an afrocentrist." Also among the converts to the afrocentrist school is Dr. Martin Bernal, professor of Government at Cornell University, who has written "that until recently many white European scholars were racists and anti-Semitic and created an Aryan model for the origins of classical Greek culture—and hence of Western civilization."

The deep and sustained involvement of Nubians in the formation and history of ancient Egypt is beyond question. Not only did the concept of kingship originate in Nubia, but the *Britannica* also reports that "written Egyptian documents date back to c.3,350 B.C., when the first Pharaohs developed the hieroglyphic script in Nubia." We also know that Nubian kings, or kings from southern Egypt with strong Nubian features, were among the greatest of the pharaohs of ancient Egypt.

However, we also know that the Nubians were Nilo-Saharan speakers, and that ancient Egyptian is currently classified as an Afroasiatic language, the language first spoken in a region between the Sudan border and the Ethiopian Highlands. It is likely therefore that when Diodorus wrote that the Egyptians "derived their beliefs concerning their burial practices and the role of priests, shapes of statues, and forms of writing from these Ethiopians," he was describing a heterogeneous group of native black Africans.

With the possible exception of classification, linguistic research in Africa is just beginning; a great deal, particularly in the area of historical reconstruction, is still not known. Significant changes are still being made even in the area of classification. The most striking examples of these changes in recent times may have been the discovery of isolated languages in east Africa and the internal reclassification of Niger-Congo. Although there may be further changes and adjustments in the future, they are more likely, as Roger Blench has written, "to be matters of detail than broad continent-spanning revisions."

What is now clear, from both the linguistic and archaeological evidence, is that the ancient Egyptian civilization, like all the others on the African continent, was developed by native black Africans; that the pillars of civilization, food production—the domestication of plants and animals—began in Africa and not in the Near East, as has long been alleged; and that, as we shall now discuss, Nubia and ancient Egypt were not the only great civilizations founded by the black emigrants from the Sahara.

When the primarily Niger-Congo-speaking emigrants from the Sahara began expanding into West Africa some 9,000 years ago, the region was already inhabited by small, red-skinned peoples whose material cultures were far less developed than the relatively sophisticated newcomers. In fact, the technological gap between the Pygmies, who were hunter-gatherers, and the Saharan farmers was so great that the Pygmies were rapidly and almost completely engulfed, and, as noted earlier, are today the only African peoples without a distinctive language. Evidence, based both on linguistic documentation and on the distribution and degree of adaptation of modern African livestock, makes it clear that the Saharans were accompanied by herds of domesticated cattle.

Animal husbandry was not the only aspect of sub-Saharan food production initiated by the immigrants. The archaeological and linguistic records also indicate that the newcomers, armed with technologically advanced, tool-polished stone axes, were able to clear the forests and to introduce agriculture into the rainforest belt between 7,000 and 6,000 years ago.

By the time of the first Arab contact, tropical Africa had already experienced more than 10,000 years of continuing development. Rapid population growth in West Africa, fed by the spread of agriculture, had led to the Bantu expansion into central, eastern, and southern Africa and to the engulfment of another group of hunter-gatherers, the Khoisans. Pre-Iron Age metallurgy begun before 900 B.C., and the first iron artifacts were found at sites in Niger and Nigeria dating before 500 B.C. Like elsewhere, based on the items found at Iron Age sites all over the region, social demand for prestige objects such as ornaments and weapons was apparently the primary motivator for the development of metallurgical technology in late Stone Age West Africa.

Despite its isolation and because of this long process of development, and in marked contrast to the reputation the region would develop during the Slave Era, by A.D. 1200 West Africa was the site of numerous dynamic and prosperous societies that compared favorably with their European counterparts. States such as ancient Ghana, in the western region of the Western Sudan, and Kanem-Bornu, in eastern Western Sudan, had by then developed strong systems of government based on hereditary kingship and centralized authority.

Relying on their own native genius tropical Africans, hundreds of years before the arrival of European slavers, had managed to build towns, cities, and even empires of considerable size and accomplishment. Written reports of Arab traders make it clear that when they first reached tropical Africa, the organization of the societies they encountered had already advanced beyond the purely tribal phase and had developed systems of monarchical government. These centers of population were supported by highly developed agricultural systems and by organized networks of market and trade. Kings, whose claim to power was based on descent from the mythical divine founding ancestors of their ethnic groups, taxed trade and levied tribute on the agricultural villages with armies of retainers, who provided their sovereigns with both a military force and a hierarchy of officials.

The little state of Kangaba in central Western Sudan, already more than two hundred years old, was getting ready to become the mighty empire of Mali. And long before the arrival of the Arab traders of North Africa, cities such as Jenne, Goa, ancient Kumbi, and later Timbuktu were centers of dynamic interregional trade between the prosperous and expanding grassland empires.

The McIntosh excavations in 1977 demonstrated that Jenne, today a small town on a tributary of the Niger, had been a settlement of iron producers and iron users as early as the third century B.C. Because of its unique history, Jenne deserves special attention here. Unlike Goa, Takrur, and ancient Kumbi, which were middlemen between the traders of the Western Sudan and those of the Sahara and North Africa, Jenne was the meeting place of the traders of the Western Sudan and the traders of the forestlands to the south. Increasingly, particularly after 1400, it was through Jenne that the gold and produce of the societies of the forest belt passed to the caravans of the trading centers. It was also through Jenne that the goods of North Africa were distributed southward into the forest societies.

When the Arabs first began trading with sub-Saharan Africa, their interest was concentrated on Kanem-Bornu (in the east, north of Lake Chad) and ancient Ghana (in the extreme west, on the borders of modern Mauritania and Mali). Ancient Ghana should not be confused with its modern namesake, which is further to the south and east. Local and Muslim sources indicate that the Kingdom of Kanem-Bornu had been formed during the early part of the ninth century A.D. as the result of interactions between Saharan nomads and agricultural village communities. There, in the lands around Lake Chad, were the southern market-centers of the trans-Saharan trade with Libya and Tunisia in the far north, Nubia in the Middle Nile, and Egypt in the far northeast.

Ancient Ghana, by the time of the first Arab contact, had already reached a level of organization that was only possible after centuries of constant development. Although very little is known about its early history, we know that it was founded by the Soninke, whose ancestors now live in the modern republic of Senegal. The *Tarikh as-Sudan*, a history book written in Timbuktu in the seventeenth century, claims that there were twenty-two kings of Ghana before the beginning of the Muslim era in A.D. 622, and twenty-two more after that. This would place the origins of Ghana at about A.D. 300. What is certain is that by the beginning of the ninth century, Ghana had become a powerful trading state, called Wagadu by its rulers, and known to the Berber traders of the Saharan market centers as Aoukar. The name Ghana, or war chief, was originally a title of its kings, but at some stage it was adopted as the name of the country. The kings were also known as Kaya magham, or lord of the gold, because they controlled its export.

The earliest Arab reference to Ghana, the earliest and the greatest of the savannah kingdoms of West Africa, dates from the early eighth century. In the middle of the eleventh century, the geographer Abu Ubayd al-Bakari described Ghana's capital, court, and trade in considerable detail. The capital was made up of two towns about six miles apart, and the territory between them was extensively developed. The Muslim traders lived in one town, and the king and the local people in the other. At the height of its prosperity before A.D. 1240, Ghana's last capital, at Kumbi Saleh (about 320 kilometers north of modern Bamako) was inhabited by more than 15,000 people. This large population was fed by produce from surrounding farms, which were supplied with water from wells.

The court reflected the power and wealth of the king, who was served and supported by numerous satellite rulers. Early Arab historians described the king of Ghana as a great king, who had gold mines in his territory and a great number of kingdoms under his control; most of his revenue came from regular taxes on trade. Muslim interest in Ghana was based primarily on its importance as a source of gold, and as early as A.D. 951, the king of Ghana was described "as the wealthiest of all the kings on the face of the earth, and as one whose forebears had reigned there since ancient times."

The wealth of the king was reflected in the splendor of his court. "When he gave audience to his people, to listen to their complaints and set them to right," al-Bakri wrote, "he sits in a pavilion around which stands his horses caparisoned in cloths of gold; behind him stands ten pages holding shields and gold mounted swords; on his right are the sons of the princes of his empire, splendidly clad, and with gold plaited into their hair.... Thoroughbred dogs that wore gold and silver collars with bells of the same metals guarded the entrance to the audience chamber. The beginning of the royal session was announced by the noise made by a drum made out of a deba."

The splendors of ancient Ghana would not fade from the memory of the peoples of the Western Sudan for hundreds of years. Some 600 years after al-Bakri had published his account, Mahmud Kati, a writer from Timbuktu, recalled the glory days of the past in his book, the *Tarikh al-Fattash*. In it, Kati tells the story of a seventh century king of Ghana who, it was said, owned 1,000 of the most pampered horses in the history of the world. Each of these horses, Kati claimed, slept only on carpet, had a silken rope for a halter, had three personal assistants, and generally was treated like it was a king. Fortunately, the generosity of the kings also extended to the people of Ghana. The kings, Kati wrote with what must have been some exaggeration, gave great banquets to 10,000 of their subjects at a time, generously dispensing gifts and justice to all whom attended.

Gold mining was important to Ghana's economy, but its prosperity depended on keeping the desert routes open. The kingdom's rise to power was due largely to its location, at the junction of the southern and northern ends of trading routes from North Africa and the Western Sudan. Ghana had become a great empire because of the trading opportunities provided, first by the trans-Saharan trade of Carthaginian and Roman times, and then by the Arab conquest of North Africa in the seventh and eighth centuries. But, the Arab conquest of North Africa also posed the great danger that this route would, eventually, be interrupted. In fact, in the eighth century, when the Umayyads had consolidated their hold on western Morocco, they launched a fierce but unsuccessful attack on Ghana between A.D. 734 and 750.

Ghana's military power was probably the most tangible expression of its wealth and political sophistication. Its immense army, which reputedly was made up of as many as 200,000 men, 40,000 of whom were armed with bows and arrows, allowed the kings to resist Berber power for hundreds of years. But, like every other civilization, however great, Ghana slowly began to decay. Mande groups to the south, many of whom had once been obliged to serve as satellite kingdoms, began to break away and to compete amongst themselves for supremacy. Eventually in 1235, after almost a thousand years of unbroken supremacy, the great kingdom of Ghana fell.

The decline of Ghana marked the rise of the empire of Mali, West Africa's second great grassland empire. Kangaba, the little state that would become the mighty empire of Mali, was already more than two hundred years old when Ghana ceased to exist. During the later years of the empire, the Mandinka people of Kangaba had been middlemen in the gold trade, supplying the rulers of Ghana and their agents with gold from the rich mines of Wangara.

The disintegration of the Ghanaian Empire ignited a fierce struggle for power, which was eventually won by Sundiata Keita, the ruler of Kangaba. After this victory, Kangaba became known as Mali, which means "where the king resides." The Keita Kings of Mali, in the green, lush, and gold-bearing lands of the uppermost Niger Valley, incorporated what was left of ancient Ghana into their own considerably more extensive state. They gained control, not only of the gold-producing lands of Wangara and Bambuk, but also of most of Diara to the northwest. They extended their power down the Niger River all the way to the shores of Lake Deba, forming one of the largest empires on the face of the earth. By the middle of the fourteenth century, Mali's kings had acquired international fame as great and powerful rulers. The North African historian Ibn Khadun, writing at the beginning of the fifteenth century, described Mali as a mighty power that all the nations of the Sudan regarded with awe.

The Moroccan scholar Ibn Battuta, who traveled through the empire about twelve years after Mansa Musa's death, found complete and general safety throughout the land. Battuta, who lived in the court of the new ruler, Mansa Suleyman, described in 1352 the Emperor as "a miserly king, not a man from whom one might hope for a rich present." Battuta had expected, as he wrote in his memoirs, "robes of honor and money as gifts," but instead he received "three cakes of bread, and a piece of beef fried in native oil, and a calabash of sour curds."

His disappointment was understandable because the kings of the western Sudan were famous for their generosity. Only a few years earlier, while traveling through Cairo on a pilgrimage to Mecca, Mansa Musa and his retinue spent so much gold they influenced the price of the Egyptian dinar. Mali gold had fueled the trade of half the civilized world, and was then providing the metal for Europe's first gold currencies since Roman times. By that time, the empire was so large, it was said that it took four months to travel its length and the same to travel its width. It was perhaps not unreasonable to expect that such a rich and powerful king could do better than bread and a calabash of curds.

While the Moroccan scholar was disappointed with the Emperor's lack of generosity, he was extremely impressed with the pomp and brilliance of his court. On the days when he sat in audience, the king was preceded by musicians playing gold-and-silver-covered guitars and attended by three hundred slaves. After a leisurely stroll around the courtyard, it was the custom of the king to stop and glance regally at the assembled crowd before sedately mounting his throne to the blare of trumpets and bugles and the pounding of drums.

The king's party at these huge assemblies would include the men of power and influence in the kingdom. Strong linage chiefs, governors of provinces, commanders of cavalry, judges, men of God, tellers of oracles, and other high officials stood somberly on both sides of the silk-emblazoned throne, while drummers or dancers performed furiously or waited to begin. The pomp included Turkish pages who had been bought in Cairo, towering guards, thoroughbred hunting dogs on leashes, strutting grooms, and splendid riding horses in resplendent harness.

As befitting its status, literacy and even scholarship became firmly established in the major cities of the empire. But to ensure the success of their empire, the Mali rulers had to maintain firm control of the Niger waterway. This meant, in turn, controlling a non-Mande people, the Songhay, who controlled the fishing and canoe transport of the middle Niger. The cultural and linguistic differences between the Nilo-Saharan-speaking Songhay and the Malians, a Niger-Congo people, made it extremely difficult for Mande to control the Songhay capital of Goa. To overcome the Mande system, which was based on Islamic universalism, the Songhay king, Soni Ali, rallied his people by appealing to their traditional paganism; he launched a ceaseless military campaign that ended with the destruction of the Mali Empire.

The arrival of the Europeans in West Africa, toward the end of the fifteenth century, only accelerated the decline of the savannah kingdoms. For centuries, the states of the forest belt had looked north, to Ghana, Mali, Songhay, Kanem, and the Hausa city-states. They, in turn, had looked further north, across the Great Desert, to the Arab and Berber states of North Africa.

But with the coming of the ships and traders of Europe, the West African seaboard ceased being what Basil Davidson described as "the edge of nowhere" and became, instead, the focus of the trading aspirations of the West African peoples.

It was, of course, a relationship that would transform Africa, Europe, the Americas, and indeed the whole world, in ways that none of the parties could have foretold. But, like almost everything involving Africa, the truth about the nature of the relationship between West Africa and Europe has been grossly distorted. The West Africans were hardly the helpless and hapless victims, as so often portrayed, of a trading relationship they did not understand. Unlike the peoples of the Congo and the East African seaboard who had been unable to repel the onslaught of the Portuguese, West African states were societies with what Davidson described as great inner-coherence, self-confidence, and social and artistic vigor; until the middle of the nineteenth century, they were never conquered from the outside. There was, Davidson has written, "a great innate sense of resistance" on the Guinea coast.

The two sides might not have trusted each other, but they were bound together by a shared interest in trade. Consequently, the history of the Guinea coast during the three hundred years between 1550 and 1850 has aptly been described as an international partnership in risk and profit.

When the Portuguese, the earliest European explorers, arrived in West Africa, Benin was the greatest of the forest city-states. By then it was the powerful capital of an empire the size of southern England and Wales, and it was ruled by a king, the Oba, who stood at the apex of an aristocratic hierarchy. Sometime around 1400, more than one hundred years before the arrival of the Portuguese, the Bini royal house had decided to replace elective succession with primogeniture, which deprived the nobility of the ability to remove the king. Although some checks and balances in policy and administration remained, by 1600 the King had acquired such enormous power and prestige that he could only be approached by other men through an elaborate ritual of ceremonial self-abasement.

So impressed were the Portuguese with this wealthy and imposing city, and with the availability of large quantities of malguetta pepper (then extremely valuable in Europe as a means of keeping meat edible), that they hurriedly began a regular trading relationship. Eager to learn more of the unknown land of the white men, the king of Benin sent an ambassador to

Lisbon. The trip was extremely successful. The ambassador, who was described in official Portuguese archives of the time as a "man of good speech and natural wisdom," was feted at the Portuguese royal court and "returned to his own land in a ship of the Portuguese king's, and at his departure they made him a gift of rich clothes."

To curious Europeans, unable to penetrate the mystery and security that surrounded the Bini monarch, the king's palace had all the allure of a forbidden city. Dutch reports, which were far more extensive than Portuguese ones, described the king's court as "very great, within it having many great four-square Plaines, which round about them have Galleries, wherein there is always kept watch; I was so far within the Court, that I passed over four such great Plaines, and whosesoever I looked, still I saw Gates upon Gates, to go into other places, and in that sort I went as far as any Netherlander was, which was to the stable where his best horses stood."

Fifty years after that report a collection of African reports by Alfert Dapper, included an engraving of the Oba riding in ceremonial procession with the densely urban city in the background, was printed and published in Europe.

Another Dutch report, from about 1602, described Benin this way: "The Towne seemeth to be very great, when you enter it. You goe into a great broad street, not paved, which seemeth to be seven or eight times broader than the Warmoes Street in Amsterdam; which goeth right out, and never crooked, and when I was lodged with Mathews Cornelison it was at least a quarter of an houres going from the gate, and yet I could not see to the end of the street. At the gate where I entered on horseback, I saw a very high Bulwarke, very thick of earth, with a very deepe broad ditch, but it was drie and full of high trees.... The gate is a reasonable good gate, made of wood after their manner, which is to be shut, and there always there is watch holden."

The citizens of Benin were described as generally very civil and good-natured, but the traders of Europe were allowed only limited freedom to move around or trade in the city. The Benin authorities not only restricted the movement of Europeans around the city, they also kept tight control of external trade. Much of this trade, the Dutch discovered, was a royal monopoly and foreigners were not allowed to bargain or buy except through the Oba's delegates or merchants. As a result, both sides were at the mercy of these agents and merchants, and sales often took months to complete.

Internal trade was not as tightly controlled, according to the same Dutch report. "They also have severall places in the Towne, where they keep their Markets; in one place they have their great Market Day and in another place they hold their little market, called Ferro....They bring great store of ironworke to sell there, and instruments to fish withall, others to plow and to till the land withall; and many weapons, as assagaies and knives.... This market and traffique is there very orderly holden."

As the Europeans became better acquainted with West Africa, they became aware that Benin was only one of several forest kingdoms. To the west of Benin lay the home of the Yoruba people, whose livelihood was based on forest farming and whose special contribution to West Africa has been said to be their remarkable urban centers, which were probably unparalleled in tropical Africa. During ancient times, the capital towns of Yoruba states were linked in a confederation under the spiritual and political leadership of the senior Yoruba ruler, the oni of Ife. But, with the rise of Oyo in northern Yorubaland during the sixteenth century, the central influence of Ife began to decline.

Yoruba states ranged across a wide swatch of territory, from Dahomey in the far west to northward through the rolling country beyond the edge of the forest, as far as the Niger, above its confluence with the Benue. There, in the north, was Oyo, founded after many of the towns to the south. Because of its advantageous trading location, it was destined to become the capital of a powerful empire. Although handicapped by the presence of two types of tsetse fly, which made it impossible to breed horses, the people of Northern Yorubaland were able to incorporate horses into their armies by buying a steady supply from north of the Niger. This allowed them to train soldiers in the tactics and techniques of cavalry warfare, which was to become the basis of Oyo power.

The Oyo were not just fearsome warriors and experienced and canny traders; they were also highly skilled in the spinning, dyeing, and weaving of cotton. By the middle of the seventeenth century, Oyo had become a great regional power, a position it would maintain for more than 100 years. After years of military expansion, and after bitter internal debate and struggle, Oyo turned vigorously to policies of economic development, especially to slave trading with Europeans along the coast. But the emphasis on trade caused the Oyo ruler to begin neglecting the real power of his central government, his army, and this led to gradual decline and eventually to collapse.

The forest states of West Africa responded to the demands of the slave trade in different ways. Benin avoided deep involvement throughout the long period of the trade. Oyo, as we have seen, resisted for a while but eventually became deeply involved. The Fon rulers of Dahomey (modern Benin) also went into the trade reluctantly, but quickly began relying on it for guns and gunpowder. That was also true for Asante (modern Ghana), where the enormously disruptive power of the slave trade was to be most dramatically manifested. Long famous for its gold, Asante, although technologically inferior to its contemporaries in Europe, had advanced like the other forest states by the time of direct contact with Europeans through what Davidson described as "perceptible stages of political, cultural and economic development."

One of the newer states of the forest belt, Asante, was organized as a militarized confederation under the unchallenged leadership of a single ruler, the Asantehene. It was created near the end of the seventeenth century as a response to the intensive raiding of scattered groups of Akan people in the Asante forest by other forest peoples, who were responding to the growing European demand for slaves. To protect themselves from the increasing threat of the slave trade, the various branches of the Asante decided to create a single state and develop military power. Because of two remarkable men, Osei Tuto and Okomfo Enokye, they would succeed brilliantly at both tasks.

Before the creation of the Asante state, the Akan groups of the central forest zone were divided into linage groups based on ancestral loyalty. To help the Akan people develop a religious and national identity, Enokye made brilliant use of the traditions of the Asante people. W.E.F. Ward described how this was done. "One Friday a great gathering was held at Kumasi; and there Enokye brought down from the sky, with darkness and thunder, and in a thick cloud of white dust, a wooden stool adorned with gold, which floated to earth and alighted gently on Osei Tuto's knees. This stool, Enokye announced, contained the spirit of the whole Ashanti nation, and all its strength and bravery depended on the safety of the stool. This was the origin of the famous Sika Agua Kofi, Friday's Golden Stool, of Ashanti, which in spite of many vicissitudes still survives today with its unifying power unimpaired."

By 1700, the Asante had defeated their previous overlord, the powerful Denkyira, and had broken through to the sea. Despite numerous setbacks, the armies and traders of Asante would never lose their hold on the direct route to the coast. But the strength and security of the Asante Union depended, from the very beginning, on the ability of its rulers to acquire large quantities of firearms and ammunition. They were, however, unwilling to sell their own people as slaves, and since muskets could only be purchased with slaves, the Asante decided to conquer other states. Since other African nations were also attacking their neighbors in order to acquire firearms to protect themselves, control of the trade routes to the coast was essential. This required even more firearms, and consequently, the ambitious and determined Asante people created what was probably the most powerful slaving nation in Africa.

Despite its late start, the Asante Union quickly became a vital component in the powerful network of commercial partnerships that made the trans-Atlantic slave trade possible. The Asante Union steadily grew more powerful and quickly became the most powerful African nation in the region. Like other regional powers before them, they conquered the smaller states on the coast and incorporated them into their empire.

For the proud Asante, their success was sowing the seeds of future disaster. Frightened and resentful of their new subservient status, the peoples of the coastal statelets turned to their European partners for help. Things were also changing in Europe. Just as the slave trade had made Asante the dominant power in West Africa, so had it increasingly concentrated the power of Europe in a single nation: Britain. Inevitably, as Britain's imperial ambitions grew, a rivalry developed between the dominant powers of Europe and Africa for control of the coast. It was a battle that the long-isolated, technologically inferior Africans could not win.

Initially, the British established diplomatic relations with the Asantehene at his capital in Kumasi in the Asante forest, but with imperialism at full tide, they invaded. The outgunned but determined and fierce Africans were not easily subdued. It required several bitterly fought wars and many setbacks before the British, despite their enormous technological advantage, were able to conquer the country. The final chapter in the story was not written until 1902, when Asante was incorporated into the British Empire. British power would not, however, long prevail in Africa. Within a mere fifty-five years, the proud people of the Asante Union would regain their freedom as part of the independent state of Ghana.

16

The Pure Race Myth and the African Origins of Modern Humans

T
he 1967 decision of South Africa's Supreme Court to uphold the classification of 11-year-old Sandra Laing as a colored person, although her parents and all of her siblings were classified as white, revealed more than the moral bankruptcy and intellectual confusion of apartheid. Even more importantly, it laid bare the fallacy that human populations can neatly and cleanly be categorized into discrete groups or races.

When she was reclassified as colored by the Race Classification Board, Laing was labeled a genetic throwback, showing strong nonwhite characteristics. After dismissing an application by her father to classify her as white, the judge attempted to reassure the family by pointing out that the girl might still become white under pending legislation that would make descent, rather than appearance and general acceptance, the standard for race classification.

To Americans and others from countries where miscegenation has long been a fact of life, Laing's story is a sad but familiar one. Our response is to immediately assume, as evidently the Race Classification Board had, that Sandra's physical appearance—her phenotype—was simply a belated but accurate expression of latent African genealogy—her genotype. Perhaps it was, but given the deep racial divisions in South Africa and the physical appearance of the rest of the family, it is more likely that the Laing case, more clearly than most, demonstrated that "similar phenotypes in the same or in different populations are not, because of that similarity, closer to each other genetically than they are to other phenotypes." More simply, external appearance alone is an unreliable way of determining genetic similarity.

This does not imply, of course, that populations cannot be grouped into larger units that share certain similarities. It does mean that the sharing of certain similarities, such as skin color and hair texture, is probably no more reliable an indicator of genetic similarity than grouping by height and body type, or by blood type and disease-susceptibility profile, or by any similar grouping. What should be considered an important part of this debate is the fact that the concept of pure races arose not as a result of dispassionate scientific inquiry, but as ideological theory driven by racial pride and political opportunism.

The truth is that modern humans are such a young species, and are therefore so closely related, that despite differences between groups in external appearance, a wide variety of genetic types is present in every existing population grouping. This is why there is greater genetic variability among individuals in any population grouping than between population groups. In fact, using sophisticated mathematical analysis, scientists ascribe more than 80 percent of the genetic differences between humans to those found among individuals, and less than 20 percent to those found between groups from major geographical areas.

The pure race concept began when European students of philology discovered, at the beginning of the nineteenth century, that there were "systematic similarities" between the ancient languages of India and Iran on one hand and the major language groups of Europe and the Romance languages developed from them on the other. Similarities in vocabulary, grammar, syntax, and phonetics between Sanskrit, Zend, Greek and Latin, and the Teutonic, Slavic and Celtic languages convinced the aspiring linguists that all the languages must have developed by gradual divergence from one original or mother language. Because the daughter languages covered an enormous geographical area, from the Ganges Valley to the border of the Bay of Biscay and the North Sea, the hypothetical mother language was named Indo-European, and the hypothetical people who spoke it were called Indo-Europeans.

While linguistic research has confirmed the common origin of the Indo-European languages, there is no evidence that the people who spoke Indo-European, and who came to be known as Aryans, ever constituted a single, "pure" race. The term Aryan was taken from the name that the Sanskrit-speaking invaders of India gave to themselves. Throughout the nineteenth century, as James C. King explained in *The Biology of Race*, "This fanciful theory was elaborated and embellished and used to support a variety of claims to national grandeur and superiority. It was used not only by the Nazis but at one time or another by English, Greek, French, and pre-German apologists as well."

Although there have been many versions of the Aryan story, a common theme united them: that of a vigorous and conquering people who traveled abroad subduing inferior peoples, bringing with them not only their language and their culture but also their intelligence, ethical sense, and superior genes. These noble souls, the fable went, were contaminated in varying degrees by the conquered peoples with whom they unfortunately intermingled. Not surprisingly, the various proponents of this myth, since they represented different physical types, were never able to agree on an exact description of an uncontaminated Aryan, and therefore never agreed on just how the nature and degree of contamination could be determined.

The notion that the speakers of a common language necessarily represent a single "pure" race has no basis in biology, history, or common sense. In the Hellenistic period, Greek, originally spoken only along the Ionian coast, spread eastward into the interior; it replaced scores of local languages, becoming during Roman and Medieval times the language of all Anatolia. After the Turkish conquest in the late Middle Ages, Turkish replaced Greek. The change in languages, from pre-Greek to Greek and from Greek to Turkish, was not accompanied by a corresponding change in the genetic character of the population. Similarly, in Roman times, the populations of Gaul and Spain became Latinized without being colonized by the Romans, abandoning Celtic and other languages in favor of Latin.

On the other hand, the people of northeastern Spain and southwestern France have retained their pre-Latin language, Basque. Today, the people of Asturias, which lies to the west of Basque territory, speak a dialect of Spanish, an Indo-European language derived from Latin. Although the Asturians spoke a pre-Latin language before the Roman period, there is absolutely no evidence that the linguistic change, from pre-Latin to Latin to

Spanish, was accompanied by genetic changes in the population; nor is there evidence that there is now any less genetic similarity between Asturians and Basques than there was before their language divergence.

Before Darwin, taxonomists in the eighteenth and nineteenth centuries believed that each species had been specially created in the remote past, and that every species had an ideal type that could only be imperfectly represented by any single individual. Derived from Genesis and Plato, these ideas not only profoundly influenced the early taxonomists, but also continue to confuse our attempts to understand animal and human variation, despite their refutation by modern science.

But in 1795, when the German physician Blumenbach decided to classify human populations, Darwin had not yet written *The Origin of Species;* indeed he would not be born for another fourteen years. Although he identified five "varieties"—Caucasian, Mongolian, Ethiopian, American and Malay—Blumenbach also pointed out that the "innumerable varieties of mankind run into one another by insensible degrees." Demonstrating a remarkably modern grasp of biological theory, he not only considered and rejected the contention that some populations of men constituted separate species, but described his own classification method, which was based on hair, skin and eye color and facial features, as "arbitrary." Nevertheless, Blumenbach would designate five skulls in his collection as ideal representatives of his five human groups.

Because the skull that supposedly exemplified the European group was that of a Georgian woman, the group would be labeled the "Caucasian variety," by Blumenbach. Describing the variety of mankind to which he belonged in lyrical terms, Blumenbach discarded any pretense of objectivity. He explained that he had taken the name from Mount Caucasus "because its neighborhood... produces the most beautiful race of men, I mean the Georgian." In a footnote he amplified these feelings by quoting from another author who had obviously actually traveled to Georgia: "The blood of Georgia is the best of the East, and perhaps in the world. I have not observed a single ugly face in that country, in either sex; but I have seen angelic ones. Nature has there lavished upon the women beauties, which are not be seen elsewhere. I consider it impossible to look at them without loving them."

Despite this, Blumenbach's book was not illustrated with pictures of living people. The beautiful women of Georgia were represented by what he described as "the most beautiful form of the skull."

For many years, European scientists would almost completely ignore Blumenbach's observation that the human races blended together. Instead, they tried to define human groups with ever-greater precision by placing greater and greater emphasis on morphology. Since there is great variability within every group, European populations began to be divided into subgroups, such as Nordic, Alpine, Mediterranean, Baltic, Dinaric, and even more obscure races and subtypes. The apex or climax of this farce was reached in 1955 when the Peabody Museum of Harvard University published the work of E. A. Hooton, who had attempted to classify the population of Ireland into eight racial categories. Although the two-volume study was based on extensive measurements and observations of the Irish population during the 1930s, the investigation offered no meaningful conclusion, and in the post-Nazi era it was largely dismissed as irrelevant by an indifferent public.

While the racial distinctions between Europeans—and, progressively, between Europeans and Asians—are increasingly regarded as insignificant and unimportant, that sentiment does not yet include Africans and other dark-skinned racial groups. That is largely true because of the understandable but mistaken view that firm and accurate conclusions about genotype—an individual's genetic makeup—can be reached by observation of their phenotype, or their physical appearance. It is true that certain ethnic groups (e.g., West Africans) are more likely than other people to possess certain physiological traits that endow some of its members with superior athletic abilities. This, however, does not negate the contention that membership in a racial or ethnic group does not imply that, individually, the members of that group are more similar to each other, in broader genetic measurements, than to individuals in other groups. Instead, it spotlights the confusion of genotype with phenotype and underlines and reinforces a central tenet of this book: the anatomical and physiological differences between Africans and other racial groups are genetically minor and biologically insignificant.

It is equally true that beneath the skin we are all the same color, and that color does not tell us what lies beneath the skin. That is, it is universally accepted that all members of a species, despite individual differences in detail, share a common genetic system. Analogous parts of the genetic information can be interchanged throughout the species; that is in fact the very definition of species. To fully understand why individuals with a common genetic system vary in appearance as much as humans do, it is important to begin with at least a basic comprehension of the laws of Mendelian inheritance.

The principle that individuals inherit characteristics through the combination of genes from both parents was discovered by the Moravian monk, Gregor Johann Mendel, the founder of the science of genetics. After entering the Augustinian monastery at Brno in 1843, Mendel unlocked the secrets of heredity by spending a quarter of a century experimenting with plants, primarily garden peas. He discovered that individuals inherit one of two alternative alleles—or forms—of a gene from each parent, which means that each person has one of the following combinations at each gene site: two dominant alleles, two recessive alleles, or one of each.

If both parents are heterozygous (that is, if they have one dominant and one recessive allele), the three genotypes will occur among the offspring with the following probabilities: one homozygous dominant, two heterozygotes, one homozygous recessive. Phenotypically (that is in appearance), the two heterozygotes will be identical to the homozygous dominant, but the homozygous recessive will be phenotypically different from the other two genotypes. One of the best-known examples of this principle is eye color. Individuals with blue eyes are only homozygous recessive, while brown-eyed individuals are either homozygous dominant or heterozygous. This explains why brown eyes are far more common than blue ones.

Because the heredity of most characteristics that account for differences between individuals—such as height, weight, body proportions, hair texture, and skin pigmentation—are controlled by polygenic systems, the laws of inheritance and development are more complex than these rules would indicate. Instead of one pair of alleles, the characteristics that vary continuously (such as weight), instead of existing in contrasting states (like eyes), are influenced by several pairs, each existing in a plus or minus form. If height, for example, were controlled by four independent loci, at each of which there are plus or minus alleles, a variety of outcomes would be possible. If every allele added or subtracted one increment of stature, individuals at the extremes of the probable outcomes would have eight minus or eight plus alleles, two at each locus, four from each parent.

Since the same principle applies to the other continuously varying characteristics, it is possible for siblings with the same parents to vary considerably in height, weight, body proportions, skin color, hair texture, etc. It is also possible for phenotypically similar sets of parents to produce very different-looking offspring. But even this model probably vastly oversimplifies reality, since few, if any, continuously varying characteristics are controlled by as few as four genetic loci. It is also true that while any one individual may have only two different alleles per locus, in the population as a whole the alleles at any given locus almost certainly vary considerably in functional efficiency; every genotype is susceptible to environmental modification. It is possible, therefore, for genotypes, through accidents of internal malfunctioning or unusual environmental pressures, to produce improbable phenotypes.

The fact that we all belong to a single species with a common genetic system, and are fashioned by a process so wondrously complex it could only have been invented by the Creator, ensures that each of us, in all our billions, is unique and special. And that is probably what the Sandra Laings are sent to remind us.

The distinguished Victorians of London's Ethnographical Society were especially proud of the liberal breadth of their international outlook. But the French gentleman invited to one of their elegant gatherings in 1861 to speak on his travels through the unexplored forests of equatorial Africa had made shocking suggestions that even they could not accept. The speaker, M. du Chailu, had dared to suggest that a tribe of naked savages, called the Mpongwa, possessed a number of redeeming features including a religion for which he expressed more than a little respect. The idea that black Africans were more than savages with brains too small for civilized development was, of course, completely unacceptable in Victorian England.

For a long time—in fact until fairly recently—the theory that "anatomically modern humans evolved from an archaic form of homo sapiens in Africa and then, about 100,000 years ago, swept out of Africa to colonize Europe, Asia, and eventually the rest of the world" was just as unacceptable to many modern anthropologists. That view of the origins of modern humans was first expressed by Dr. Christopher B. Stringer, of the Natural History Museum in London, during a debate among anthropologists about the relationship between modern humans and Neanderthals.

One school of thought, led by Dr Stringer, contended that Neanderthals were driven to extinction and replaced by modern humans who originated in

Africa about 200,000 years ago. The other school, headed by Milford Wolpoff of the University of Michigan, argued just as passionately that modern humans evolved from Neanderthals in Europe, and from other archaic species of *Homo sapiens* in other parts of the world.

The theory that modern human races were created separately is, of course, not new. In 1962, the anthropologist Carleton Coon argued that modern man was "born" several times in different parts of the world. And in the nineteenth century, the so-called polygenists held that human races were separate biological species, the descendants of different Adams. As another form of life, black Africans, they contended, did not have to participate in the equality of man. The other, softer, or more liberal school adhered to the biblical view that the races had a single source. The monogenists, as they were called, also believed that human races are a product of degeneration by different degrees. Not surprisingly, even these "liberals" believed that black Africans had declined the most and Europeans the least.

Since the question of racial ranking has, unfortunately but consistently, poisoned the debate about the origins of modern humans, it is not surprising that for a long time most white specialists (and almost all the specialists are white) proposed a European origin for modern humans. So while some experts proposed, as early as 1975, a unique origin for modern humans in sub-Saharan Africa, even today people like Dr. Wolpoff still argue that Neanderthals were, at least in part, the ancestors of modern humans.

Nevertheless, both modern schools agree that man's earliest ancestors appeared in Africa more than five million years ago and eventually evolved into a prehuman creature called *Homo erectus*. Some populations of *Homo erectus* then migrated out of Africa into the rest of the Old World and evolved in different places into various archaic versions of *Homo sapiens,* including the Neanderthals. The disagreement over the Neanderthals' relationship to modern humans is, as the *New York Times* explained, "about what happened after that."

The Stringer School has embraced what has been called the "Garden of Eden" theory, that a founding population of *Homo erectus* evolved into anatomically modern humans in Africa, and then replaced primitive types all over the world. Perhaps, most controversially, at least at the time, they also believed that there was little or no interbreeding between these conquering Africans and archaic forms of Homo sapiens like the Neanderthals.

The Wolpoff school scornfully rejected that view. They proposed instead a "multi-regional" model of modern man's origins. In that view, modern man evolved independently in different parts of the world, with some interbreeding between the various groups. By this formulation, the African *erectus* fathered modern Africans, the Chinese *erectus* fathered modern Chinese, the European *erectus* fathered modern Europeans, and so on. That meant, of course, that Neanderthals, not invading Africans, were the immediate ancestors of modern Europeans.

It is not difficult to believe that many of the proponents of the "multi-regional" model are racially motivated, since the theory bears a striking resemblance to the one proposed by Carleton Coon in 1962. In his book, *The Origin of Races,* Coon insisted that modern humans had not appeared suddenly "fully formed as from the brow of Zeus" in one place, and that the "visible and invisible differences between living races could be explained only in terms of history." Each major race, he insisted, "had followed a pathway of its own through the labyrinth of time." Coon then openly discarded the veil of scientific objectivity by suggesting that African civilization was less advanced because black people were the last to evolve into modern humans. While conceding that the first hominids may have arisen in Africa, Coon argued that the evolution of modern humans seemed to have occurred first in Europe and Asia. "If Africa was the cradle of mankind it was only an indifferent kindergarten," he concluded.

Coon has since been proven wrong even by the paleoanthropological evidence. Fossils subsequently discovered in Africa are now widely believed to be from modern humans living there about 100,000 years ago. These bones represent the earliest known modern humans. Before the discovery of these fossils, as *Newsweek* pointed out in a 1988 article, "it was assumed that modern humans didn't evolve until 35,000 years ago, which is when they first appear in the European fossil records. So blacks were clearly not the last group to reach modernity."

A concern about racial ranking is not the only consideration influencing the debate about the origins of modern humans. To some extent it is also being shaped by a struggle between competing scientific disciplines. For a long time, the practitioners of the softer sciences, such as paleoanthropologists, drove and dominated the debate about man's origins. And for centuries before that, the creation myths of the major religions had been taught and accepted as the literal truth. Until the second half of the nineteenth century, the vast majority of scholars, laymen, and clergy believed that the creation story of the Bible literally and accurately recounted the prehistory of the world.

As C.L. Brace and M.F. Ashley Montagu explained in *Man's Evolution*: "All attempts to view the present state of the world as the outcome of the operation of natural forces were viewed with suspicion, hostility and fear, as contrary to the teachings of the scriptures. The suggestion that man himself might have developed in a similar manner was regarded as blasphemous."

It was in that intellectual atmosphere that Darwin wrote *The Origin of Species*. Although the epochal work had very little to say about man himself, it explained the mechanism through which evolution worked and injected new direction and energy into the science of anthropology. The work of the Leakeys in East Africa in the 1950s first gave credibility to the theory that mankind may have originated in Africa. Their flair for publicity and the development of fairly reliable potassium-argon dating methods not only dramatically increased the level of financial support for archeological activity, but also brought a flood of young and idealistic students into the field. As a result, until the 1980s, explanations of humankind's progression from ape to modern man were the unchallenged province of paleoanthropologists and their Y-shaped trees.

That changed forever in 1983. Men and women in white lab coats launched a major invasion of the previously exclusive and unassailable terrain of the fossil hunters. The assault began on the very first day of the year in the form of an article in *Nature*. The piece, titled "Mitochondrial DNA and human evolution," was both highly technical and, to paleoanthropologists, extremely startling. The essence of the challenge to the paleoanthropologistic view of human origins was contained in just two brief sentences: "Mitochondrial DNAs from 147 people, drawn from five geographic populations, have been analyzed by restriction mapping. All these mitochondrial DNAs stem from one woman who is postulated to have lived about 200,000 years ago."

Although *Nature* has an international circulation of just 40,000, the opening salvo of the war reverberated around the world. Despite its limited circulation, *Nature* is the most prestigious scientific publication in the entire world; almost every new biological, astronomical, chemical, and anthropological announcement is made in its pages. It is where the first identification of the AIDS virus was announced, where the discovery of lasers was first explained, and where James Watson and Francis Crick had first outlined the very structure of DNA itself. It was also where the Leakeys announced many of their great fossil finds. Intense debate was often sparked by technical reports that were not much more than a page in length, or by mere letters to the editor.

The authors of the article were Allan C. Wilson and Mark Stoneking of the University of California at Berkeley, and Rebecca L. Cann of the University of Hawaii. They had discovered that mitochondrial DNA provided "new perspectives on how, where and when the human gene pool arose and grew." Mitochondrial DNA, unlike nuclear DNA, is inherited only maternally and, except for occasional minor mutations, is passed intact from great grandmother to grandmother to daughter without the complication of recombination. For that reason, the paper explained, mitochondrial DNA, unlike nuclear DNA, where recombination does take place, was a powerful new tool "for relating individuals to one another."

But mitochondrial DNA has other advantages for genetic sleuthing. While the nuclear DNA, which is contained in the nucleus of the cell, is composed of perhaps 60,000 genes, the DNA from the mitochondria, the energy-producing compartments of the cell, contain only thirty-seven genes, all inherited by both sexes solely from their mothers. The human race is therefore connected, Wilson explained, "by an unbroken chain of mothers—whether you're a son or a daughter—back into the past. And what we're interested in doing is building up a genealogical tree that connects these maternal chains."

Not only does the mitochondrial DNA allow geneticists to look straight into the female past, it also provides an unparalleled view of genetic diversity, because mutations accumulate much faster in mitochondrial DNA than they do in the nucleus. Since mutations in the mitochondrial DNA occur at a set rate of two to four percent every million years, the changes in mitochondrial DNA throughout the ages are a kind of molecular clock. Wilson argued that neutral mutations accumulate at approximately the same rate in all organisms, from bacteria to humans. "The same basic rate of ticking, the same rate per year, is observed in all of these creatures, so in this vast array of organisms, we have a timepiece ticking away in a statistical fashion, and allowing us the possibility of being able to put a time scale onto all of evolution, regardless of whether the species have a fossil record."

A measure of the confidence the geneticists had in the new technique was the claim made by Cann that it was "entirely possible that we could identify Cleopatra's mitochondrial genes in modern people and, at least theoretically, also specify her entire mitochondrial genotype." More to the point, the technique allowed scientists to study racial groups and accurately determine which group has accumulated the most mutations. The group with the most mutations is the most divergent among each other and is assumed to be the oldest; because the longer a population has been around the more mutations it would have accumulated.

To conduct the historical experiment that would lead to the discovery of the mitochondrial Eve, the geneticists first had to persuade 147 women to donate their placentas to the project. This part of the experiment was headed by Cann, and she selected American women with ancestors from Africa, Europe, the Middle East, and Asia. She also had collaborators in New Guinea and Australia who found Aboriginal women in these countries. After the babies were born, the placentas were gathered, frozen, and sent to Wilson's lab in Berkeley for tissue analysis. There, as described by *Newsweek*, "the tissues were ground in a souped-up Waring blender, mixed with a cell-breaking detergent, dyed fluorescent and spun in a centrifuge again." The result was a clear liquid containing pure mitochondrial DNA.

Mitochondrial DNA, as already noted, is not affected by recombination, but it is altered by mutations that are sudden, random mistakes in copying the genetic code. These "mistakes" are then passed on to the next generation. Each random mutation then produces a new type of DNA as distinctive as a fingerprint. And since there is an almost incalculable number of ways to rearrange the units of the genetic code, the odds against two identical mitochondrial DNAs appearing are almost non-existent.

To study these mutations, the Berkeley researchers then cut each sample of DNA into segments that could be compared with the DNA of other babies. The results were surprising, even shocking. The differences, although clear, were unexpectedly small, without even telltale distinctions between the races. As Stoneking explained, "We're a young species, and there are really very few genetic differences among cultures. In terms of our mitochondrial DNA, we're much more closely related than almost any other vertebrate or mammalian species. You find New Guineans whose DNA is closer to other Asians than to other New Guineans.

"This is so," Stoneking continued, because many racial differences "represent trivial changes. Skin color, for instance, is a minor adaptation to climate—black in Africa for protection from the sun, white in Europe to absorb ultraviolet radiation that helps produce vitamin D. It takes only a few thousand years of evolution for skin color to change. The important changes—in brain size, for instance—can take hundreds of thousands of years."

Despite the surprisingly small differences, the geneticists concluded that the DNA of the babies seemed to form a family tree rooted in Africa. *Newsweek* reported that "The DNA fell into two general categories, one found only in some babies of recent African descent, and the second found in everyone else and the other Africans. There was more diversity among the exclusively African group's DNA, suggesting that it had accumulated more mutations because it had been around longer—and thus was the longest branch of the family tree, and then at some point a group of Africans emigrated, splitting off to form a second branch of DNA and carrying it to the rest of the world."

The DNA of the babies, the geneticists discovered, could all be traced back, ultimately, to one woman. This was not surprising to statisticians familiar with the vagaries of genetic inheritance. As Wilson explained, "there must be one lucky mother. Although, to a layman, it may seem highly unlikely that the source of all the mitochondrial DNA in the entire world was a single woman, it is a well-known outcome of the laws of probability." The disappearance of family names is a similar phenomenon. These, like mitochondrial DNA, are generally passed along by only one sex—in this case, male. As the *Newsweek* article pointed out, "if a son marries and has two children, there's a one-in-four chance that he'll have two daughters. There's also a chance that he won't have any children. Eventually the odds catch up and a generation passes without a male heir, and the name disappears."

To John Avise, a geneticist at the University of Georgia, "it's an inevitable consequence of reproduction. Lineages will be going extinct all the time." To demonstrate his point, Avise pointed to the history of Pitcairn Island in the Pacific, which had been settled in 1790 by thirteen Tahitian women and six British sailors who had mutinied on the Bounty. Half of the original names had disappeared after only seven generations, and if the island had remained isolated everyone on the island would, eventually, have the same last name. A visitor would then conclude that all the inhabitants had descended from one man—call him the Pitcairn Adam.

Although traditional anthropologists found it difficult to deny the possibility of a mitochondrial Eve, they were startled at the projected date of her birthday, which the geneticists calculated by counting the number of mutations in her DNA. They took the oldest branch of the human family tree—the one with the DNA types that differed most from each other—and then figured out how many years it would have taken for the mitochondrial Eve's original DNA to mutate into those different types. On the basis of this molecular calculation, the Berkeley researchers concluded that the mitochondrial Eve must have lived somewhere between 140,000 and 290,000 years ago.

The announcement stunned the paleoanthropological community. Not only was the new technique unfamiliar to the vast majority of anthropologists, but it also seemed frighteningly complex and precise. As Michael Brown noted, "there is nothing more controversial to a paleoanthropologist than a claim that someone can precisely describe when and where and how man arose from a primordial, ape-filled past. As frequently as not, paleoanthropologists can't even agree on the most basic things. Often they see different traits, different species, and far different implications—sometimes even a different genus—in the very same cranium."

Anthropologists are notorious, even amongst themselves, for their highly opinionated and individualistic way of interpreting fossils and presenting evolutionary trees. So much so that on those rare occasions when two or three of them agree on an issue (or even a part of an issue), the agreement becomes, it has only partially in jest been suggested, a theory or school of thought. The eminent paleoanthropologist Clark Howell concurred with this relatively negative assessment of his colleagues: "You can't really tell who thinks what this week or last month. The consensus is who shouts the loudest."

Suddenly, anthropologists who had rescued the debate about the origins of man from the stifling embrace of religion were faced with the very real prospect of losing the initiative to a new kind of scientist. This new breed worked in air-conditioned American laboratories instead of desiccated African rift valleys, and were trained in molecular biology instead of anatomy. While paleoanthropologists had generally concluded that the oldest of the man-apes and ape-men had been born in Africa, there was no consensus on just where the next major stage in human development, the formation of anatomically modern man, had taken place.

As expected, anthropologists were divided on this subject. There were those who, like Wolpoff and his allies, were convinced that *Homo sapiens* had evolved independently in many different places and were connected to each other only by occasional sexual intermixing. Others were just as convinced that a select population of *H. erectus* evolved into *Homo sapiens* in one region, and then replaced the more primitive types in the rest of the world.

Although the evidence of the fossil records was overwhelmingly in favor of Africa as the single point of origin, the bones said different things to different anthropologists. To many of them, Africa figured only in the distant past. Howell, then at Berkeley, and an extremely influential paleoanthropologist, strongly believed that "The idea of an African origin for anatomically modern man was still not quite there." While willing to concede that there was the "conceivable possibility," he maintained that the "the evidence was so equivocal or unconvincing or inadequate, that people were probably unwilling to hang their hats on that stance. Eurasia was still a consideration. India was a possibility talked about."

Despite the virtual absence of meaningful evidence, Europe remained, in the minds of some anthropologists, a feasible candidate as a region where *H. erectus* had evolved into anatomically modern man. But the real debate pitted Asia against Africa, although the evidence for Asia was only marginally stronger than it was for Europe. The real problem was explained very clearly by Brown: "Africa was fine as the rootstock of man-apes and ape-men but the delicate evolution to *homo sapiens*—millions of years after the first australopithecines had been spawned—seemed better placed in areas where civilization was most advanced."

For many, the very idea that modern man not only originated in Africa but then also replaced all primitive types living in Asia and Europe was too traumatic to even contemplate. To do so would be to give up long-cherished notions of white superiority and entitlement, and to indict hundreds of years of European history. Given the racial bias against Africa, the sentiments for Asia as the cradle of mankind would remain strong, as long as nobody could disprove that it was not. The standards of proof for Africa and Asia, anthropologists made very clear, were very different. William H. Howells, another major anthropologist, explained the difficulty facing those who would attempt to disprove that Asia was man's first homeland. "Paucity of fossils and infirmity of dates remain a central problem," he wrote.

But the men and women in the white coats faced no such restriction. They, as reported by *Newsweek*, "looked at an international assortment of genes and picked up a trail of DNA that led them to a single woman from whom we're all descended." The evidence produced by the geneticists was both staggeringly detailed and compelling. A genealogical tree, which resembled a huge, encrypted horseshoe, replaced simple line charts, with 134 little twigs representing the mitochondrial mother. It was a bewildering maze. The ancestral lines could easily have been mistaken for the diagram of an electric plant. A long and undecipherable block of code numbers listed polymorphic restriction sites. It looked like something only a computer could read.

The geneticists were openly disdainful of the old-school paleoanthropologists and the limitations of fossils. Rebecca Cann observed that "Besides the likelihood that the most sought after bones will not materialize, there is the problem of properly identifying the fossils that are found. It is hard to know, by bone shape alone, whether a fossil represents a species already identified or whether it is different enough to represent a species of its own. Then there is the difficulty of knowing whether the fossil was left by a human ancestor or by a related primate that became extinct. All in all, it is too much to hope that the trickle of bones from the fossil beds of eastern Africa will, in itself, provide a clear picture of human evolution any time soon."

She pointedly added: "As molecular biologists, we at least knew that the genes available from present-day specimens came from some ancestor. In contrast, paleoanthropologists can never be certain that a given fossil has left descendants." Wilson was even more blunt: "Some people don't like our conclusions, but I expect they will be proved wrong again."

Wilson was referring to an earlier skirmish with the paleoanthropologists. For many years, most anthropologists had held that hominids started evolving away from the forebears of our closest relative, the chimpanzee, at least fifteen million years ago. But in 1967, geneticists led by Wilson and Vincent Sarich introduced contradictory evidence into the debate. Using blood drawn from baboons, chimps, and humans, they studied the molecular structure of a blood protein that was believed to change at a slow, steady rate as a species evolved.

As the geneticists expected, there were major differences between the molecules of chimps and baboons, confirming that the two species had been evolving separately for thirty million years. The difference between humans and chimps was, however, surprisingly small—so small that Wilson and Sarich concluded that humans and chimps parted company only five million years ago. Other geneticists, using different methods, concluded that the separation had taken place seven million years ago.

Traditional anthropologists, not surprisingly, resented being told their estimates were wrong by eight or ten million years. As a result, the genetic calculation was dismissed and ignored for more than a decade, to Wilson's considerable displeasure. Cann recalled that Wilson, who won a MacArthur "genius grant" in 1986, "was called a lunatic for ten years." But eventually the geneticists were vindicated by the bones themselves. Anthropologists finally realized, as more fossils turned up, that the 15-million-year-old bones did not belong to a human ancestor and that chimps and humans did indeed diverge much more recently.

Despite their earlier defeat, the anthropologists were not about to sit by and allow the upstarts in the white coats to take over their traditional turf without a fight. They blasted the Berkeley researchers for getting most of their African DNA samples from American blacks, whose ancestors could have mixed with Europeans and American Indians. The criticism seemed valid. Cann explained there hadn't been the money to get a good sampling from the African continent and that there were "political" problems getting blood or placentas in Africa. Despite their trepidation, Cann, Stoneking, and Wilson decided to go ahead with the experiment, even if the only samples available were from American blacks. They reasoned that black Americans would have African mitochondrial genes because sex between the races had been primarily between white men and black women.

The assumption was widely attacked, but Stoneking countered by describing the objections as irrational. He reminded the critics that mitochondrial DNA is maternally inherited and that because, until recently, interracial interactions in the United States would have been restricted almost exclusively to white males with black females, it was unlikely that there would be any contribution of Caucasian mitochondrial DNAs to the black American mitochondrial DNA gene pool. He also pointed out that there were a number of restriction site polymorphisms that appeared in the black American sample which were characteristic of native African populations.

Despite their confidence in the methodology and the conclusions of the first experiment, the Berkeley researchers decided to do it all over again—

this time with many samples from native sub-Saharan peoples. The second experiment included mitochondrial DNA samples from 189 people, including the King of Botswana; the eastern Pygmies of Zaire and the western Pygmies of the Central African Republic; the Yorubas of Nigeria and several other African populations; Europeans, Asians and American blacks. The results, as reported in *Nature*, also concluded that the common ancestor of modern humans lived in Africa very recently, between 166,000 and 249,000 years ago.

Dr. Linda Vigilant, who helped write the report and began her studies under Dr. Wilson (who died before the paper was published), claimed that the new paper had made a major advance in firming up the placement of an ancestor in Africa. "We have done the work much more rigorously than before, and now the statistical methods are there for people to make their own independent assessments."

The new paper, which even Wolpoff praised for its technical elegance, made converts of some former skeptics. Chief among them was Dr. Douglas C. Wallace of Emory University in Atlanta, a highly respected molecular geneticist who had also compared mitochondrial DNA of different human populations. Wallace, the *New York Times* reported, insisted that the only possible interpretation of the data was that modern humans came from Africa relatively recently and did not intermix with others. Wallace explained that while he did not know what happened to *Homo erectus*, "our mitochondrial DNA data indicate a single flowering of *Homo sapiens* in Africa about 150,000 to 250,000 years ago. I don't feel there's any question about that. I've seen some of the fossils Wolpoff has, and they're interesting and provocative, but I don't feel they're compelling enough to sway me against the molecular data."

But to the strongest critics of the out-of-Africa theory the new evidence was still not enough. Wolpoff, who clung to his belief that our common ancestors lived about a million years ago, derisively dismissed the theory of the geneticists by suggesting that if Eve's descendants had wiped out all rivals, the new theory should be named after her murderous son, Cain. To separate himself from the openly racist Coon, Wolpoff rejected not only the "Garden of Eden" theory but also Coon's so-called candelabra theory. He compared his to a trellis: "the separate races gradually evolving along parallel lines but connected by a network of genes flowing back and forth. The Neanderthals turned into modern Europeans, while Peking Man's descendants were becoming modern Chinese. Immigrants brought in new genes, but the natives' basic traits survived. This would explain why both the Neanderthals and the modern Europeans have big noses, why Peking Man and current residents of Beijing have flat faces, why today's aboriginal Australians have flat foreheads like Java Man."

Other anthropologists found these similarities unconvincing. It might, they explained, just be a coincidence that modern Europeans have big noses like the Neanderthals; they were, after all, subject to the same or similar environmental conditions. More striking to the "Garden of Eden" proponents were the differences between ancients and moderns. Modern Europeans, they argued, are much less stocky than Neanderthals; their arms and legs are proportioned far more like those of humans from the tropics. Not only is there no clear sign in the fossil records of a transition from Neanderthals to modern man, they pointed out, but scientists have now firmly established, for the first time, that Neanderthals lived in Western Europe as recently as 36,000 years ago, several thousand years after the first modern humans are believed to have appeared there.

That development was announced in an article in the *New York Times* on June 27, 1992. The article, based on a report in *Nature*, reported that French scientists had confirmed that a "Neanderthal skeleton discovered at an archeological site near the village of St. Cesaire, north of the city of Bordeaux, is the most recent identified so far." Because the radiocarbon dating is ineffective with objects as old as the skeleton, the scientists used another dating technique, thermo-luminescence, on the flint tools found with the skeleton. The technique, which involves an analysis of light released when the flint is heated, yielded an age of 36,000 years, with a margin of error of plus or minus 2,700 years.

The paper was authored primarily by Norbert Mercier, a physicist at the Center of Low-level Radioactivity at Gif-sur-Yvette, France. It pointed out that despite the relatively late date of the St. Cesaire remains, the skull "has classic Neanderthal features," which, as the *New York Times* explained, is "beetle-browed, with a low forehead, deep eye sockets and an extremely elongated face." Because the St. Cesaire skull shows no evidence of evolution in the direction of modern humans, the authors concluded that the idea that Neanderthals became extinct by evolving into modern humans "becomes chronologically untenable at least in Western Europe." Dr. Richard

B. Klein, a paleoanthropologist at the University of Chicago, noted that even allowing for some error, Neanderthals and moderns were too close together in time to allow for one to evolve into the other.

The *Times* reported Klein's view that the Cro-Magnons, or first moderns, "were set apart from the Neanderthals by their superior culture, especially the ability to innovate and to create a wide variety of stone, bone and horn tools that were as different from Neanderthal tools as saws and screwdrivers are from simple straight-edged scrapers." Klein also noted that the site, along with the Neanderthal remains, yielded tools that appeared to be a step beyond what Neanderthals were accustomed to, but not as advanced as the Cro-Magnons. That indicated, he suggested, that the Neanderthals "were trying to imitate" the latecomers' technology, but "not quite making it"

Although the oldest remains of fully modern people in Europe date to only 30,000 years ago, archaeologists believe that they were there at least 10,000 years earlier. Advanced tools that could only have been made by modern people have been uncovered in a number of Western European sites dating to 40,000 years ago. That demonstrates, Stringer explained, "that modern humans and Neanderthals must have co-existed for several thousand years." But, as Klein pointed out, there is no evidence—zilch—of Neanderthal-modern hybrids. Stringer was not quite so adamant. He was content with the observation that "the Neanderthal contribution to the evolution of modern people is negligible."

It takes very little imagination to hear in this debate, albeit with an ironic twist, echoes of the one about the contribution of Africans to western civilization. Stringer and others, who believe that Neanderthals were an evolutionary dead-end, claim that modern humans did not supplant Neanderthals by conquering or killing them, just that they had an edge in technological or demographic competition. To Stringer, the Neanderthals lost out because they were inferior, although not massively so. He has also written that Neanderthals were slowly displaced to environments where the supplies of food were less reliable and where, consequently, "their dwindling numbers would have suffered greater attraction from the vagaries of fluctuating climates and food supplies, as well as disease."

To demonstrate how Neanderthals may have been gradually supplanted, Egon Zubrow, an anthropologist at the State University of New York at Buffalo, has calculated that an increase of even two percent in the mortality rate of Neanderthals, caused by either disease or lack of food, could have led to their extinction in only 1,000 years, or thirty generations. And Dr. Jeffrey T. Laitman, an anthropologist at Mount Sinai School of Medicine, believes that the shape of the Neanderthals' upper respiratory tract, which evolved to aid nasal breathing in a cold, dry climate, may have predisposed them to serious respiratory infections, putting them at further disadvantage.

The proponents of the "Garden of Eden" theory clearly believe that Neanderthals perished because they were biologically inferior to the newcomers from Africa. Some of them have theorized that perhaps the most distinctive difference between Neanderthals and modern humans was neither in physique nor in intelligence, but in the ability to speak. Laitman believes that the Neanderthal larynx was higher than that of modern humans, limiting the Neanderthals' speaking ability. And Cann is confident that language gave the moderns a competitive edge. This competitive edge was particularly important, she has proposed, because it made them better at remembering things, such as why they were not supposed to play with those big woolly animals, or how to get back when they're out wandering in the woods. She believes that communication by spoken word was probably an explosive stage. Language, Cann argues, allowed the moderns to communicate the locations of watering holes or better warn one another of lurking dangers.

Comparative studies tracing the evolution of the human supralaryngeal vocal tract through the fossil record, and analysis of classical Neanderthal fossils, have confirmed the theory that human speech was beyond the anatomical capacity of Neanderthals. Although they had large brains and developed a relatively advanced culture, Neanderthals retained certain primitive features, including the archaic features of the general mammalian basicranium, which was specialized for chewing at the expense of phonetic efficiency. Because the cranial nerves and the brain's blood supply enter and leave the skull through the basicranium (the skull base), it was, in an evolutionary sense, extremely conservative because uncoordinated changes in its form would have had profound consequences.

The long mandibles (the bones of the lower jaw) that are characteristic of the general mammalian basicranium maximized chewing efficiency by providing plenty of space for teeth and kept the tongue within the oral cavity. The restructuring of the modern human basicranium, which significantly shortened the length of the jawbones without reducing the size of the primitive tongue, was accompanied by a descent of the larynx to a position opposite the fourth, fifth, and sixth cervical vertebrae. To accommodate the size of the tongue in the reduced area of the oral cavity in modern man, the tongue, instead of being long and thin, is curved and positioned partly in the mouth and partly in the pharynx.

Despite earlier claims that Neanderthals had normal adult vocal tracts, it is now clear that because of the high position of the Neanderthal larynx—relative to their palate and tongue—the modern human supralaryngeal vocal tract could not have developed within a classic Neanderthal skull.

The descent of the larynx in anatomically modern humans made breathing, swallowing, and chewing less efficient. In comparison to the relative straight airways of animals, the human airway is a tortuous channel. The pattern for swallowing in modern adult humans, which involves the passage of food over the opening of the larynx, sometimes causes choking and even death. In all other animals, including the Neanderthals, this is not possible because the pharynx (throat) lies behind the larynx. And, of course, shorter jawbones reduced the number of teeth and therefore the efficiency of chewing.

Given these facts, it is clear, as Philip Lieberman explained in *The Biology and Evolution of Language*, that the selective forces that led to the restructuring of the human basicranium must have had extremely high selective value. Lieberman identifies "encoded, high-speed vocal communication" as the selective advantage that "outweighed the vegetative advantage of the nonhuman supralaryngeal airway." The ability to speak became more important than the ability to chew efficiently.

While the preponderance of the evidence strongly suggested for some time that Neanderthals were indeed an evolutionary dead-end, Wolpoff and his colleagues were hard to convince. They argued that the fossil evidence from Central Europe clearly established that early modern humans still displayed many traits that are obviously Neanderthal in character, and therefore evolved from them. They claimed that many early modern skulls display a telltale bone near the place where the mandibular nerve enters the jaws. Dr. David Frayer, a physical anthropologist at the University of Kansas, contended that the bone is a well-established characteristic of Neanderthal skulls. Additionally, according to Dr. Fred H. Smith of the University of Illinois (who believes that Neanderthal genes live on today in many Europeans), the backs of most Neanderthal skulls look "as if a little bun were stuck there."

That little bun, which Smith says is also found on the skulls of early modern humans found in Czechoslovakia, is found in neither the Neanderthals nor the earliest moderns in Israel. "How did the earliest modern humans in Europe get it unless they got it from Neanderthals?" Smith asked. To Smith the question was purely rhetorical. To him it was obvious that the earliest modern humans in Europe inherited the little buns on the backs of their skulls from what he insists were their Neanderthal ancestors.

Smith has suggested what he describes as a "possible scenario" to explain the disappearance of the Neanderthals. He claims that the physical characteristics of the Neanderthals enabled them to adapt well to the cold of ice age Europe. An example, according to Smith, was the unusually large size of Neanderthal babies that made them better able to survive the cold. The last Ice Age lasted from about 120,000 to about 18,000 years ago. According to Smith's scenario, during a warm interlude early modern people from elsewhere, who lacked the Neanderthals' physical adaptation to cold, drifted into Europe and interbred with the Neanderthal population. The Ice Age, Smith says, reasserted itself for a time, but by then the surviving population had developed better clothing, more efficient fires and better houses to withstand the cold.

Because of these developments, Smith theorized, a robust body adapted to the cold became less important and even a liability because it required more energy. As the generations passed, he claims, the human population lost its Neanderthal features under the culling of natural selection. But although the Neanderthal physical type disappeared, "the breed did not go extinct in the classical sense." Rather, Smith insisted, Neanderthal genes live on today in Europeans and those who, like most Americans, trace their lineage to Europe.

In the years since the debate began, evidence has continued to mount that Neanderthals were, indeed, an evolutionary dead-end. On March, 29, 2000, the *New York Times,* announced that "New DNA evidence, extracted from the ribs of a Neanderthal infant, one of the last of its kind, supports the thesis that these hardy, beetle-browed people left little or no genetic legacy in today's populations." Neanderthal DNA had been first isolated in 1997, from bones first found in the Feldhofer Cave in the Neander Valley in 1856. Those DNA findings, which showed a pattern very different from modern humans, were greeted skeptically by supporters of the Neanderthal-human assimilation theory.

The confirmation from the second sample forced even Smith to concede, grudgingly and carefully, that the new DNA data were "incredibly important and significant," and that it "certainly strengthens the fact that there is quite a gap between Neanderthals and recent humans in terms of mitochondrial DNA." But he and others remain emotionally attached to the proposition that some interbreeding did take place between Neanderthals and modern humans.

Despite beliefs of that type, there can be little doubt that both the fossil record and molecular data point overwhelmingly to Africa as the cradle of mankind, and that the molecular data strongly suggests that anatomically modern man migrated out of Africa about 50,000 years ago, gradually replacing the more primitive types then living in Asia and Europe. Geneticists have been able to construct human family trees, using both mitochondrial DNA and the Y chromosome.

The most detailed of the trees to date is one constructed by Dr. Douglas Wallace of Emory University on the basis of mitochondrial DNA. Wallace discovered that while all other populations were split into various lineage groups, in Africa there is a single main lineage, which he designated L. This L lineage divided into three branches and the youngest branch, L3, which is common in East Africa, is believed to be the source of both the Asian and European lineages.

Wallace also concluded that the most ancient human populations are the Vasikela Kung of the northwestern Kalahari Desert in southern Africa and the Biaka pygmies of Central Africa. Wallace's theory, which is consistent with the linguistic evidence, was substantially confirmed by another study, this time of the male or Y chromosome. Conducted by Dr. Peter A. Underhill of Stanford University and published in *The American Journal of Human Genetics* in December 2001, the study reported that the earliest mutations in the Y chromosome tree are found at high frequency among the Khoisan and among the Oromo and Amhara peoples of Ethiopia.

Although the mitochondrial DNA and Y chromosome trees led, in some instances, to slightly different African populations, both pointed to the Khoisan since Kung speakers are members of the Khoisan language family. The discrepancy is hardly surprising, as Underhill explained, because many of the earliest lineages in the ancestral population are likely to have been lost and survival was based purely on chance. Far more relevant is Underhill's observation that the earliest Y chromosome lineages are only found in Africa and are apparently associated with hunter-gatherer-forager lifestyles.

He believes that the men carrying these lineages began spreading across Africa somewhere between 130,000 and 70,000 years ago. Then, about 50,000 years ago, a new lineage arose and a population derived from this lineage left Africa for southern Asia and Australia. Finally, another population from the Asian lineage moved into Europe some 30,000 to 20,000 years ago.

Belatedly, and often skeptically, archaeologists are beginning to catch up with the biologists. After years of objection and denial, some of their most influential members have recently conceded that not only did anatomically modern man emerge from Africa, but that he did so after more than 30,000 years of modern behavior. The impetus for the change was artifacts discovered at Blombos Cave, 200 miles east of Capetown, South Africa. The people who occupied this cave on a high cliff overlooking the Indian Ocean more than 70,000 years ago were, they have concluded, definitely anatomically modern humans capable of abstract and creative thought, and, very likely, communications, through articulate speech.

Previously, many of the experts in this field were convinced that modern human behavior was a relatively recent development, one that began in a kind of "creative explosion" in (where else?) Europe. Evidence for the European origin of modern behavior was said to be the fine tools and cave art of Upper Paleolithic Europe. Explaining why he no longer accepted the "creative explosion" concept of modern human behavior, Dr. Rick Potts, director of the human origins program at the Smithsonian Institution, told the *New York Times:* "I think the nails are going into the coffin of that hypothesis. We are seeing many elements of modernity that were developing much earlier in Africa, and more gradually."

There can be now no doubt that these new Africans, with their lighter skeletons, larger brains, softer brows, and newly developed ability to speak, were the first truly modern people. Probably initially numbering no more than a few hundred hunter-gatherers, they would overcome in the centuries ahead every challenge to their survival and multiplication. Slowly, but relentlessly, they would spread across the face of the earth, subduing climate, beasts, and more primitive types of man. And like the other L lineage groups, they were, at the start, dark-skinned and woolly-haired.

Not much more than a hundred years ago, anthropologists, reeling from Darwin's shattering of the creationist myths, desperately searched for a theory that would accept mankind's common but distant ancestry, while affirming that the racial groups had been separated long enough to develop major and intrinsic differences in talent and intelligence. George Stocking, a historian of anthropology, wrote that "the resulting intellectual tensions were resolved after 1859 by a comprehensive evolutionism which was at once monogenist and racist, which affirmed human unity even as it relegated the dark-skinned savage to status very near the ape." Stephen Jay Gould explained that, in an effort to guarantee irrefutable precision for the new theory, "evolution and quantification formed an unholy alliance; in a sense, their union forged the first powerful theory of scientific racism."

The child of the union was craniometry, or the measurement of the skull and its contents. The leaders of craniometry were not, as Gould pointed out, "conscious political ideologues. They regarded themselves as servants of their numbers, apostles of objectivity. And they confirmed all the common prejudices of comfortable white males—that blacks, women, and poor people occupy their subordinate roles by the harsh dictates of nature."

Eventually craniometry and other pseudo-sciences, such as psychometrics, were thoroughly discredited and exposed as advocacy masquerading as objectivity. The relentless march of science has ruthlessly stripped away, layer by layer, the encrusted prejudices that once relegated black Africans and their descendants throughout the world to subhuman status. Even now, racial considerations continue to obscure the debate on man's origins. There are no Africans, or black Americans, or any black person of any kind, among the principals in this debate, and therefore there is no racial reason for geneticists to select Africa as the cradle of mankind. Even the most persistent critics of the out-of-Africa and replacement theories admit that the new technique of mitochondrial analysis is the wave of the future. Those anthropologists who, like their nineteenth century counterparts, continue to insist that the races separated at least a million years ago, are clearly motivated by more than pure science.

It would be easy, even understandable, for black Americans so long abused to see in the facts presented in this book as proof of their own biological superiority, and to view European hegemony as, historically, brief and temporary. Africans were, after all, the first modern humans, and they created the world's first great civilization, which was the springwell of modern civilization. They not only survived the horrors of slavery and the humiliations of segregation and discrimination, but they have grown in strength and prosperity. And they are, of course, the world's greatest athletes, and their greatest athletes are the very examples of physical perfection.

It is tempting to see Europeans, with their paler skins, shorter limbs and softer bodies, as having degenerated from Africa's perfection. But that is not what the evidence indicates. Athletic ability is of very little real consequence. The biological differences between the races matter only in the highly specialized world of professional athletics and the differences between the greatest athletes of all races, even in activities involving speed and power, is often just a matter of inches. And sports, lest we forget, is mere entertainment. What the evidence shows, and what I believe in, despite the title of this book, is the profound unity of the human family. The differences between the races are so minute that the traits that matter—intelligence and courage and the capacity for love and empathy—are evenly distributed across all racial and ethnic groups.

Hopefully, this book, by establishing that black athletic superiority is the result of biologically meaningless physical differences between themselves and other racial groups and by helping to erase the historical slander of black African intellectual inferiority, will play a role, however small, in convincing those who read it that the human family is just that: a family.

The final word should go to the biologists, many of whom have discovered that their reconstruction of the human past has a value that transcends mere genetics. They have learned, from constructing their linage trees, that most of the differences between the lineages lie in areas of the DNA that do not code for genes, and, therefore, have no effect on the body. To Dr. Underhill, the message is clear: "We are all Africans at the Y-chromosome level and we are really all brothers." After more than two decades of working on mitochondrial DNA, Dr. Wallace had this to say: "What I have found astounding is that it clearly shows we are all one human family. The phylogeny in Africa goes back to the origin of our species, but the fingers of L3 are touching Europe and Asia, saying that we are all closely related."

Selected Bibliography

Aaron, Hank, with Lonnie Wheeler. *I Had a Hammer: The Hank Aaron Story*. New York: McMillan, 1990.

Ashe, Arthur, with Kip Branch, Oceania Chalk, and Frances Hanes. *Hard Road to Glory: A History of the African American Athlete*. New York: Warner Books, 1998.

Banton, Michael. *Racial Theories*. London: Cambridge University Press, 1987.

Berger, Lee R., with Brett Hilton-Barber. *In the Footsteps of Eve: The Mysteries of Human Origins*. Washington D.C.: National Geographic Society, 2000.

Blench, Roger, with Kevin C. MacDonald. *The Origins and Development of African Livestock*: *Archaeology, Genetics, Linguistics and Ethnography*. London: UCL, 2000.

Brace, C. Loring, with M. F. Ashley Montagu. *Man's Evolution: An Introduction to Physical Anthropology*. London: Macmillian, 1969.

Brown, Jim, with Steve Delsohn. *Out of Bounds*. New York: Kensington Publishing, 1989.

Brown, Michael H. *The Search for Eve*. New York: Harper Perennial, 1991.

Bruce-Chwatt, Leonard Jan. *The Rise and Fall of Malaria in Europe*. London: Oxford University Press, 1980.

Carlson, Dennis G. *African Fever: A Study of British Science, Technology, and Politics in West Africa, 1787-1864*. New York: Science History Publications, 1984.

Chadwick, Bruce. *When the Game was Black and White: The Illustrated History of Baseball's Negro Leagues.*

Coon, Carleton Stevens. *The Origin of Races*. New York: Knopf, 1973.

Crosby Alfred W. *Ecological Imperialism: The Biological Expansion of Europe, 900-1900*. Cambridge University Press, 1986.

Dean Cromwell, with Al Wesson. *Championship Technique in Track and Field*: *A Book for Athletes, Coaches, and Spectators*. New York: Whittlesley House, 1949.

Darwin, Charles. *The Origin of Species*. Danbury: Grolier Enterprises Corp. 1988.

Davidson, Basil. *The African Genius: An Introduction to African Cultural and Social History*. Boston: Little, Brown & Co., 1970.

Davidson, Basil. *The African Slave Trade*. Boston: Little, Brown & Co., 1970.

Diamond, Jared M. *Guns, Germs and Steel: The Fates of Human Societies*. New York: W.W. Norton, 1997.

Diop, Cheikh Anta. *The African Origin of Civilization*. Chicago: Lawrence Hill Books, 1974.

Drimmer Melvin. *Issues in Black History: Reflections and Commentaries on the Black Historical Experience*. Dubuque, Iowa: Kendall/Hunt Publishing Co., 1987.

D'Souza, Dinesh. *The End of Racism: Principles for a Multiracial Society*. New York: Free Press, 1995.

Ehret, Christopher, with Merrick Posmansky. *The Archaeological and Linguistic Reconstruction of African History*. Berkeley: University of California Press, 1982.

Ellis A. B. *The Tshi-Speaking Peoples of the Gold Coast of West Africa*. London: Chapman and Hall Ltd., 1887.

Faust, Drew Gilpin. *James Henry Hammond and the Old South*. Baton Rouge: Louisiana State University Press, 1985.

Faust, Drew Gilpin. *James Henry Hammond and the Old South*. Baton Rouge: Louisiana State University Press, 1981.

Fredrickson, George M. *The Arrogance of Race: Historical Perspectives on Slavery, Racism, and Social Inequality*. Middleton, Conn.: Wesleyan University Press, 1988.

Gould, Stephen Jay. *The Mismeasure of Man*. New York: W. W. Norton & Company, 1981.

Gould, Stephen Jay. *Ever Since Darwin*. W. W. Norton & Company, 1979.

Grier, Rosey, with Dennis Baker. *Rosey, an Autobiography: The Gentle Giant*. Tulsa: Honor Books, 1986.

Halberstam, David. *The Breaks of the Game*. New York: Knopf, 1981.

Halberstam, David. *Playing for Keeps: Michael Jordan and the World He Made*. New York: Random House, 1999.

Halberstam, David. *Summer of '49*. New York: W. Morrow, 1989.

Hamer, Dean. *Living with Our Genes*: New York: Doubleday, 1998.

Hart, Betty, with Todd R. Risley. *Meaningful Differences in the Everyday Experience of Young American Children*. Baltimore: P.H. Brookes, 1995.

Heine, Bernd. *African Languages: An Introduction*. Edited with Derek Nurse. Cambridge: Cambridge University Press, 2000.

Hernstein, Richard J., and Charles Murray. *The Bell Curve: Intelligence and Class Structure in American Life*. New York: Simon and Schuster, 1996.

Hoberman, John. *Darwin's Athletes*. Boston: Houghton Mifflin Co., 1997.

Holoway, John. *Voices from the Great Black Baseball Leagues*. New York: Dodd, Mead, 1975.

Judson, Horace Freeland. *The Eighth Day of Creation: Makers of the Revolution in Biology*. New York: Simon and Schuster, 1980.

July, Robert William. *A History of the African People*. New York: Scribner, 1980.

King, James C. *The Biology of Race*. Berkeley: University of California Press, 1981.

Kingsley, Mary H. *Travels in West Africa*. London: Phoenix Press, 2000.

Lieberman, Philip. *The Biology and Evolution of Language*. Cambridge, Mass.: Harvard University Press, 1984.

Malthus, Thomas. *On Population*. New York: New American Library, 1960.

Mansfield, Peter. *A History of the Middle East*. London: Viking, Penguin Books, 1991.

McKelvey, John J. *Man Against Tsetse: Struggle for Africa*. Ithaca: Cornell University Press, 1973.

McNeill, William H. *Plagues and People*. New York: Anchor Books, Doubleday, 1989.

McMahon, Thomas A. *Muscles, Reflexes, and Locomotion*. Princeton: Princeton University Press.

Morgan, Joe, with Richard Lally. *Long Balls, No Strikes: What Baseball Must Do to Keep the Good Times Rolling*. New York: Crown Publisher, 1999.

Pannikar, K.Modhu. *The Serpent and the Crescent: A History of the Negro Empires of Western Africa*. New York: Asia Publishing House, 1964.

Patterson, Orlando. *The Sociology of Slavery*. Kingston: Granada Publishing, 1974.

Rader, Benjamin G. *Baseball: A History of America's Game*. Urbana: University of Illinois Press, 1992.

Restak, Richard M. *The Brain: The Last Frontier*. New York: Warner Books, 1980.

Roberts, Randy. *Papa Jack: Jack Johnson and the Era of White Hopes*. New York: Free Press, 1983.

Rutkoff, Peter M. *Cooperstown Symposium on Baseball and the American Culture*. Jefferson, N.C.: McFarland and Co., 2000.

Shaw, Thurston. *The Archaeology of Africa: Foods, Metals, and Towns*. London: Routledge, 1993.

Sowell, Thomas. *Ethnic America*. New York: Basic Books, Inc. 1981.

Sowell, Thomas. *The Economics and Politics of Race*. New York: William Morrow and Company, 1983.

Snowden, Frank M. Jr. *Before Color Prejudice*. Cambridge: Harvard University Press, 1991.

Tanner, J.M. *The Physique of the Olympic Athlete*. London: G. Allen and Unwin, 1964.

Tucker, William H. *The Science and Politics of Racial Research*. Urbana: University of Illinois Press, 1994.

Tygiel, Jules. *Baseball's Great Experiment: Jackie Robinson and his Legacy*. New York: Oxford University Press, 1977.

Voight David Quentin. *Baseball, an Illustrated History*. University Park: Pennsylvania State University Press, 1987.

Wertheim, L. Jon. *Venus Envy: A Sensational Season Inside the Women's Tennis Tour*. New York: Harper Collins, 2001.

Will, George F. *Men at Work: The Craft of Baseball*. New York: McMillan, 1990.

Williams, Doug, with Bruce Hunter. *Quarterblack: Shattering the NFL Myth*. Chicago: Bonus Books, 1990.

Williams, Eric. *Capitalism and Slavery*. London: A. Deutsch, 1964.

Wilmore, Jack H. *Training for Sport and Activity: The Physiological Basis of the Conditioning Process*. Boston: Allyn and Bacon, Inc.

www.ingramcontent.com/pod-product-compliance
Lightning Source LLC
Chambersburg PA
CBHW061717270326
41928CB00011B/2021